International Conflict Resolution

D0048385

International Relations for the Twenty-first Century

Series Editor: Charles Hauss,
Alliance for Peacebuilding
George Mason University

Ranging from international political economy to security, migration, human rights and the environment, this series is designed to explore the issues that make International Relations such an exciting, controversial and, at times, confusing field in a world undergoing unprecedented change.

The books in the series are designed as core texts for advanced undergraduate and specialized graduate courses. Each volume introduces general theories and concepts as well as carefully selected case studies that students can use to deepen their understanding of the theoretical issues. Also included are bibliographies and addresses of useful websites.

Published titles in the series
International Conflict Resolution, first edition by Charles Hauss
International Law and International Relations by Craig Barker

INTERNATIONAL CONFLICT RESOLUTION

Second Edition

Charles Hauss

Alliance for Peacebuilding
George Mason University

continuum

NEW YORK • LONDON

The Continuum International Publishing Group Inc
80 Maiden Lane, New York, NY 10038

The Continuum International Publishing Group Ltd
The Tower Building, 11 York Road, London SE1 7NX

www.continuumbooks.com

Copyright © 2010 by Charles Hauss

All rights reserved. No part of this book may be reproduced, stored in a retrieval system, or transmitted, in any form or by any means, electronic, mechanical, photocopying, recording, or otherwise, without the written permission of the publishers.

Library of Congress Cataloging-in-Publication Data
Hauss, Charles.
  International conflict resolution / Charles Hauss. – 2nd ed.
    p. cm. – (International relations for the 21st century)
  Includes bibliographical references and index.
  ISBN-13: 978-0-8264-8910-4 (hardcover : alk. paper)
  ISBN-10: 0-8264-8910-9 (hardcover : alk. paper)
  ISBN-13: 978-0-8264-8911-1 (pbk. : alk. paper)
  ISBN-10: 0-8264-8911-7 (pbk. : alk. paper) 1. Pacific settlement of international disputes. 2. International relations. 3. Conflict management. I. Title. II. Series.

  JZ6010.H38 2010
  327.1'7–dc22

                                                                2009012180

ISBN 978-0-8264-8911-1 (PB)
      978-0-8264-8910-4 (HB)

Typeset by Newgen Imaging Systems Pvt Ltd, Chennai, India

To Nicole Dial, my friend and colleague,
who was killed in Afghanistan while building peace in 2008.

Contents

List of Figures

List of Tables

Acknowledgments

I have written more than my share of books.

I think I have learned to write better and have a firmer grasp of my subject each time out. However, I also have learned that each time out my debt to friends, colleagues, and experts I've never met gets bigger and bigger.

As the dedication to the book suggests, my biggest debt is to my friends in the conflict resolution field. That has always been the case, but I have learned a lot more from them in the decade since I made conflict resolution and peace-building the core of my political and professional life. There is not room to list them all here, but those of you who aren't personally thanked will undoubtedly have seen your impact on the evolution of my thinking.

First, I have to thank the two NGOs I've worked for since 2000. Search for Common Ground is the largest conflict-resolution NGO in the world. As I will suggest in the last few pages of the book, Search is also the most creative organization. At Search, Roger Conner and Rob Fersh tried to be my boss. John and Susan Collin Marks were mentors and helped me find balance between my political obsessions and the rest of life. In fact, I saw them at a party the day before I wrote these words. John and I talked about sports.

Along those same lines I have to thank the Alliance for Peacebuilding, which gave me a home where I could more easily pursue my interests in working with the Defense Department, and with national security in general. CEO Chic Dambach has become not only a trusted colleague but a fast friend. The rest of our staff—all women under 35—give me hope for the future, not to mention the occasional reality check.

Second, there is what I jokingly refer to as the Oberlin mafia. For reasons none of us understand, an amazingly large number of conflict resolution scholars and practitioners went to that tiny college in Ohio. An even more amazing group were there when I was, including four people who shared a house with me in my junior year. Bernie Mayer is arguably the best theorist in the field. Peter Woodrow knows more about evaluating conflict resolution programs than anyone in the world. Bill Kramer devotes his energy to sustainable development. Paul Osterman is a dean at MIT's business school and works on the community organization movement that gave rise to President Obama.

Roger Conner, again, has to be mentioned. He was a political adversary when I was majoring in ending the war in Vietnam. But in our time together at Search for Common Ground, Roger forced me to think about how we can do this work and be advocates for changing foreign policy. Walt Galloway introduced me to appreciative inquiry. David Smock knows more about the link between religion and conflict than anyone I know. Kate Howard and Jake Kramer-Duffield survived working with me as interns and are now making their marks in related fields. YB (Yeworkwa Belechew—hence YB) runs the Oberlin Center for Dialogue and Communication. She invited me to teach a class a few winter terms ago. Despite the fact that she made me live in my freshman dorm, it was an experience I'll always cherish.

A few other individuals deserve mention, none more than my wife, Gretchen Sandles. An accomplished political scientist in her own right, Gretchen has been my strongest supporter and worst critic. She has spent her career as an intelligence analyst, which makes us an odd couple. So, we have decided to write a book together on rethinking national security. Her daughter, Evonne Fei, has also been a great help, especially now that she is counseling returned veterans from Iraq and Afghanistan. And, our beloved dog Jessie is my most enthusiastic critic. Whenever I hit a writing block, we go for a walk and talk it through.

Almost as important is Dick O'Neill. Dick and I met either in nursery school or kindergarten. We were good friends through college, but we drifted apart as I pursued my left-wing career and Dick became a Navy intelligence officer. We were reintroduced by a high-school classmate just before 9/11. Dick had set up a think-tank to help the Pentagon think outside the clichéd box, and we worked together a bit before 9/11. Dick came to the launch party for the first edition of this book on 9/13. It was a tough time. But this career peace worker and his friend the career military officer handled the questions and answers together. Since then, Dick has been my main entry point into the national security community.

Joel Peters taught me more than he realizes about the Middle East. He got me to East Jerusalem to run workshops on conflict resolution for young Palestinian professionals. Peter Dixon of Concordis International has done more to help the situation in Darfur than anyone on the planet. Larry Wright of the *New Yorker* made me think about what we could and should do about terrorism. Susan Collin Marks shared her experience in the transition from apartheid.

Finally, I want to thank the serving and former military and intelligence officers who contributed so much to the last five chapters of the book. I cannot name most of them. You know who you are.

Charles Hauss
Falls Church, VA
January 2009
chiphauss@gmail.com

Prologue

Authors rarely write about the changes they made from one edition of a book to the next in the body of the text. Readers won't have read the previous edition, and should care less about what was in it and how this new one is different.

In this case, you should understand two ways in which this book is different from the one I finished in late 2000.

The World Has Changed

In a perverse quirk of fate, the first edition of this book was published in early September 2001. The book launch party for it occurred on 9/13 (see the final chapter).

Those of us who work on conflict resolution knew that terrorism was an issue and that Afghanistan and Iraq were countries we needed to pay attention to. But, we frankly had no clue that jetliners would fly into the World Trade Center and the Pentagon on 9/11. Once we came to grips with the crumbling and burning towers and the new world they unfortunately ushered in, my colleagues and I had to rethink our personal and political priorities.

Critics of conflict resolution work (including my 87-year-old-mother) tell us that war has been and always will be a part of the human landscape.

I can't disagree.

But, in the first as well as this edition of the book, I've tried to make the case that opportunities for easing and even solving conflict exist.

Many disputes that seemed unsolvable twenty years ago are close to being permanently settled today, as we will see in considering South Africa and Northern Ireland. Others, where conflict rages again, still have the possibility of a peaceful resolution, as, again, we will see, with the Israelis and Palestinians.

In short, this edition of the book will focus on what has gone well and what has gone wrong. Most people who write about conflict resolution focus on the former. That said, we actually learn the most when we concentrate on what didn't work, which in this case will mean chapters on Iraq, the war on terrorism, and Darfur.

I Have Changed

Academic books also rarely revolve around what their authors do outside of the classroom or their book-lined study.

In that sense, too, this edition will be different.

I am deeply involved in the efforts to solve the conflicts discussed in Part 3.

Before the first edition of this book was published, I was a grassroots activist who worked on conflict resolution part-time. But in the late 1990s, when my wife and I lived in the outer suburbs of London, I was twice asked to teach young Palestinian professionals about conflict resolution.

When I returned from Palestine the second time, I realized that I could not do this work well only as an academic and freelance consultant.

One day shortly thereafter, my phone rang. It was an old friend and political adversary from my undergraduate days who had been hired to set up a conflict resolution program for American politics at Search for Common Ground, and wanted me to come on board. We did work on consensus-building for health care, the faith-based initiative, prisoner re-entry, HIV/AIDS, and our relations with the Muslim world.

In the process, I met most of the people I quoted in the first edition. Their wisdom and friendship have enriched the pages that follow.

While at Search, I built on a friendship with someone from nursery school days to reach out to the military. Much to our surprise, we found that in the post-9/11 world we agree far more than we disagree. The military-NGO connection was better managed through the Alliance for Peacebuilding, where I work today.

In the process, I became a Washington insider.

Your Challenge

I have written other textbooks in which I exhort readers to figure out how they can make a difference in shaping the world my generation is leaving them. I should not have to make that case here. The problems we face and the failures of my generation, and those that came before us, will be obvious in the pages that follow. So, also, should be our accomplishments.

It is your challenge to figure out how to do what we've done, better.

PART 1

Introduction

CHAPTER ONE

Passion, Argument, Evidence, Insight

Decimation means the killing of every tenth person in a population and in the spring and early summer of 1994 a program of massacres decimated the Republic of Rwanda. Although the killing was low-tech—performed largely by machete—it was carried out at dazzling speed; of an original population of about seven and a half million, at least eight hundred thousand were killed in just a hundred days. Rwandans often speak of a million deaths, and they may be right. The dead of Rwanda accumulated at nearly three times the rate of Jewish dead during the Holocaust. It was the most efficient mass killing since the atomic bombings of Hiroshima and Nagasaki.
—Philip Gourevitch

In April 1994 two momentous events occurred. On April 6 the airplane carrying the presidents of Rwanda and Burundi was shot down, killing all aboard. The crash was the catalyst for the genocide in Rwanda described in the passage by Philip Gourevitch (1998) that begins this chapter. Three weeks after the crash, South Africa held its first democratic election, which swept Nelson Mandela into power and marked the end of apartheid and one of the greatest strides toward peace in decades.

Those two events symbolize what this book is about.

The killings in Rwanda and Burundi are but the tip of a much larger iceberg of war and violence in the post-Cold War world. Many academics look longingly back to the Cold War, when geopolitical pressures at least seemed to impose some limits on human cruelty. Others go further, like the journalist Robert Kaplan (1994, 1996), who warns of a "coming anarchy" in which the combination of crime, poverty, environmental decay and war will make our world a far more volatile and violent place.

The experience of South Africa suggests that political life does not have to remain as violent as that. Those of us involved in the 1980s campaign to force American universities and pension funds to divest their stock in companies that cooperated with the South African government frankly worried that we might never see the end of an apartheid regime that still seemed so very strong. Yet, just as the 1990s dawned, the South African government released Mandela after 27 years in prison. He and his former jailers then led negotiations that produced the transition to majority rule. The former inmate became one of the world's most respected and adored political leaders. That said, South Africa remains very troubled, with more than its share of political violence and one of the highest murder rates in the world. Nonetheless, an important corner toward peace and reconciliation has been turned, presenting a model that many of us are convinced can be adapted and used elsewhere to gradually redirect the world away from what Robert Kaplan called the coming anarchy.

As optimistic as I am, it is impossible to ignore the pain and agony and *lack* of progress concerning many contemporary conflicts. As I write, wars continue to ravage Iraq,

Afghanistan, Palestine, and dozens of other countries. The number of wars may have decreased and, with the exception of Iraq, Afghanistan, Congo and Darfur, their human toll may have lessened as well (Mack 2005). But, the problems posed by international conflict should not be ignored. To cite but one example, the star of the hit film *Hotel Rwanda*, Don Cheadle (Cheadle and Prendergast 2007), has become a major voice demanding the end of genocide in Darfur in western Sudan, which has taken a quarter million lives.

In short, we face the same problems we had in 2000 when I finished the first edition of this book. Too much conflict. Not enough good ideas or tools for ending it.

To get out of that bind, we need to take the words of the title of this chapter seriously. We are interested in conflict resolution because of the passion it provokes. But we also need to be disciplined and craft ever better arguments, and buttress them with evidence. Then we can arrive at insights that, in turn, can help inform and improve the work we do on the basis of our passion.

Passion

Most academic books are dispassionate. Their authors weigh evidence and arguments in a reasoned way, downplay their own values, and reach what they believe to be rational conclusions given what they know.

We cannot, however, ignore either our values or our emotions in trying to come to grips with international conflict and its resolution. As Gourevitch implies, it is usually something like revulsion against the killings in places like Rwanda that draws most of us to the subject in the first place.

We know that the stakes of international conflict are high. The twentieth century was the most violent on record. The final report of the Carnegie Commission on Preventing Deadly Conflict (1997) shows that more than 100 million people died in wars during those bloody one hundred years.

Over the last thirty years, somewhere between twenty and thirty-five wars were being fought at any one time. During most years, forty million people flee their countries as refugees. Ethnic cleansing in the former Yugoslavia brought genocide back onto the political agenda. The first war crimes tribunals since the end of World War Two were created, which in turn led to the creation of a permanent international criminal court to deal with crimes against humanity.

Today's violent conflicts also take a terrible toll on civilians. In World War One, nine soldiers were killed for every civilian who got caught in the crossfire. Now that ratio is reversed. Civilian casualties dwarf those of soldiers. The devastation among civilians is doubly tragic because it undermines the economies and environments of the countries in which these wars are fought. Some estimates put the cost of the war in Iraq at $3 trillion, to cover everything from rebuilding that country to the health care coverage of American and other allied soldiers who were wounded and survived.

Today's conflicts also are different from those at the heart of academic international relations. Most at least started as domestic rather than international wars, though many have spilled across national boundaries. Most revolve around emotionally charged "identity" issues involving religion, ethnicity, language and race, which are much harder to resolve than the geopolitical issues that sparked most earlier wars. Today's wars are also what we call asymmetrical conflicts, because one side is seemingly much stronger than the other. Yet, the supposedly weaker side often seems to not only hold its own, but even to prevail.

Although the media tend to focus on the violence, there are thousands of people who have dedicated their intellectual and political lives to finding a better way of settling international disputes. Especially since the end of the Cold War, there has been an upsurge of interest in positive-sum or win-win conflict resolution that leaves all parties satisfied and open to cooperative problem-solving in general. In time, that kind of dispute resolution can lead to what Kenneth Boulding (1979, 1988) called stable peace, a state in which war is all but impossible because the parties to past violence have learned to settle their differences without considering the use of force.

Such prominent politicians as former US President Jimmy Carter and senator George Mitchell have built new careers as mediators in international disputes. Similarly, Bernard Kouchner moved on from his post as head of *Médecins sans frontières* to become first a socialist cabinet minister in France, then head of the UN's reconstruction efforts in Kosovo, and now foreign minister in a conservative government. Even more impressive is the new group of former national heads of state and other eminent persons, The Elders, who have pledged to spend their retirement years to work for world peace (www.theelders. org).

Attempts to resolve conflict non-violently often come from previously unexpected sources—and with unexpected enthusiasm. Peacekeeping and peace-building are now part of the training of all senior officers in the Canadian and Scandinavian militaries. The US is following suit, though it will take time for such changes to ripple through such a huge organization. A decade ago, one European think tank identified more than 500 NGOs (nongovernmental organizations) that devote all or part of their efforts to international conflict resolution (Miall, Ramsbotham, and Woodhouse 1999: 37). Now, there are tens of thousands of people who have full-time careers in governments, NGOs and consulting firms specializing in conflict resolution.

Argument

But, this *is* an academic book and thus cannot rely on passion alone. It is based on the premise that students and other readers can make the most sense of international conflict resolution by using theoretical arguments to sift through the evidence and reach deeper and more insightful conclusions.

There is no shortage of general analyses that can help people come to grips with international conflict and its resolution. However, those theoretical works have only been put to limited use because their authors have focused all but exclusively on the optimistic or the pessimistic sides of the field. Some see international conflict and violence as an inescapable part of the human condition. Others conclude that there are better ways of settling our disputes that puts them to rest once and for all.

I will make the case for at least giving serious consideration to new approaches to conflict resolution that stress win-win outcomes, reconciliation, and stable peace. Those ideas are not new. There was a burst of optimism at the end of the nineteenth and beginning of the twentieth centuries similar to what exists now. Moreover, the "new" theories to be discussed in Chapter 5 have roots in the world's major spiritual traditions, which means they can be traced back for thousands of years. If I am right, the changed nature of conflict today and our growing, though still limited, experience with these strategies and techniques suggest that it would be foolhardy not to take the new forms of conflict seriously.

That does not mean that the realists and others who argue for the continued use of traditional analytical models and foreign policies are wrong. While today's conflicts are qualitatively different from those that traditional international relations theory is based on, the next period in international relations could be one in which states, geopolitics and wars fought by conventional arms are again the norm. More important, win-win conflict resolution is still very much the exception to the rule. To understand why that is the case, we will explore both the more traditional theories and the less optimistic conclusions they typically lead to.

In short, I do not want to seem too optimistic. Conflict is an inescapable part of our lives at every level from the interpersonal to the international. And, if the first analyses of globalization are true, there could well be more conflict, not less, in the years to come.

Nonetheless, I will be insisting that there is what I have elsewhere called a rational basis for hope for the medium to long term (Hauss 1989). As we gain more experience using the new approaches to conflict resolution to be described in later chapters, we should be able to learn to use them more effectively, and to build more support for them in the process.

There is no single theory that covers all of the cases and outcomes covered in Part 2. The "real world" is too complicated for that. Instead, most of the prominent theories in international relations and conflict resolution help illuminate some, but not all, of the cases that follow.

In academic life, there is a tendency to pit theories against each other in a "debate" over which of them is correct. I will not do so. I do have a strong personal preference. I very much want to live in a world in which win-win conflict resolution becomes the norm because individuals, organizations and states learn to settle their disputes "better." However, my task here is to help the reader understand the way conflict is addressed today. That is a very different matter. Writing this book convinced me more than ever that we need both the new and the traditional theories in trying to explain conflict and its resolution, because they *complement* more than they *contradict* each other.

Evidence and Insight

Theory is important, but it is not enough. Our goal may be to reach general and even abstract conclusions that shape both our analyses and our actions. However, research by scholars who study how people learn suggests that few of us can assess theory by working solely at an abstract level.

Therefore, this book draws on relevant case studies to allow readers to test the theories and reach their own conclusions. Part 3 presents six examples that illustrate the variety of conflicts, from those in which major strides toward resolution have occurred, to those in which the dispute festers and ongoing violence is the norm. Together, they allow us to get a first glimpse of the conditions under which win-win conflict resolution and stable peace are most—and least—likely to occur and, as a result, where traditional and new approaches to international relations are most and least effective. The cases therefore are presented in order from the most to the least successful, which should help you see more clearly what does and does not "work" in the field.

The case studies are:

- the transition to democratic rule in South Africa
- efforts to end the "Troubles" in Northern Ireland
- the peace process between Israelis and Palestinians
- the so-called global war on terrorism
- the two wars the United States has fought in Iraq
- the genocide in Darfur.

The rest of this book will demonstrate that combining theory and case studies leads to new insights about conflict resolution and the state of international relations in general. Outlining them here, however, would be premature. The conclusions depend on the joint consideration of theories and cases, and it only makes sense to defer discussing specific insights until the end of the book. Each case study chapter will start with theoretical questions and end with what we practitioners call "lessons learned" about conflict resolution in general that can be derived from that example.

Conflict Resolution on the Web

Beginning with this one, each chapter will have a box with useful websites for the material covered in it. They will allow you to go beyond what is in the book, and stay up to date on the issues or country discussed in that chapter.

The best place to begin is Beyond Intractability, an online handbook for all forms of conflict resolution: www.beyondintractability.org.

As is almost always the case in academic life, the Virtual Library has an outstanding and well-documented collection of sites: www2.etown.edu/vl/peace.html.

Also helpful are the Centre for Security Studies and Conflict Research in Switzerland, <http://www.fsk.ethz.ch>, and INCORE on ethnic conflict based in Northern Ireland: http://www.incore.ulst.ac.uk.

Most American-based conflict resolution NGOs belong to the Alliance for Peacebuilding (where I work): www.allianceforpeacebuilding.org.

The Alliance, and Beyond Intractability, co-host a service that posts jobs, information about conferences and other events, a news service, and a discussion forum. It can be reached through either website's home page.

I can be reached at chiphauss@gmail.com.

Each chapter also has a list of references that includes everything cited in it. The bibliographies are not meant to be exhaustive lists of books and articles at the cutting edge of scholarship. Rather, they direct you primarily to works that are particularly useful to people who are not specialists in either international relations theory or on the conflicts covered in Part 2.

Staying with Conflict

While writing this book, I had the pleasure of reading Bernard Mayer's *Staying With Conflict* (2009). Bernie and I have been friends since we were undergraduates, and have worked together ever since.

What he argues in his new book will soon become obvious to you. We have to "stay with conflict." There is no quick fix to any of the cases included in Part 3, or any of those others I could have written about.

A mutual friend was running a workshop in Northern Ireland in 1990. He was asked how long it would take to forge peace there. He asked his questioner when the conflict began. He was told it was at the Battle of Boyne in 1690. Our friend said that the citizens of Northern Ireland should expect another three hundred years before things were worked out.

My guess is that we can speed things up to some degree. But even the two success cases in this book—Northern Ireland and South Africa—still have a long way to go before they reach anything like reconciliation.

Select Bibliography

Boulding, Kenneth (1978). *Stable Peace*. Austin, TX: University of Texas Press.

—(1988). "Moving from Unstable to Stable Peace." In *Breakthrough: Emerging New Thinking: Soviet and American Scholars Issue a Challenge to Build a World Beyond War*, ed. Martin Hellman and Anatoly Gromyko, 157–67. New York: Walker.

Carnegie Commission for the Prevention of Deadly Conflict (1997). *Preventing Deadly Conflict*. New York: Carnegie Commission. Also available at <http:www.ccpdc.org>.

Cheadle, Don and John Prendergast (2007). *Not on Our Watch*. New York: Hyperion.

Fisher, Roger, and William Ury (1981). *Getting to Yes*. New York: Penguin.

Gourevitch, Philip (1998). *We Wish to Inform You That Tomorrow We Will Be Killed with Our Families*. New York: Farrar, Strauss and Giroux.

Hauss, Charles (1989). "A Rational Basis for Hope." In *Peace: Meanings, Politics, Strategies*, ed. Linda Rennie Forcey, 203–18. Westport, CT: Praeger.

International Committee of the Red Cross (1999). *People on War: General Report*. <http://www.onwar.org>. Accessed December 20, 1999.

Kaplan, Robert D. (1994). "The Coming Anarchy." *Atlantic* (February).

—(1996). *The Ends of the Earth: A Journey at the Dawn of the 21st Century*. New York: Random House.

Mack, Andrew (2005). *The Human Security Report*. www.humansecurityreport.info/

Mayer, Bernard (2009). *Staying With Conflict*. San Francisco, CA: Jossey Bass.

Wallensteen, Peter, and Margareta Sollenberg (1995). "After the Cold War: Emerging Patterns of Armed Conflict." *Journal of Peace Research* 23: 345–60.

CHAPTER TWO

Understanding Conflict

In the years ahead crises and threats will grow more numerous, not less, and will pose significant threats to international peace and security and to the interests of many nations.
—*Michael Lund*

It is tempting to leap right into the theories we will use to explain international conflict and its resolution. Doing so, however, would be premature.

Instead, we have to start with a more basic question. What is international conflict like? How observers answer that question is actually an important first step in seeing why they reach different theoretical conclusions about to solve it.

As Michael Lund suggests in the quotation that begins this chapter, conflict is inescapable. It is a normal part of our daily lives where we live and work, as well as in political life. Our challenge as students, scholars and citizens is to figure out how to deal with it, presumably better than we have throughout history.

That conflict is all around us is obvious. I finished this chapter on January 4, 2009. That morning, the *New York Times* and the *Washington Post* together ran several articles on conflicts in Iraq, Iran, Afghanistan, Pakistan, Israel, Northern Ireland and Sudan. Some of the stories were optimistic. Iraq, for instance, had just gained sovereignty over the Green Zone.

But, most of the stories were anything but hopeful. The most depressing of them was about the renewed fighting between Israel and the Hamas-led government in the Gaza Strip, a story which had dwarfed all other international coverage for the past several days.

The Nature of Conflict

Until recently, scholarship on international conflict focused on wars fought between countries. Indeed, the definitions of war used most frequently a generation ago were based on battle deaths in fighting between the armies of internationally recognized states.

Since the end of the Cold War, our attention has been riveted on civil and other primarily intrastate wars. Interstate wars have become the exception rather than the rule, especially those between major powers that have been at the heart of traditional international relations theory and analysis. Depending on how you count, at least 80 percent of the violent conflicts since 1945 have been intrastate. We just did not focus on them as such until the 1990s because we tended to see them as proxy battles in the Cold War, rather than disputes to be analyzed in their own right.

About two-thirds of these wars have taken place in the world's poorest countries. Only one (Russia) of the bottom 43 countries (that is, below the United States) in the 2008 Global Peace Index is from Europe or North America (www.visionofhumanity.org). The GPI and other statistical attempts to chart violent conflict in this decade point to a syndrome of problems such countries face.

Many of the countries that have been the site of these kinds of conflict have been labelled failed or failing states because they have lost all or most of their ability to maintain order, let alone forge policies to help their societies and economies develop (Ghani and Lockhart 2008; www.fundforpeace.org). Wars not only kill soldiers and civilians but also make life intolerable for the millions of people who struggled to survive even before the fighting began.

It is hard to underestimate the physical toll these conflicts take. For instance, ten percent of the Rwandan population was killed in eight weeks. Well over half the ethnic Albanians living in Kosovo were forced to flee their homes in a shorter period. The fighting in Rwanda and the former Yugoslavia was so appalling that the United Nations established war crimes tribunals for them, an institution that had been put in political mothballs once the trials after World War Two were completed. Now most of the world's countries have a signed the treaty that created a permanent International Criminal Court, though it is by no means clear how effective it will be since the United States and a few other key countries have refused to join.

Research in 15 of the most deeply affected countries that was conducted for the International Committee of the Red Cross (1999a: vii–xi) is especially telling. Just about one-quarter of the combatants have been either killed or injured. One in six were imprisoned. Of them, about 20 percent claim to have been tortured. The two most commonly used adjectives to describe the fighting were "horrible" and "hateful." That is hardly surprising. The majority of the casualties have been civilians. Almost a third of the respondents reported having had at least one close relative die. Forty percent cited having permanently lost touch with at least one family member, many of whom, of course, are dead but not accounted for. A third had their homes destroyed, while another quarter had their property looted. In perhaps the most tragic example of all, hundreds of thousands of children as young as ten years old are fighting on the world's battlefields today.

These are not easy conflicts to resolve. In the twentieth century as a whole, about half the interstate wars ended as a result of a mediated settlement. For civil wars, the figure was only 15 percent (Stedman 1999: 16). That is the case because their roots lie in what we call identity issues—race, language, ethnicity, and religion—that make negotiations more difficult than in most "traditional" wars. As we will see time and again in Part 2, it is harder to reach a compromise on questions that revolve around "who I am" than on where the borders between two countries should be.

These are not high-tech wars in which Humvees and precision-guided missiles are the weapons of choice. While they are made more tragic by a massive and often illegal market for machine guns and other weapons, these wars have almost nothing in common with those fought by the United States and its allies since the 1990s. More often than not, ill-disciplined groups of guerrillas do much of the fighting, much of which seems like little more than random acts of violence against citizens who they think are members of the groups they oppose.

In the insurgencies in Afghanistan and Iraq, the rebels do not wear uniforms and easily blend in with the population as a whole. In Rwanda, most of the hundreds of thousands of victims were hacked to death by Hutu militants wielding machetes. Often, too, it is hard to differentiate purposive political violence from organized crime, especially in cases like the combined war being fought by revolutionaries and drug lords against the government of Colombia.

Useful Websites

The Conflict Information Consortium at the University of Colorado has two sites. CRINFO is mostly a compendium of links: www.crinfo.org.

Beyond Intractability is an online handbook about the field and is a wonderful complement to any book: www.beyondintractability.org.

The Alliance For Peacebuilding has links to all of its member organizations' sites and beyond: www.allianceforpeacebuilding.org.

The Fund for Peace annually compiles, publishes and analyzes a failed states index that documents the countries with the least effective governments that are also among the most prone to conflict. This is their home page. The specific page for the index changes each year when it is updated. Go to their publications page and navigate from there: www.fundforpeace.org.

The Institute for State Effectiveness is a new NGO created by two veterans of post-conflict Afghanistan. Ashraf Ghani and Clare Lockart set up the Institute to help countries overcome the problems the Fund for Peace focuses on: www.effectivestates.org.

The Global Peace Index also ranks countries not on the degree to which their states are failing but on their peacefulness. The United States ranked #95 in 2008: www.visionofhumanity.org.

The Center for Security Studies and Conflict Research in Switzerland maintains an exhaustive set of links to other sources of material on international conflict, especially to sites outside the United States: www.fsk.ethz.ch.

Perhaps the most tragic aspect of conflict today is the widespread use of child soldiers, which UNESCO defines as anyone under 18 who is a combatant. No one knows how many children as young as eight or nine have been forced to bear arms and kill. The best estimate is that there are more than 400,000 of them. The use of child soldiers not only disrupts societies but almost always deprives the children of anything resembling a normal life, as the memoir by Ishmael Beah (2006) and the video by the Invisible Children project have poignantly pointed out (www.invisiblechildren.org).

Finding solutions to these conflicts is made more difficult by the fact that most of them are "asymmetric." One side has a lot more power, however we choose to define that term.

As we will see in the next chapter about realist theory, the powerful are reluctant to give up their advantages to groups they have looked down on for decades, if not centuries. Sunni Arabs dominated the Shi'ite and Kurdish majority in Iraq long before Saddam Hussein came to power. Protestants in Northern Ireland outnumbered Catholics and controlled every major institution in the province, from the corporate boardrooms to the police force.

By contrast, the weaker side seeks what peace studies scholars and others call social justice. That means not just stopping the conflict but also ending the political, economic and other inequalities which, they think, gave rise to the conflict in the first place. And even more importantly, that means redistributing income and the other determinants of power that created and sustain the inequality.

The neo-conservative journalist, Robert Kaplan, has described the dismal picture of asymmetric conflicts in the best summary I have read:

> It was in Sierra Leone that I first considered the possibility that just as states and their governments were meaning less and less, the distinctions between states and armies, armies and civilians, and armies and criminal gangs were also weakening. (1996: 45)

The International Dimension

We should not conclude that these are purely domestic conflicts. International factors are almost always among their causes and consequences. And, perhaps most important of all for our purposes, the international community is increasingly involved in trying to solve them.

On a few occasions the actions of other states are consciously intended to provoke or sustain conflict, as was the case with Soviet aid to the Palestine Liberation Organization and the African National Congress for much of the Cold War, and American support to Iraq during its war with Iran. More frequently, the impact is indirect and unintentional. The economic dislocations caused by the international financial institutions' demands for structural adjustment have exacerbated tensions in much of the Third World and contributed to the escalation of many of the conflicts in sub-Saharan Africa.

Even the provision of humanitarian aid can make things worse. In such places as Bosnia and Rwanda, the food, clothing and medicine the international community sent in served to strengthen the resolve of one side in the conflict, and thus helped to prolong the fighting.

Many wars spill across national borders, as we will see especially in the case studies on terrorism and Darfur. Most conflicts produced waves of refugees, which were estimated to top seven million in Africa alone in mid-1999. In some cases, the fighting itself spread to neighbouring countries or drew other regional powers into the struggle.

The international community has played an increasingly active role in trying to resolve these disputes. While the United Nations has received the most attention—and criticism—for its involvement, it is often not a major factor, since it lacks either the legal right or the economic and human resources to intervene. Rather, as we will see in Part 3, most of these efforts are spearheaded by private citizens, nongovernmental organizations (NGOs), individual states, or regional alliances.

The Life Cycle of International Conflict

As many experts see it (Lund 1996: 38; Miall, Ramsbotham, and Woodhouse 1999: chs 3–7) conflicts have a life cycle spanning four stages. Not all conflicts pass through each one of them. Nonetheless, the onset of each phase does make the next one more likely. More importantly for our purposes, the stages offer us a useful way for making sense of the evolution of any dispute and, as we will see in the rest of this book, why all conflict resolution techniques work better in some situations than others.

Crisis Creation

In the first stage of a conflict, tensions deepen to the point that violence becomes a possibility. In considering conflict resolution at this stage, political scientists have begun regularly using a term we borrowed from the physicians. Almost all doctors now practice preventive medicine, trying to convince their patients that they should lose weight or change their diets to reduce their risks of heart attack, stroke, and other debilitating conditions.

Thus, we now speak of "preventive diplomacy" in which states, NGOs or international bodies try to literally prevent a conflict from turning violent. To that end, we frequently cite the OSCE mission sent to Macedonia in the early days of the fighting as Yugoslavia fell apart. It has largely succeeded (so far at least) in its "trip-wire" mission to detect and react to signs that the fighting might spread into Macedonia. Such operations provide an opportunity to avoid the outbreak of fighting and move directly into a situation in which it is possible to reduce tensions in the short term and, over time, to (re)build stable peace.

For reasons that will become clear below, politicians rarely are able to summon the political will to exercise preventive diplomacy: they more often make weak or belated efforts. Thus, the Serbs had been eroding the rights of Kosovars and laying the groundwork for rebellion for almost a decade before the international community made a serious attempt to find a negotiated settlement.

There is little doubt that early intervention in a looming crisis saves everything from lives to money. The problem is that it is hard to persuade politicians to summon up the political will to get involved before the fighting breaks out. At the Alliance for Peacebuilding, we have created the BEFORE project for early warning and prevention of fighting in Guinéa and Guinéa-Bissau, but we have a long way to go . . .

Turning to War

As with preventive diplomacy, there is reason to believe that timely intervention when the fighting begins can lead to a quick cessation of hostilities. However, as noted above, the parties to the conflict and the international community rarely commit themselves to any sort of conflict resolution until the fighting has become intense. Indeed, the failure to intervene proactively has been one of the most consistent criticisms of leaders of the world's major powers during the 1990s. In perhaps the most tragic example, Romeo Dallaire, the Canadian head of the UN peacekeeping mission in Rwanda, was convinced that he could have stopped the genocide as it began if he had been given a few thousand more soldiers. The Security Council refused.

To its credit, the international community tends to concentrate on helping people who are caught up in the fighting once it begins. In recent years, the United Nations and other international organizations, NGOs and national governments (including their militaries) have stepped up their humanitarian intervention in what has come to be known as the Right to Respect (Weiss 1999; Weiss and Collins 1996). NGOs and the military have historically had a rocky relationship, but the United States Institute for Peace has worked hard to create a way for the two parties to work together in dangerous settings (www.usip.org).

Perhaps because development agencies and dozens of NGOs are already working in troubled states when the fighting starts, they have become the vehicle through which food, medical supplies and other aid is channeled in attempts to ease the damage during what are euphemistically known as "complex emergencies." One sign of how such efforts have grown is the fact that Bernard Kouchner, one of the founders of *Médecins sans frontières*, is currently the left-wing foreign minister in President Nicolas Sarkozy's conservative government in France. Those of us in the NGO community do not readily accept the role the military could and should play in any phase of peace operations. Nonetheless, as we will again see in the final chapter, cooperation between NGOs and the military is growing throughout the Western world.

A New Taxonomy

In 1992 United Nations Secretary-General Boutros Boutros-Ghali issued a report, *An Agenda for Peace*. He pointed out that in the early 1990s, the UN (and by implication, other international organizations) had gone beyond the peacekeeping role that it had used most frequently during the Cold War years. Since then, other writers have suggested changing some of his terms or adding some new ones. For our purposes, his list and terminology are good enough:

- peacemaking—the attempt to bring fighting to an end using peaceful means
- peace enforcement—the armed effort to stop the fighting
- peacekeeping—monitoring and reinforcing a ceasefire that is already in place before the UN or other forces come in
- peacebuilding—steps taken to settle the disagreements that led to the fighting in the first place, which entails building stable peace.

Stopping the Fighting

Until recently, political scientists have been convinced that it is all but impossible to stop the fighting until the parties reach what I. William Zartman (1989) and Richard Haass (1990) call a "mutually hurting stalemate." At that point, serious negotiations can begin, often mediated by a neutral third party drawn from international organizations or the growing group of former politicians who have taken on international conflict resolution as a retirement job (www.theelders.org).

Historically, too, the most attention has been focused on peacekeeping by the United Nations and regional international organizations, such as the European or African Union. The UN's lightly armed "blue berets" were only introduced once a ceasefire agreement was reached, and they have normally played a limited role—preventing the resumption of the fighting after an agreement was reached. However, in the last decade, more heavily armed UN troops have been deployed in East Timor and Kosovo, and given the unusual authority to defend themselves and fire on adversaries if need be.

In other words, the international community is now willing at times to send in troops even while the fighting is still going on. They are not the lightly armed or unarmed "blue helmets." In these new kinds of intervention, forces expect to have to do some fighting and take some casualties. In such circumstances, the international community is not neutral but weighs in against a government whose human rights violations sparked the mission in the first place. As I write, the debate over what should be done about Darfur continues to rage. Those of us who have advocated more intense engagement there and elsewhere understand that any UN or African Union mission will face violence in ways that "blue helmets" have rarely faced in the past.

Building Stable Peace

During the Cold War, political scientists typically stopped their analyses of peace processes with peacekeeping and its less-than-stellar track record. The events of the last 20 years, however, have led some observers to give new attention to the areas of the world in which stable peace is the norm. Though rare in the Third World, there is little doubt that stable peace is the rule rather than the exception among industrialized democracies. Although they use the term "zone of peace" instead, conservative analysts Max Singer and Aaron Wildavsky (1996) make a convincing case that war between the major Western European, East Asian, Antipodean and North American states is all but impossible.

Other observers have looked at domestic and international efforts to create what comparative politics specialists call civil society, and also at the other preconditions for a system in which people use nonviolent means to settle their disputes. The most widely cited such example is the remarkable ongoing transition in South Africa. When the 1990s began, the country still had a repressive, white-dominated regime. When the decade ended, it had held its second all-race election following six years of reasonably successful democracy and black majority rule. One of the highlights of those years has been the efforts by leaders—black and white alike—to overcome the horrors of the past, and build true reconciliation between their communities.

In that sense, stable peace is the only true form of conflict resolution. Literally speaking, resolution is the harmonious solution to a problem, as when a resolved chord ends a piece of music. To achieve stable peace, states and other actors must find ways to solve the problems that gave rise to the violence so that people no longer consider it an option, because it is no longer needed.

Stable peace does not mean that conflict disappears or that citizens of the societies involved like each other. Thus, when I lived in France and in Great Britain, it was rare to find French or British citizens of my generation (born shortly after World War Two) who had nice things to say about Germans. Nonetheless, relations between these powers are now good enough that there no longer is any real chance that they would turn to violence to solve the conflicts over trade, foreign policy or immigration that are still a common feature of their joint political lives.

Stable peace is rare. It takes the kind of time and patience that is uncommon in political life. Still, there are signs that the international community is taking the idea more seriously than ever before, and is experimenting with new strategies to take societies closer to it.

South Africa is the most prominent example of a country whose leadership has tried to ferret out the truth about the political crimes of the past as a first step toward building reconciliation between former adversaries. It requires a very different attitude. In the words of the seventeenth-century philosopher, Baruch Spinoza:

> Peace is not an absence of war; it is a virtue, a state of mind, a disposition for benevolence, confidence, justice.

We have also seen new tools to help build lasting peace. The most famous of these was the Truth and Reconciliation Commission in South Africa, which we will explore in Chapter 6. All in all, there have been 20 such commissions at the national level and at least one at local level: in Greensboro, NC, on the twenty-fifth anniversary of a Klan attack that had the tacit support of the police and which killed a number of left-wing activists.

No two of these commissions are alike. Some have focused all but exclusively on finding the truth about what happened. Few have been as ambitious as South Africa's, which aimed to heal a lot of the country's deep, historical wounds. Critics of these bodies have properly pointed out that they have not definitively settled any of these disputes. Given how divided these countries have been, it could hardly be otherwise. Nonetheless, as we will see in the chapter on South Africa, the nation learned just about everything there was to be learned about human rights abuses during the more than 40 years of apartheid. As the documentary *A Long Night's Journey Into Day* and first-hand accounts of people who participated in the process (Marks 2001) show, remarkable progress was made in a very short time.

Most of these efforts have one goal in common, something legal scholars call restorative justice (Amstutz 2005, Philpott 2006). Traditionally, courts have tried to hold officials responsible by punishing them, something lawyers call retributive justice. And there are certainly people who needed to be held accountable in those terms, including the late leaders Slobodan Milosevic and Saddam Hussein.

The logic behind restorative justice is quite different. The parties to the conflict find ways of working together and building trust so that they can literally restore their relations in a more constructive way. Some examples are quite simple. A teenager in my neighborhood steals my car and has an accident. There will probably have to be some kind of formal legal action. But in addition, in restorative justice proceedings, my family would sit down with the teenager and his or her family and try to reach a legally nonbinding agreement that would satisfy us all and that might even include my mentoring the youngster in choosing a college (a service I actually provide for any friend's child who asks).

The roots of restorative justice lie primarily in traditional legal systems in poor, Third World countries that do not have a strong rule of law as we know it in the West. The most striking example is the use of *gacaca* proceedings in post-genocide Rwanda. The country is so poor that it had no chance of prosecuting the 200,000 or so people who were incarcerated for their role in the 1994 massacres. Instead, the authorities have drawn on this traditional technique that has Hutu murderers meet with Tutsi survivors in their villages (the two have traditionally lived together in the same communities) and find ways of reintegrating these mostly young men.

Before going further, it is important to point out that none of these systems are perfect. Humanity has been fighting wars for thousands of years. We have only consciously sought ways of building stable peace for a few decades. Indeed, the first major book, graduate degree program and major NGO in the field date from the early 1980s. In short, we still have a lot to learn.

Conflict Resolution: An Ambiguous Track Record

It is easy to reach pessimistic conclusions about conflict resolution. After all, as I write, there is widespread violence in many parts of the world. Even more depressing is the fact that somewhere between a third and a half (depending on how you count) of the countries that reach a ceasefire or other basic agreement revert to fighting within five years. You can make the case that this has happened at least twice in the dispute between the Israelis and Palestinians in this decade alone. Yet, as Andrew Mack (2005) and his colleagues have pointed out, between 1993 and 2005 the number of conflicts declined by 40 percent, the number of genocides by eighty percent. For good or ill, the conflicts that ended, and especially those that haven't broken out, don't get as much publicity as those marked by intense fighting. Still, the conflict resolution community writ large must be doing something right . . .

Select Bibliography

Amstutz, Mark (2005). *The Healing of Nations*. Boulder, CO: Rowman and Littlefield.

Beah, Ishmael (2005). *A Long Way Gone*. New York: Farrar, Straus and Giroux.

Boulding, Kenneth (1978). *Stable Peace*. Austin, TX: University of Texas Press.

—(1988). "Moving from Unstable to Stable Peace." In *Breakthrough: Emerging New Thinking: Soviet and American Scholars Issue a Challenge to Build a World Beyond War*, ed. Martin Hellman and Anatoly Gromyko, 157–67. New York: Walker.

Boutros-Ghali, Boutros (1992). *An Agenda for Peace*. New York: United Nations, 1992.

Ghani, Ashraf, and Clare Lockhart (2008). *Fixing Failed States*. New York: Oxford University Press.

Haass, Richard (1990). *Conflict Unending*. New Haven, CT: Yale University Press.

International Committee of the Red Cross (1999). *People on War. General Report*. <http://www.onwar.org>. Accessed December 20, 1999.

Kaplan, Robert D. (1996). *The Ends of the Earth: A Journey at the Dawn of the 21st Century*. New York: Random House.

Lund, Michael S. (1996). *Preventing Violent Conflict: A Strategy for Preventive Diplomacy*. Washington, DC: United States Institute for Peace.

Mack, Andrew (2005). *The Human Security Report*. New York: Oxford University Press.

Miall, Hugh, Oliver Ramsbotham and Tom Woodhouse (1999). *Contemporary Conflict Resolution*. Oxford: Polity.

Minow, Martha (1998). *Between Vengeance and Forgiveness: Facing History after Genocide and Mass Violence*. Boston: Beacon Press.

Philpott, Daniel (ed.) (2006). *The Politics of Past Evil*. South Bend: University of Notre Dame Press.

Singer, Max, and Aaron Wildavsky (1996). *The Real World Order*. 2nd edn. Chatham, NJ: Chatham House.

Stedman, Stephen (1999). *International Actors and International Conflicts*. Rockefeller Brothers Fund, Project on World Security.

United Nations (1996). *The Blue Helmets: A Review of United Nations Peace-Keeping*. 3rd edn. New York: United Nations.

Weiss, Thomas (1999). *Military-Civilian Interactions: Intervening in Humanitarian Crises*. Lanham, MD: Rowman and Littlefield.

Weiss, Thomas, and Cindy Collins (1996). *Humanitarian Challenges and Intervention: World Politics and the Dilemmas of Help*. Boulder, CO: Westview.

Zartman, I. William (1989). *Ripe for Resolution*. 2nd edn. New York: Oxford University Press.

PART 2

Theory

CHAPTER THREE

The Role of Theory

I pass with relief from the tossing sea of Cause and Theory to the
firm ground of Result and Fact.
—Winston Churchill

People who actually try to solve international disputes rarely think about the role that theory plays in their work. Many go so far as to reject one of the underlying premises of this book—that theory matters at all.

Winston Churchill certainly did that, in the statement that begins this chapter. More recently, the same sentiment found its way into the second paragraph of Richard Holbrooke's memoir about the diplomatic initiatives that led to the Dayton Agreement ending the war in Bosnia: "This was not a theoretical game between nation states, but a dangerous and unpredictable process" (1998: xv). John Marks, the founder and CEO of Search for Common Ground, often quotes Napoléon Bonaparte as saying, *"on s'engage, après on voit."* One gets involved, then one figures out what to do.[1]

The likes of Churchill, Holbrooke or Marks can, of course, be excused for not worrying about theory at the most charged moments of their political lives, when the pressure of events simply did not leave them the time to do so. That is not true for academics, however. In the kind of teaching and research most of us do, we cannot make much progress without theory.

In fact, everyone uses theory all the time whether they realize it or not. While we may not be aware of how they shape our thoughts or even that we are using them, theories serve as the mental lenses through which we view and interpret the world. As such, they determine how we make the judgments that govern how we act—average citizens and policymakers alike. Churchill's implicit theory revolved around the need for democracies to remain resolute in the face of totalitarian regimes such as that of Nazi Germany. Holbrooke's expectations were different, reflecting the more optimistic times of the first years after the end of the Cold War. Marks' statement acknowledges the fact that no two conflicts are alike, and therefore NGOs have to use somewhat different approaches to each of them.

---

[1] There is no evidence that Napoléon ever uttered exactly these words. Whether accurate or not, the quote does summarize the way that Search for Common Ground and other NGOs start their projects.

What is Theory?

As with everything else in academic life, there is no simple or universally accepted definition of theory. As it will be used here, a theory is an attempt to reach general conclusions about a broad body of material.

There are two main types of theories (Viotti and Kauppi 1999; Dougherty and Pfaltzgraff 1996; Booth and Smith 1995). Empirical theories seek to explain why certain phenomena occur and, therefore, focus on cause and effect relationships. Normative theories are designed to prescribe what we should do in dealing with those phenomena. Thus, empirical theories of conflict resolution analyze why at some times we can settle our disputes peacefully, while at others we turn to violence and war. A normative theory would lay out options we should use in trying to reach a certain goal, such as a nonviolent outcome that satisfies all parties to the conflict.

The two types of theories will be treated separately here. However, keep in mind that no theory is entirely empirical or normative. Theories that purport to be empirical invariably reflect the ideological and other biases of their creators. Similarly, the best normative theories are based on solid analyses of "what is" as well as of "what ought to be."

We should not expect any theory to satisfy everyone. There are gaping holes in what we know about international relations, especially about what motivates leaders to act as they do. Those uncertainties are especially important during times like ours, when things are changing so fast that some pundits claim change is the only constant in our lives. Furthermore, we disagree too much about normative goals and how to achieve them. And those disagreements get in the way of reaching agreement on empirical issues as well, something we will see time and time again in the case studies in Part 3.

Using Theory

Still, we should never underestimate the importance of theory, because it is by contrasting different theories that we make most progress in understanding a contentious field like international relations. That is the case because of four ways we can use theory in empirical analysis.

First, we need theory to help us organize what we think we know. The *New York Times* masthead proclaims that it includes "all the news that's fit to print." In fact, that isn't true. The *Washington Post*, for instance, gives American national politics far more attention. The *Times* includes all the news that its editors think is worthy to print and that fit into the number of pages they have available for the paper that day. They make their decisions using some simple rules about what they think is important and what will sell newspapers, rules which form a rudimentary theory of what it takes to run a successful "quality" daily paper in these times when fewer and fewer newspapers are making a profit.

At the very least, then, theories help us to organize information. They point us toward some pieces of evidence and away from others. They give us intellectual cubbyholes (for example the domestic news, foreign news, sports, business, and other sections of a newspaper) into which to put the information we gather, and they supply an order in which to analyze it.

Different theories do that in different ways. Realists have us focus on the international system, the balance of power, geopolitical issues, and the (hoped-for) rational actions of leaders. Their mainstream critics, usually dubbed pluralists, liberals or ideal-ists, draw our attention to the often-complicated and anything-but-rational nature of domestic politics. Globalization theorists broaden our horizons even further by includ-ing international organizations,* multinational corporations, and nongovernmental organizations.

Secondly, theory allows us to think at a more general and abstract level. Educational theorists argue that one of the toughest challenges students have to face is learning to take a concept encountered in one context and apply it in another. What does learning about the Holocaust teach me about genocide in general? Can I use the insights gleaned from the dreadful history of the Third Reich and its "final solution" to help me under-stand ethnic cleansing in Bosnia or Darfur?

To do that, Rosenau and Durfee tell us we have to move up an intellectual "ladder of abstraction." We do so by asking the syntactically awkward question "Of what is this an instance?" (2000: 3). The Holocaust was an instance of European fascism. Even more gen-erally, it was an example of genocide, the most horrific kind of human rights violation.

Put in slightly different terms, a theory helps us understand common patterns, or similarities and differences we find in a large number of related phenomena. Why is it that the most authoritarian regimes engage in massive abuses of human rights? By con-trast, why is it that democracies rarely—if ever—do so?

Thirdly, empirical theory can be a powerful tool for reaching conclusions in what may strike you at first glance as an odd way. No theory can ever be proven true.

Useful Websites

After years of looking, I still have not found any outstanding websites dedicated to international relations theory.

That does not mean that the internet is of no use to people studying international theory. If you go, for instance, to the Virtual Library's site on international relations, you will find that almost all the entries will provide some links to theoretically rich sites: www.etown.edu/vl/.

Realistically, however, you are most likely to find useful material from sites such as CIAO (Columbia International Affairs Online), Infotrac, ProQuest, Project Muse, Jstor, and similar reference sources that include full texts of journal articles. I have not provided the URLs for these sites here, since they are typically services that can only be reached through a library or research institute that has paid the relevant subscrip-tion fees.

Researchers can gather an enormous amount of evidence. However, it is always possi-ble that they missed a case in which they would have found that the theory's predictions and explanations were inaccurate. Similarly, researchers can never be certain that there will not be some future event that undermines the theory.

Thus, the critical characteristic of a theory is that we can falsify it or show that its pre-dictions or explanations are wrong. Once we have done that, we can take an even more vital step, and ask ourselves why the theory failed in the cases under consideration. In so doing, we can improve both the theory and our overall understanding of the subject under consideration.

To see what it means to falsify a theory, start with Thomas Friedman's variation of the controversial theory that democracies do not go to war with other democracies because of the values, cultures and other phenomena they share. In early 1999, he argued that "no two countries that both had McDonald's had fought a war against each other since each got its McDonald's" (1999: 195). He claimed that what he called the "golden arches theory of conflict prevention" existed because of the economic, cultural and other "globalizing" links that drew such societies together and raised the cost of going to war with each other.

Fortune Cookies

It's not just Big Macs that are important here from a culinary and theoretical perspective.

Jennifer 8 Lee (2008) has written a masterful book, *The Fortune Cookie Chronicles*, in which she demonstrates that fortune cookies are almost certainly the creation of Japanese Americans living in California. There is no General Tso's chicken anywhere in China. The cheap Chinese bus that runs between New York and Washington was created to transport restaurant workers, almost all of whom are from Fujian province.

The specifics of her book are not important, especially for someone who likes General Tso's chicken. Rather, what Lee tells us is to take conventional wisdom (fortune cookies are Chinese) and question it. Then you learn things.

8 is in fact her middle name. It signifies beautiful in Chinese.

Friedman understood that his theory had its share of limitations, because he went on to point out that someday there would be a war between countries with McDonald's. In fact, it happened in the first weeks after his book was published. The heavily McDonaldized NATO powers went to war with Yugoslavia, whose seven McDonald's were shut when the war broke out but were back in business within a few days.

To see where falsification can take us, consider a more intellectually contentious example—the contemporary critiques of realism. Traditional realists claim that wars arise when states cannot otherwise adjust to changes in the balance of power among the leading states. Thus, they focus on such trends as the shifting European balance of power after the Napoleonic wars, and the events leading up to the two world wars. Similarly, realists account for superpower involvement in many of the regional conflicts between 1945 and 1990 as proxy struggles between the superpowers.

Realists, however, have had a much harder time categorizing the wars of the last 20 years. I am not saying that they have failed completely. We can develop realist analyses of recent conflicts. They are all, alas, an intellectual stretch. As a result, some international relations analysts have decided that realism has been falsified. As I will argue in the next chapter, I don't agree. I prefer other theories, but realism has its place.

The next step is not in itself empirical, since we cannot determine what is wrong with a theory simply by looking at the facts. Instead, the theorist has to take a step back from the data, and use his or her intuition and creativity to amend the old theory or develop a new one altogether. In this case, because the state is no longer the most important unit in international political life, we have to concentrate on domestic politics, ethnicity, and other factors in explaining what gave rise to most of today's most vexing conflicts.

Theory and Cases

This book is also written on the assumption that most people can easily deal with theory by moving up Durfee and Rosenau's ladder of abstraction from specific examples to general conclusions. That approach, however, flies in the face of scientific orthodoxy, which is deductive. Most experts are convinced that, because we need theory as an intellectual road map and as a tool for falsification, we need to start with it and then assess it in the light of the data we uncover.

Unfortunately, most professors find that students have a hard time getting beyond the theory if we focus only on abstract issues. To get around this problem in my classes, I rely heavily on the case study method, which is widely used in business and other professional schools. With it, I guide the class through a discussion of the critical issues in the case so that that I can move students up that ladder and get them to see the general arguments that flow from it. Unfortunately, a book is more linear than a classroom discussion. It has to go from page 1 to page 2, Chapter 1 to Chapter 2, Part 1 to Part 2, and simply cannot be as flexible as a teacher in a classroom. Therefore, this book is structured more along the theory-to-cases-to-revised-theory lines of conventional scientific work than are my classes.

Select Bibliography

Booth, Ken, and Steve Smith (1995). *International Relations Theory Today*. Cambridge: Polity Press.

Dougherty, James, and Robert Pfaltzgraff (1996). *Contending Theories of International Relations*. Boston, MA: Addison-Wesley.

Durfee, Mary, and James Rosenau (2000). *Thinking Theory Thoroughly: Coherent Approaches in an Incoherent World*, 2nd edn. Boulder, CO: Westview.

Friedman, Thomas L. (1999). *The Lexus and the Olive Tree: Understanding Globalization*. New York: Farrar, Straus and Giroux.

Holbrooke, Richard (1998). *To End a War*. New York: Random House.

Lee, Jennifer 8. (2008). *The Fortune Cookie Chronicles*. New York: Twelve Books.

Viotti, Paul, and Mark Kauppi (1998). *International Relations Theory*. Boston, MA: Allyn and Bacon.

CHAPTER FOUR

International Relations Theory and Conflict Resolution

You can never solve a problem on the same level you created it.
—Albert Einstein

Albert Einstein's statement above tells us a lot about conflict resolution theory. As we will see throughout this chapter and the rest of the book, disruptive disputes require new, creative, "outside the box" solutions. That does not mean, however, that the international relations theory I was exposed to as a student, most of which still dominates that field, is of no value. Rather, both traditional and new approaches to conflict resolution *together* can take us to a level other than the one at which the problem was created. We will start with traditional approaches, and then consider the newer ones.

Traditional Perspectives

Our opinion of the gods and our knowledge of men lead us to conclude that it is a general and necessary law of nature to rule whatever one can. The strong do what they have the power to do and the weak accept what they have to accept.
—Thucydides

Very few conflict resolution practitioners have advanced degrees in political science. That is both understandable and unfortunate. It is understandable because dozens of graduate programs that specialize in conflict resolution and peace-building have been created since the early 1980s outside the area of political science. It is unfortunate because traditional international relations theory can help us understand a lot about conflict resolution, especially the cases that most observers would cite as failures on our part.

International relations is one of the theoretically richest parts of political science, and the study of conflict has been at the heart of the field for well over two thousand years. That does not mean, however, that there is a large and sophisticated "mainstream" literature on international conflict *resolution*, because scholars have typically focused more on the conflict than on its resolution. (See the box on frames of reference.) Indeed, the best brief book on the subject (Nye 2008) focuses on the causes of major international disputes, and did not even have an entry in its index for "resolution" until the fifth edition was published a few years ago. Therefore, as in the next section on new approaches to conflict, we will have to extrapolate from a series of underlying theoretical principles to specific factors that could affect the ways international disputes are settled.

Different Frames of Reference

There are many reasons why the theorists covered in this chapter reach such different conclusions, but also why their ideas complement more than they contradict each other. None is more important than the issues or "dependent variables" they focus on.

Analysts who rely on new approaches to conflict resolution concentrate on strategies for ending disputes before they reach crisis point, and on building stable peace once a conflict has run its course.

By contrast, the theorists we will consider in the next few pages focus on why some crises turn to war and how the fighting is (finally) stopped.

Realism and Its Intellectual Cousins

Given the long-standing interest of international relations experts in war and conflict, no author can hope to do justice to the diversity of their analytical approaches in one part of a short chapter. Therefore, I have chosen to concentrate only on the central aspects of the two most widely used theories—realism and pluralism (also referred to as idealism and liberalism)—that are of most use in understanding how disputes are settled.

Realism is by far the oldest and most widely used theory in international relations. Indeed, its lineage can be traced back to Thucydides' *Melian Dialog*, an extract from which begins this section. Realists reach more pessimistic conclusions about the possibility of win-win conflict resolution, reconciliation, and stable peace than the theorists considered below because, like Thucydides, they are convinced that international relations is power politics. As Hans Morgenthau, the founder of modern realism, put it:

> All history shows that nations active in international politics are continuously preparing for, actively involved in, or recovering from organized violence in the form of war. (Kegley and Raymond 1999: 3)

As recently as the ongoing Iraq war, the United States and its allies demonstrated that Thucydides' simple statement still carries plenty of weight in explaining the outcome of conflict. This state of affairs is no accident. Originally, realists and similar theorists saw it as a reflection of our human nature. Today's neo-realists, however, emphasize how the nature of the international system makes conflict, violence and war so common in political life (Waltz 1959; Buzan 1991).

States do many things. To realists, however, protecting national security, which they define in terms of key geopolitical and other vital resources, is by far the most important challenge any state faces. If political leaders fail in this, they put their people and the very existence of their state at risk. Because such resources as wealth, population and territory are in short supply, states invariably compete with each other for them.

That competition is different from other forms of conflict, because the international system is anarchic. Realists do not use the term anarchic to suggest that states are at each other's throats all the time. Rather, they mean that there is no international state, no equivalent of the government in Washington or Warsaw, that can maintain order, enforce the law, or regulate interstate competition. Realists often call this a "self-help system" in which states have to look out for their own interests, or work with allies in a hostile environment.

The Gulf crisis of 1990–1 is instructive. There was no international state the Kuwaiti authorities could turn to in order to stop Iraq from invading. Similarly, while far too weak to halt Baghdad on its own, Kuwait did have allies who could build a coalition that eventually forced Iraq to withdraw.

The stakes of a conflict can be magnified by security dilemmas in which the actions of one state to protect its own security actually serve to weaken that of its opponents. Thus, as Yugoslavia was falling apart, Croats tried to protect their compatriots living outside the republic, which threatened the Serbs and thus helped fan the flames of their already considerable nationalism (Rose 2000).

The State as Level of Analysis

Most of the case studies in Part 3 are not primarily interstate in nature. It could also be argued that some of them do not involve the vital interests of the world's leading powers.

Therefore, the purest of realists might not include them in a list of conflicts they would focus on. However, given the changes and uncertainties of the last few years and the disruptive potential of each one, there are very few realists who have not expanded their frame of reference to include conflicts such as these.

In sum, conflict is an inescapable feature of international political life. And because the international system is anarchic, there is no equivalent of a national state that can routinely adjudicate disputes. Furthermore, because no state is likely to give in willingly to its rival(s), competition between states can become extremely tense. Therefore, states usually have to look out for their own interests on their own.

As a result, states also have to resort to the use of power, which political scientists typically define as one side's ability to get its opponent to do *what it otherwise would not do*. Those six italicized words in the definition of power are all-important here. The exercise of power is an attempt to get another state to act contrary to its own wishes and interests. It requires one state to try to exert its power by at least threatening the use of force. That does not necessarily require recourse to violence and war. Deterrence, alliances, and other strategies that the realists stress, can prevent fighting from starting. In fact, as the quantitative studies of warfare have shown, well under a quarter of the world's intense conflicts in which one side or the other threatens to use force actually lead to a full-scale war.

This is the case because realists expect states to behave rationally by calculating the likely costs and benefits of the various courses of action open to them. They should, thus, only use force when the likely gains in terms of vital national interests outweigh the losses they could realistically expect to incur.

These last few paragraphs suggest why cooperative problem-solving is so difficult to achieve in international relations. Once in a conflict, realists do not expect states to seek any sort of resolution as long as one of them is convinced it can win or at least avoid losing.

Win-win outcomes are possible only when both sides have reached the mutually hurting stalemate discussed below (Zartman 1989). More often, they keep the conflict going until one side wins and the other loses in so-called win-lose or zero-sum outcome.

To see this from a different angle, consider a recent typology of six types of security arrangements listed in Table 4.1. Each type depicts a way in which states and their allies go about trying to ensure their security. At one end of the spectrum is the creation of the security community. At the other are situations in which force is "needed" because the parties cannot readily reach agreements due to their own insecurity, ongoing tensions, and imbalances in the distribution of power.

The security arrangements at the top of the table do not lend themselves to win-win outcomes because of the particularly tense and unequal relations among the states involved in them. The closer you get to those in the bottom rows, the easier it is for states to cooperate and resolve whatever conflicts arise without coming close to the use of force. But, as realists would be quick—and correct—to point out, the "need" for win-win conflict resolution is greatest in cases shown near the top of the table, where it is least likely.

The focus on vital national interests also leads many realists to be skeptical about the kind of military involvement the United States and many other major powers have engaged in since the end of the Cold War. From the United States' point of view, prudent leaders are concerned only about their direct, national interests. The business of international relations is dangerous and risky, and states should focus only on their most vital interests in protecting their territory, population, and other critical resources. And, while it is tempting for a state like the United States to want to intervene when another state or states is engaged in immoral or inhuman activity, as was the case in, for instance, the former Yugoslavia and Rwanda, doing so does not make sense unless those critical interests are threatened.

Table 4.1 Patterns of International Security

Security Situation	Characteristics	Examples
Insecurity	Open hostility, or approaching it	The former Yugoslavia after 1991
Balance of power	Security through deterrence, or use of arms	India and Pakistan for most of the period since 1947
Spheres of influence	Coercive leadership by a strong power	Russia with Belarus today
Concert of states	Loose cooperation among somewhat differing regimes	NATO and the Partnership for Peace
Hegemonic community	One state dominates a cooperative alliance	NATO
Security community	Voluntary alliance, stable peace, cooperation	European Union

Source: Adapted from Kolodziej (1998: 18)

The Mainstream Critics

Realism's mainstream critics also stress the difficulties in forging win-win agreements to end conflict, albeit for markedly different reasons. As noted earlier, they have a number of labels. I have chosen to use pluralism because it reflects their major contribution to international conflict resolution in drawing our attention to the complexities of domestic political life, which make rationality and the associated pursuit of interests difficult, if not impossible, to achieve. It also does the same for win/win conflict resolution.

Values

That is the case, first of all, because values and beliefs always have an important role in the way international conflict is addressed (Moravcsik 1997). To see this, let us start with a statement by Kevin Toolis, a not unsympathetic observer of Irish republican politics, if not of the Irish Republican Army (IRA):

> In their hearts, the IRA's Volunteers saw themselves as defenders. It did not matter that there could never be a military victory. "Standing up to the British," standing up to the Protestants by bombing and killing, served its own purpose by maintaining the spirit, the very possibility, of resistance in the face of an overwhelming enemy. (Toolis 1995: 82)

People who take part in the kinds of conflict considered in this book believe very strongly in the justice of their cause in the ways Toolis suggests. Their commitment is not likely to waver if the possibility of a compromise to end the fighting is on the political horizon. More generally, goals other than the rational pursuit of either a win-win or win-lose outcome may matter most to them. For the working-class Catholics Toolis studied, standing up to the British and to the Protestants was a worthy end in and of itself, even if they had next to no chance of winning.

Participants in at least the weaker side of intense conflicts have deep feelings of injustice and persecution. Many have suffered and made tremendous sacrifices. Thus, the Rev. Frank Chikane endured far more hardship, during the apartheid years in South Africa, than most of us can conceive of. After 1977 he survived six rounds of detention, countless hours and unspeakable methods of torture, a year of hiding during the 1986 state of emergency, and finally in 1989, an assassination attempt that very nearly succeeded. Over the years, such abuse left him at various times paranoid, confused, and unable to walk, sleep or speak. Yet every physical and verbal assault only seemed to fuel his determination to fight back with his whole being (Goodman 1999: 31).

More recently, the statements made by Al Qaeda leaders demonstrate a strong belief in Islam and Islamic control of its traditional lands. Those ideas may not make a lot of sense to Western observers. That is not the point. What matters is the fact that those beliefs, rather than the realist's rationality, guides their behavior.

Psychological Dynamics

The same holds for three overlapping psychological dynamics that tend to drive the parties to a dispute farther apart.

The first is the image of the enemy (White 1984; Keen 1986; Frank and Melville 1988). While there is now impressive evidence that such negative attitudes can be overcome, there is equally impressive evidence that when they exist, they make it hard for adversaries to deal with each other in any sort of constructive way. Under conditions of anarchy and scarce resources, people often think of conflict in "we versus they" terms. We attribute "good" motivations to ourselves. More important for our understanding here, we tend to see our opponents as wholly evil, or at least as wholly responsible for the problem. Leaders use rhetoric about "the focus of evil in the world," "the Great Satan," or "the next Hitler." As we use stereotypes and assume the worst of our opponents, it becomes harder and harder to sit down and talk, let alone act rationally from a realist's perspective.

Second, political leaders are like the rest of us. They make mistakes of judgment and interpretation. At times, their political vision is clouded by biases introduced by the kind of stereotypical thinking discussed above. At others, they simply make mistakes based on limited or faulty information about the other side's capabilities or intentions (Jervis 1968). Such misperceptions are most likely to occur and have serious consequences at the height of a crisis, when leaders have to make momentous decisions quite quickly.

The third factor is "groupthink," or the tendency on the part of small and relatively isolated groups to make a decision and then never consider evidence that might lead them to question that initial choice (Janis 1983). The classic example comes from the Johnson administration's internal discussions on the Vietnam War. Advisers such as George Ball who voiced doubts about the administration's policies were shunted into the background. Others who began to question the conduct of the war, including Secretary of Defense Robert McNamara, were reluctant to air them for a variety of reasons, ranging from loyalty to the president to fear of losing their jobs and influence.

If the George W. Bush administration's critics are to be believed (Ricks 2007), the most recent tragic example of groupthink was the decision to invade Iraq in 2003. The administration received intelligence reports and recommendations that cast doubt on all of its major justifications for going to war. However, the president and his closest advisers only took seriously the advice that confirmed their own point of view, thereby plunging the United States into what would become the longest war in its history.

These psychological dynamics can pose particularly difficult obstacles to successful negotiations (let alone reconciliation) when cultural differences among the countries are involved (Cohen 1997; Avruch 1998). A country's culture consists of the general and often unspoken values and assumptions that "set the political stage." Raymond Cohen, in particular, has demonstrated that the greater the cultural differences between parties to a negotiation, the harder it is for them to reach agreement. Americans, for instance, have a legalistic approach that leads them to focus on "making a deal," whereas many people in Asia and the Middle East focus instead on the relationship that emerges in the discussions, on saving face, and on obtaining respect. At the very least, it behooves negotiators to know as much about the culture and values of the people they are dealing with as possible, something that all too rarely happens in practice. Indeed, cultural differences can be a problem within societies as well, something we will see later in how little direct experience whites had of black living conditions in South Africa, or Protestants of Catholics' lives in Northern Ireland, at the time serious discussions about ending those conflicts began.

Values and psychological dynamics are part of even broader trends in domestic politics that almost always comes into play in international conflict resolution. Realists are frequently criticized for treating the state as a "black box," the insides of which do not matter. Similarly, many advocates of win-win conflict resolution are so taken by their new approaches that they often fail to explore the "real-world" obstacles to their use. What the pluralists show us is that what happens "on the ground" invariably makes political life more complicated, and successful conflict resolution more difficult.

This is most obvious in the United States, whose political system based on the separation of powers makes any sort of rational decision-making difficult. Thus, in fall 1999, the late Senator Jesse Helms (Republican: North Carolina) finally allowed hearings on the nomination of Richard Holbrooke to be ambassador to the United Nations to proceed after delaying them for more than a year. Meanwhile, in the annual budgetary give-and-take, the Congress refused to appropriate funds the Clinton administration had pledged to help implement the Wye River Accord negotiated the previous autumn between Israel and the Palestinian Authority, although it did finally cave in during the final negotiations with the White House.

Not all states face the same degree or type of pressure from outside the foreign ministry, but all do to some extent. For our purposes, the degree to which they do is largely determined by the interplay of two main factors:

- How divided is the society over foreign policy and other matters?
- How open are the governing institutions to such pressures?

Democratic states provide at least some channels through which individuals and interest groups can influence the making of foreign policy. Polls have shown that the average voter in most countries is more interested in domestic politics than international relations. Nonetheless, there have been periods when public opinion has had a major impact on the way a conflict was settled.

Authoritarian regimes offer few opportunities for public participation, as we will most clearly in the chapter on Iraq. Nonetheless, at various times during Saddam Hussein's rule, angry Kurds and Shiites rose up in revolt.

Whatever type of regime a country has, the state will face the most pressure if it is deeply divided, as the United States and its allies have been over the Iraq war. Indeed, most observers think that opposition to the war from within his own party forced British Prime Minister Tony Blair's decision to retire in 2007.

There will be less pressure when the divisions are not very intense. That has been the case for most of the post-war years in Japan, especially regarding trade policy. It also was true of the United States during the early Cold War years, when Senator Arthur Vandenberg made his famous statement that "politics stops at the water's edge."

That said, most states involved in an intense international conflict will face significant pressures from their own societies. For example, protests from the Protestant community delayed implementation of parts of the 1998 Good Friday Agreement in Northern Ireland for more than a year. Similarly, many observers worry that sooner rather than later the African National Congress government will have to provide more jobs and services for blacks, a change which, at present, can only come at the expense of the white minority. Most recently, of course, the insurgency in Iraq has made a tough task all the more difficulty for the American military and the new Iraqi regime.

Useful Websites 1

There will be two of these boxes in this chapter. This one focuses on traditional approaches. The next one will do the same for newer ones.

The Conflict Processes Section of the American Political Science Association has a site with research papers presented at its sessions along with a series of links to home pages with other data and research findings: <http://wizard.ucr.edu/cps/cps.html>.

The Institute for Security and International Studies has one of the best general websites among the think tanks: <http://www.isis-online.org>.

The Carnegie Endowment for International Peace in Washington DC has long sponsored high quality research on a number of issues, especially nuclear non-proliferation: <http://www.ceip.org>.

The University of California's campuses cooperate with the Institute for Global Conflict and Cooperation: <http://www-igcc.ucsd.edu>.

The Canadian military provides an excellent site that, not surprisingly given Canada's history, emphasizes peacekeeping as well as conflicts themselves: <http://wps.cfc.dnd.ca>.

Professor Rudolph Rummel of the University of Hawaii has by far the most extensive site, with data and findings on the controversial theory linking democracy and peace: <http://www2.hawaii.edu/powerkills>.

The Democratic Peace

There is one finding from the pluralist literature that could provide some support for analysts or activists who believe in win-win conflict resolution and stable peace. There is now strong support for theories about the "democratic peace" (Russett 1993; Weart 1998; but for a contrary view, Gowa 1999). Democracies rarely, if ever, go to war with each other. They fight other kinds of regimes, and many have acted oppressively toward some of their own citizens, a point we will see in the Northern Ireland and Israeli cases. Nonetheless, virtually every observer is convinced that there is a link between democracy and peace.

There is far less agreement about why the "democratic peace" exists or what its implications are for conflict resolution. One version holds that the tolerance and compromise that are a central part of domestic political life in a democracy carry over into international affairs (Muravchik 1996). If that proves to be the case, it may well be that if democracies continue to take root in the former Soviet bloc and the Third World, we will see a decline in the number of violent international conflicts.

Eight Factors

This has been a long section that, at times, had to be rather abstract. Therefore, it is important to highlight eight factors from the foregoing that will be important in Part 3, before turning to newer theoretical perspectives. The eight fall into two categories.

The first three focus on why win-win conflict resolution and stable peace are so difficult. The others involve opportunities to make progress in settling a dispute, though—reflecting the pessimism of most international relations theorists—doing so falls far short of the kind of conflict resolution discussed in the previous chapter.

Obstacles

1. Institutions of global governance may be more active now than they were twenty or thirty years ago. However, they are still rather ineffective when it comes to intense conflict, because of their own weakness and the anarchy of the international system as a whole. In short, The UN and other international organizations can have an impact, but they do so largely on the margins.

This point can be seen in the rise and decline of UN operations since the 1990s. In the first half of that decade, the UN was involved in more missions than in the first forty years of its history combined. What's more, some of those missions went well beyond traditional peacekeeping efforts. Yet, when it came to the civil war that ripped apart Yugoslavia and the 2003 invasion of Iraq, the UN could not muster the support needed in the Security Council to act decisively. In this decade, the UN has often found itself without the funds to take on all the missions it might have wanted to. More importantly, because it lacked troops of its own it has had to rely on soldiers from member nations, many of whom are at best ill-disciplined, as we have seen in sexual and other scandals in the Democratic Republic of Congo.

2. Longstanding disputes are most often resolved only after they have reached a hurting stalemate, at which point the parties realize that the costs of continuing the fighting far outweigh any potential benefits, because victory has come to seem all but impossible. Not surprisingly, the parties to the dispute become more amenable to negotiations once that point has been reached.

However, the years of conflict and combat also leave the participants bitter. As we will see in Northern Ireland, that does not mean that they become easily open to reconciliation and the other parts of the peacebuilding process. More worrisome is the fact that so many conflicts reignite within a few years of an agreed ceasefire. That has led some observers to speak of "orphaned agreements" that wither and die because leaders lack the political will to push beyond an initial treaty or agreement.

3. Domestic politics almost always makes the search for win-win conflict resolution more difficult. There is no need to repeat the specific points made earlier, except to reinforce the pluralists' caution that the complexities of domestic political life render the pursuit of stable peace—and any other goal—extremely difficult in the short as well as the long run. The only exception comes in those rare moments when the active members of a society reach what Daniel Yankelovich (1999) calls public judgments on new principles, and agree to set off in a wholly new political direction. Those moments have been extremely rare in foreign policy.

Opportunities

4. The least intrusive of the policies that can reduce tensions is humanitarian intervention, in which the international community provides aid to civilians and refugees who have been caught up in the fighting. This kind of intervention is not new, having been

formally begun with the creation of the International Committee of the Red Cross (ICRC) in 1864.

The ICRC's charter defines what humanitarian intervention has traditionally entailed. It obliges the organization to be strictly neutral, and to aid all sides in a conflict. That role is vitally important in today's complex emergencies, because the fighting leads to social, economic, demographic and environmental problems, as well as to bloodshed and physical destruction. Indeed, armies are often used to distribute food, medicine and other material, and to protect aid workers who distribute them in the combat zone.

Most important for our purposes, the UN's various aid agencies and many non-governmental organizations have begun to see humanitarian relief as part of a broader peace process. It may be a political "carrot" they can use to try to persuade the antagonists into negotiation. Still, the "right to respect" is now enshrined in international law. This was easiest to see in the reaction to the tsunami that devastated much of the coastal regions of southeast Asia in 2004. What is not clear yet is how humanitarian relief (a matter on which most people agree) can be translated into concrete political steps toward conflict resolution—an issue which is far more controversial.

5. There are two political "sticks" to go along with the "carrot" of humanitarian relief. States and alliances have long used the threat of force to induce their adversaries to go along with their wishes, which Alexander George and his colleagues called "coercive diplomacy." As George defined it:

> Coercive diplomacy bears a close resemblance to the ultimatum. [It involves] a specific demand on the opponent, a time limit for compliance, and a threat of punishment for noncompliance. (1994: 2)

Until recently, coercive diplomacy had been used primarily for conventional foreign policy goals, not as part of a strategy for achieving stable peace. That has begun to change with, for instance, the growing imposition of sanctions by either ad hoc collections of states, the United Nations, or other international governmental organizations.

Sanctions typically take one of two forms:

- an arms embargo that blocks the transfer of weapons to either a state or all parties to a conflict
- broader bans on trade and other economic transactions, such as freezing the overseas bank accounts of individuals and/or organizations in the offending states.

Given their apparent failure to force Iraq to pull out of Kuwait in 1990, or to compel Saddam Hussein to cooperate with weapons inspectors in 2002 and 2003, many realists think sanctions are not likely to work. However, more systematic research has shown that sanctions, other threats, and skilful diplomacy have shown that coercive diplomacy can be effective. To do so, sanctions must be enforced effectively, imposed on economic sectors that can truly harm the leaders who are being targeted, and given enough time to have an effect. If the South African case is any indication, that time period can last years rather than merely a few weeks or months.

6. The second "stick" is the use of armed force through what is euphemistically called peace imposition. Obviously, the use of force is not new. However, in the past the international community rarely intervened in the domestic politics of states—even those that

had been deemed to have violated international norms or law. Though anticipated by the UN Charter, the Cold War superpower rivalry made such intervention difficult, if not impossible, between 1945 and 1990.

Now, however, intervention has become a far more frequently used device. On occasion, the UN and other international bodies have gone beyond traditional peacekeeping and taken a far more proactive stance towards some particularly violent conflicts, as in East Timor in 1999 and 2000. In most such conflicts, fighting is still occurring or could break out again at a moment's notice. In most recent cases, the international forces have intervened over the objections of at least one of the parties to the conflict.

Peace imposition operations are different from traditional forms of international intervention in another way, reflected in a term often used to describe such interventions: "peacemaking." As the NATO allies loudly proclaimed in the spring and summer of 1999, they did not launch the air war on Serbia just to stop the ethnic cleansing and other abuses in Kosovo. Rather, they viewed the fighting as the first step in a campaign to move toward something like stable peace.

There are, however, serious doubts about both the cost and potential effectiveness of peace imposition. The wars against Iraq involved vast numbers of American and other allied forces, but those victories were limited at best. Saddam Hussein, Slobodan Milosevic (until his defeat at the polls in late 2000) and their regimes remained in power. In Iraq, human rights abuses and violations of internationally imposed weapons bans continued. Even otherwise supportive observers have questioned the scale of the interventionist attacks, worrying that they may have violated the Geneva Conventions and the more general principles of just war theory in both conflicts. Meanwhile, few efforts at reconciliation were made, since the allies had demonized their erstwhile opponents, whose own indignation toward the West only increased. Put simply, the actual use of force can make long-term peace-building difficult, especially if one of the major intervening states plays a major role in reconstruction and stability.

That is especially true of the United States. To use the words of the 1960s folk singer, Phil Ochs, the United States and their allies sometimes acted as if they were the "cops of the world," without either fully taking on the role or considering the negative consequences for long-term peace and stability of having done so.

7. There has also been increased interest in holding the men and women responsible for genocide and other offenses legally accountable for their actions. But this is another area where the realists and other mainstream international relations theorists point out the relative powerlessness of the United Nations and other transnational bodies. Few observers object to the strengthening of international criminal courts, but skeptics are quick to point out that they are still extremely weak. Relatively few of the most heinous violators of international law have been brought before international tribunals. To make matters worse, the United States has refused to ratify the ICC treaty; it also independently prosecuted Saddam Hussein and his colleagues on its own, along with a new Iraqi government which it totally controlled.

8. As we will see in the next section, even some conservative analysts have argued that the spread of democracy to almost all of Europe has made war in those countries all but unthinkable. Critics, however, have pointed out two problems with democratization. First, as noted earlier, we really do not understand what makes the democratic peace work. It may not involve democracy at all, but perhaps cultural norms common in Western

Europe and North America that cannot be readily exported, whatever institutions a country adopts. Second, and probably more important, building democracy is a lot like eroding the image of the enemy. It takes a decade or more of the smooth and proper functioning of elections and representative institutions before most political scientists are prepared to acknowledge that a country has a stable democratic regime. And, as we have seen time and time again, the parties to a dispute who have reached a tentative peace agreement rarely allow that kind of time.

New Theory

> *Stable peace can almost be measured by the amount of dust on the plans*
> *for the invasion in the various war offices.*
> —*Kenneth Boulding*

This section outlines new theories that show us why win-win conflict resolution and stable peace are at least possible. As noted in Chapter 1, the new and traditional schools of thought will not be treated as opposites. Instead, we will use the case studies in Part 3 to show that they help us understand both the nature of international conflict and how we end it.

We do not have sophisticated theories that explain why win-win conflict resolution occurs. That should not be surprising, since it has only been in the last generation that scholars have begun examining international conflict beyond the initial ending of the fighting. (See Fisher 1969, however.) That does not mean that there are no useful analytical perspectives for us to use. In fact, there are three broad schools of thought we can draw on. However, as is often the case in any new field of inquiry, their intellectual roots lie in other fields than international relations.

Overlaps With Traditional Theory

Some actually have close ties to the theories considered in the previous section, and two of those overlaps will be important in the rest of this book.

First, not all theorists who would have placed themselves in the realist camp think we have to live in a dog-eat-dog world. One group, largely inspired by the late Headley Bull of Oxford, argues that there is what he called an "international society." Bull was a committed realist, but also argued that states and other actors could overcome anarchy and create arrangements through which policy-makers can reach agreements that fall short of violence. More recently, Steven Krasner and others have highlighted the importance of international regimes. Krasner, who served as director of the State Department's Office of Policy Planning, claimed that states reach formal and informal agreements to build something akin to Bull's international society. Such theorists point to effective international organizations whose roots can be traced back to the International Telecommunications Union formed in the 1860s. They may not have military forces to enforce their rules, but nonetheless their member states and other organizations obey them. To see their influence, consider how easy it is to send snail-mail and emails, or to have your possessions follow you in an international move. In our case, all of our belongings were packed and moved without incident between the United States and the United Kingdom in the late 1990s. We did have the benefit of diplomatic rules. But at the same time that we moved back from the UK, our best friend moved from the UK to Israel as a non-governmental employee, and had no more trouble moving his books, computers and furniture than we did.

Second, some conservative scholars have charted the progress made since the end of the Cold War in shaping either international society or regimes. The first team was led by Aaron Wildavsky and Max Singer, as mentioned above. Often connected to the "neo-con" movement in the United States, they persuasively made the case that as the EU and NATO expanded, the "zone of peace" in which war was implausible, and the "zone of conflict" where people still fought with each other, expanded. A decade after they first wrote, Thomas Barnett published *The Pentagon's New Map* (Barnett 2003). Barnett had spent his whole career charting new challenges to American security. But in this book, he showed that the real new world division is between what he called the "integrated core" and the "disenfranchised gap." Analysts disagree about which states should be in the zone of peace or the integrated core, but wherever the lines are drawn, there is a tremendous potential for bringing states in those two regions together. And, as with the arguments about the democratic peace, none of these observers dig deeply enough into why this has occurred; nonetheless, the fact that zones of peace and an integrated core have emerged opens doors to other ways of resolving long term and intense conflict.

Systems Theory

But in a few important new ways, the new theories are qualitatively different from those that grow out of realism and its intellectual cousins. The first is based in systems theory, and its spin-offs in chaos and complexity studies (for non-scientific audiences, the best introductions are to be found in Capra 1982; Senge 1990, 1999; Gleick 1987; Waldrop 1992), and among journalists studying globalization (Horsman and Marshall 1995; Friedman 2007).

Systems theory uses interdependence as an intellectual starting point, and leads us to win-win conflict resolution and stable peace as possible empirical as well as normative outcomes. As such it offers a new paradigm not just for conflict resolution but for international relations as a whole, a point we will return to in the conclusion of the book.

Because a system is completely interdependent, the analyst has to explore how the behavior of each actor affects every other actor. (See box below.) This has vital implications for such basic concepts in international relations as the national interest. Thus, if a state tries to get what it wants but provokes a powerful response from its adversaries, its apparent pursuit of its self-interest can turn out to be highly counterproductive, as we will see in the case of Iraq's invasion of Kuwait.

Systems theory also gives a prominent role to "feedback," or how my actions today shape what you do tomorrow. If my actions harm you, you are likely to be resentful and want revenge. But if my actions seem to help you, the opportunities for building a better relationship grow. In a larger system such as an international conflict, everyone affects everyone and everything else. Or as the cliché has it, "what goes around comes around."

Systems and the Systemic Level of Analysis

There is a potential point of terminological confusion here. Many realists and other traditional international relations theorists often work at what they call the "systemic" level of analysis. In so doing, they focus on the interaction of states with each other.

Systems theory goes much farther in three respects. First, it leads us to consider all actors, not just states. Second, it forces us to focus on all international political issues and not just geopolitical ones. Finally, because it brings feedback into the intellectual picture, it forces us to use a much longer-term perspective in which the rationality of traditional theories in general, and zero-sum decision-making in particular, lose a lot of their luster.

Systems theory also leads us to take into account the medium- and long-term effects of our actions on the entire system. Thus, we cannot understand today's events without exploring their historical roots, often stretching back for many generations. Traditional international relations theories are mostly based on short-term analyses that are like intellectual snapshots. Systems theory provides the intellectual equivalent of a videotape, and an extended-play one at that.

That does not mean that systems theorists always anticipate positive outcomes. In fact, many proponents of it use the two Chinese characters for the English term "crisis" in discussing how a system works. The first character represents "danger," the meaning most Westerners have in mind when they think about a crisis. The second is "opportunity." To use a different metaphor drawn from complexity studies, a system can behave like a vicious circle and deteriorate. By contrast, it can behave like a virtuous circle and improve its performance over time. Many of these theorists talk about "complex emerging systems" whose structures and behaviors only develop over time, and can evolve in a wide variety of different ways.

The potential for decay can be seen most easily in environmental studies. As most ecologists see it, the earth is a single life-support system. If it is disrupted in one place, unpredictable and often undesirable consequences can occur everywhere, something we see most clearly in the threats posed to ecosystems by the accumulation of greenhouse gases producing "global warming," so powerfully discussed in former Vice-president Al Gore's film and book, *An Inconvenient Truth* (2006).

By contrast, management theorists have pointed out that systems can also improve over time through what they call "social learning." The executives and workers of successful companies take the feedback or information about past events, and develop new strategies to build on prior successes and overcome earlier failures (Senge 1990, 1999).

The capacity for growth and decay, plus the need to consider the long term, have profound implications for international relations and conflict resolution. Put simply, anything other than a win-win outcome tends to produce systems that decay at least over the medium to long term.

From a systems perspective, win-lose or lose-lose conflict resolutions tend at best to produce temporary victors, while the vanquished lick their wounds and sow the seeds of more—and often more intense—conflict at some later point. There are times when win-lose outcomes are so definitive that the relationship starts again from scratch afterwards, as was the case between the Allies and Germany and Japan after 1945. However, such cases are few and far between in international relations today.

Seen in these terms, win-win outcomes *can* set the participants off in a very different and more constructive direction, by using feedback and other features of the complex relationships involved to find leverage points that seem to lend themselves to more constructive solutions. The word "can" was emphasized in the preceding paragraph because even the most optimistic advocates of systems theory acknowledges that interdependence and win-win outcomes do not always produce a more harmonious relationship.

Conflict Resolution Theory

The literature on conflict resolution takes us a lot farther and in a different direction (Yankelovich 1999; Fisher and Ury 1991; Mayer 2009). Win-win conflict resolution is now the "dominant paradigm" in interpersonal and corporate relations. That does not mean that theorists working in the field think it is the norm. Instead, most acknowledge the difficulties of reaching win-win outcomes that grow out of cultural differences, time pressures, dysfunctional relationships between those involved, and other issues that make cooperation difficult.

Scholars working in other fields argue that it is almost always possible to envision a win-win outcome that would satisfy all parties to a conflict. Some conflict specialists argue that win-win outcomes should not always be our goal, as in the case of an abusive husband or, for our purposes, where a conflict involves genocide. Nonetheless, for most international conflicts, progressing toward win-win outcomes is preferred by scholars and practitioners working from this perspective. Making it happen can be very difficult, but is most likely to occur when all or most of the parties:

- understand that it is in everyone's long-term interest to reach a mutually satisfying agreement.
- look for new and creative solutions to their problems. This is especially important for the more powerful party in an asymmetric relationship, that typically has the most room for maneuver and most resources to offer.
- focus on their general goals, not their specific demands.
- treat each other with dignity and respect.
- use trained mediators or other "third parties" to help antagonists see new options and reach an agreement.
- see the conflict as part of a larger relationship that can improve or deteriorate over time, depending on the choices they make.
- perhaps most importantly of all, understand that no complex conflict can be settled with a single agreement.

Two Motivations

Although they do not explicitly draw on systems theory, Hugh Miall, Oliver Ramsbotham and Tom Woodhouse (1999: 5–9) have developed a simple chart (reconfigured here as Table 4.2) that highlights much of what we know about how win-win conflict resolution can occur, but also why it happens so rarely.

Table 4.2 Approaches to Conflict

Concern for self	Concern for others	
	LOW	HIGH
HIGH	Aggression	Cooperation
LOW	Withdrawal	Capitulation

Source: Adapted from Miall, Ramsbotham, and Woodhouse (1999: 6)

Participants in conflict can be influenced by two main sets of motivations. They tell us to focus on two of our own concerns. The first is how much I care about what happens to me as a result of the conflict. The other is how much I care about what happens to you. These motivations do not ask how much you care about what happens. Instead, they have me focus on the stakes *I* have in what happens to you. As noted earlier, traditional international relations theory focuses all but exclusively on the former, while systems analysis compels us to consider the latter as well.

The combination of these two sets of motivations typically produces four types of outcome:

- Withdrawal from the conflict is most likely to occur in conflicts that are not high-priority matters to both parties.
- Capitulation more often occurs when the issue does not matter much to one party, and that person or group has a deep concern about what happens to the other side.
- Aggression is a common outcome when one party feels its own interests are at stake and has little concern for what happens to the other side.
- Cooperation is most likely when both sides have a strong self-interest and a strong concern for the people they are in conflict with.

The table reinforces a central conclusion in the literature on interpersonal conflict resolution that often gets short shrift from critics. Effective conflict resolution, reconciliation, and the creation of stable peace, do not simply involve being "nice." People cannot ignore their own self-interest, however one chooses to define the term. Giving in to the other side tends to leave the party who did so feeling as dissatisfied as someone who actually lost, and can thus also lay the foundation for future conflict. As noted earlier, successful conflict resolution requires meeting everyone's needs at least in the medium to long term.

The need to meet every party's needs also reinforces the importance of thinking about how one's actions affect everyone else in the system, including one's opponent. This may be a relatively new idea in international relations. It is not, however, unprecedented in other areas of political science. Other analytical schools (for example, those focusing on the link between political culture and democracy) emphasize less selfish actions in which incentives such as the good of the community as a whole come into play.

Effective win-win conflict resolution occurs when the parties to a dispute reach an agreement that satisfies them all. In the best of circumstances, they are able to resolve the conflict once and for all by eliminating the issue(s) that gave rise to it in the first place.

More often, all a single win-win outcome does is provide some of what both sides seek, thereby reducing tensions between them. If done "right," win-win decisions can also build trust between the parties, thus making it possible for the parties to go further and faster toward ending their dispute once and for all later on.

Many political scientists focus on compromise. Win-win conflict resolution is more than that. In a compromise, the various sides grudgingly give up some or all of what they seek, making an agreement that hurts them all the least. In win-win conflict resolution, all parties are happy with the outcome because, at least over time, they all will benefit from it.

Win-win conflict resolution does not appear magically out of thin air. It requires hard work, creativity, and flexibility on the part of everyone involved. The solution itself typically involves stepping back from the specific demands each side has, to consider broader concerns which they both share. It also requires at least one of the parties taking the initiative to seek an outcome that works better for them all. The party that takes the initiative often is the one with the most power in the relationship and realizes that it will have to share some of that power, as we will see in the chapters on South Africa and Northern Ireland. Finally, all parties need to understand that no single agreement will solve the problem overnight.

As a political scientist who works in Washington DC, I know that concern for other parties is in short supply, especially in intense conflicts. Similarly, many politicians who worry about their standing in the polls and how they will do in the next election find it hard to take the long-term consequences of their actions into account when making foreign policy.

Ten More Factors

The principles of systems theory, and insights drawn from the conflict resolution literature, can be distilled into the following ten factors that will be combined with the eight discussed earlier in the case studies and conclusions that follow. Because the authors whose work underlies these ideas believe strongly in win-win conflict resolution and reconciliation, their emphasis is on factors that contribute to cooperative problem-solving. However, given the "danger" as well as the "opportunity" side of systems theory, the factors are presented here to suggest that they can hinder, as well as bolster, win-win conflict resolution.

1. The most momentous changes in the international system over the last generation have put conflict resolution more prominently on the world's political agenda. The end of the Cold War did away with the old bipolar distribution of power that made intervention by the international community into domestic political life and disputes extremely difficult. The terrorist attacks of 9/11 and their aftermath also dramatically altered the political landscape in ways that made government–NGO cooperation more feasible. Meanwhile, globalization in all its guises has both shown people the horrible consequences of war even in such faraway places as Somalia or East Timor, and convinced many of us that we can and should be involved in trying to improve such dire situations.

In sum, the world's new geopolitical arrangements have provided governments, international organizations and NGOs with unprecedented opportunities to intervene and try to solve conflicts. In contrast, the sheer number and severity of those conflicts have also made it abundantly clear that the international community lacks the experience, expertise or resources to intervene effectively on a consistent basis.

2. It is not difficult to find an intellectually plausible win-win solution for just about every international conflict on the world's political agenda today. For instance, the status of Jerusalem has long been a major stumbling block in the Arab-Israeli peace process. There are, however, dozens of proposals on the table to turn Jerusalem into an international city, or for the Israelis and Palestinians to share it in some way as a joint capital of what would be two states.

The hard part lies in finding the political will to put these proposals into practice. Indeed, there are some issues that are so divisive that such win-win outcomes are not given serious consideration.

3. Many academics stress the importance of preventive diplomacy, which works best before a conflict turns violent or otherwise gets out of hand. Nonetheless, the international community in any of its guises is rarely able to address a conflict before the fighting starts. The Alliance for Peacebuilding recently began early-warning and prevention projects in Guinéa-Bissau and Guinéa, and would like to expand that work to more of the 25 or so states that seem most likely to explode.

Few observers doubt the value of preventive diplomacy. However, it is simply not something that politicians rely on very often or very effectively for two main reasons. First, a simmering crisis is not likely to reach their busy agendas, which are filled with what seem to them much more pressing needs, both at home and abroad. Second, even if diplomats or politicians see the need for early action, it is not easy (at least in democratic states) to raise the money or gain the popular support to put its soldiers in harm's way.

4. Win-win outcomes only occur if the parties involved can break down their image of the enemy, and hatred of them, and deal with other psychological factors that lead the parties to demonize each other. Psychologists have demonstrated that attitudes that blame our problems on the other side, and portray ourselves as wholly virtuous, are a major reason why so many conflicts escalate into violence. From this perspective, conflict resolution advocates have to replace those attitudes with new ones that reflect the concern for others discussed above, reassure worried adversaries, build on positive incentives, create trust, and transform the relationship into one in which cooperation and win-win outcomes are at least possible.

But even the relatively successful examples we will consider also illustrate one of the major problems associated with such attempts at conflict resolution. It usually takes a long time to change people's attitudes and values, because the most effective work is done on a person-by-person basis.

5. The fourth factor points to the fifth. Leadership is critical. In the last few years, we have seen an unusual number of political leaders who took risks to increase the possibilities for peaceful conflict resolution: Mikhail Gorbachev and others who brought East and West closer, Nelson Mandela and F. W. de Klerk who ended apartheid, or the British and Irish politicians who made the 1998 Good Friday Agreement possible. Sometimes the "leaders" are not prominent individuals, as we have seen in the roles that the activist John Prendergast and the actor Don Cheadle have played in making Americans aware of the genocide in Darfur.

Moreover, some negotiation theorists now argue that the diplomatic challenge requires more of our leaders than was the case before the end of the Cold War, because building stable peace requires much more than simply stopping the fighting. Rather, we need new types of diplomacy and leadership that address the fundamental injustices and inequalities that gave rise to the conflict in the first place. This is never easy. It is especially difficult when states have different priorities and resources, which means that they often end up talking past each other. What's more, today's negotiations are much more complicated even than those of the Cold War years, when two states with their national security interests dominated so much of international life. Now we have to deal with literally dozens of issues, nearly 200 world states, and countless other parties.

Conversely, history provides us with even more examples of intransigent leaders such as Saddam Hussein or the ruling elite in Sudan, who make reaching agreements exceptionally difficult. Even politicians who talk about building bridges in such places as Israel or Palestine often deepen divisions instead, because the rhetoric they use is often interpreted by the other side as biased and insensitive.

6. There is even more compelling evidence that the parties to intense conflict rarely settle their disputes on their own. One example is South Africa in the early 1990s. Mandela, de Klerk and their supporters were able to reach their landmark agreement without significant outside support. More often, however, the services of a neutral third party are critical, especially in the pre-negotiation stage during which it is difficult to bring the antagonists to the table.

Third parties are most effective if they have no vested interest in the outcome of the conflict. With time, they can use their impartiality and their negotiating skills to ease the tensions that typically accompany this kind of bargaining by, among other things, instilling trust.

Sometimes, little-known ordinary citizens working through NGOs play an important role in helping to solve conflicts on a local or regional basis (Mathews 1997). Traditionally, NGOs were not involved in politics and concentrated on providing relief, development aid, and other support to societies in conflict and crisis. Over the last twenty years, however, hundreds of new NGOs that focus exclusively on conflict resolution have been formed, including two I have worked for.

But third parties are not a panacea. To begin with, despite the recent rapid growth of university and non-academic training programs, there are not enough mediators. Furthermore, it is often difficult to find a third party that is both influential and impartial enough. That is particularly true when the United States is involved. It often has to play a role, given its strengths and interests, as is the case in the Middle East. However, it is often too closely identified with one side of the dispute, and its representatives find it difficult to establish a trusting relationship with the other party.

7. The mass media—especially television—can also facilitate conflict resolution. At a time when news services from CNN to al-Jazeera have reporters working almost everywhere, it has become much easier to follow global events. Because CNN was the first global news network, the impact of the media is sometimes known as the "CNN effect" (Strobel 1997).

While it is hard to pin down with any accuracy, it seems certain that televised reports of the tumult in post-Saddam Iraq fed opposition to the war in the United States, while visits of the likes of Prendergast and Cheadle to Darfur helped build support among the American people to do *something*. The CNN effect, however, cannot be taken for granted. There are quiet crises in places like Sierra Leone or Eritrea that rarely make it into the pages of the *New York Times*, let alone the nightly news. Moreover, while the CNN effect may have shrunk the world so that we can get more information, it has also increased our expectations. As the news becomes available to us instantaneously, there is a parallel expectation that problems can be solved immediately.

Furthermore, the media can be part of the problem rather than the solution. News coverage of setbacks in Somalia in the early 1990s, for example, prompted the international community to withdraw rather than to intervene more forcefully.

The media are never unbiased, either in what they cover or in how the stories are presented. Thus Tim Pat Coogan, only half-jokingly, refers to the British and Irish press having looked at each other across the Irish Sea during the Troubles using "telescopes with the cap on" (1996: 296). The English government frequently put pressure on the press not to carry favorable coverage about the nationalist cause, let alone about the Irish Republican Army. The Irish press just as frequently chose to carry only stories that stressed the extremism of the Protestants in Ulster, or the intransigence of the authorities in London.

8. Stable peace cannot be built as the result of a single win-win decision. Instead, it entails a much longer and more difficult period of peace-building. In Fen Osler Hampson's words, peace has to be "nurtured." As the South African leadership has understood as well as anyone, a permanent end to a conflict requires transforming the relationship between the antagonists into one of cooperation through reconciliation. In the most comprehensive book on reconciliation, John Paul Lederach (1997: 29) argues that reconciliation includes the following steps that, in time, can alleviate the root cause(s) of the conflict:

- **Truth**—acknowledging the wrongs that have been committed
- **Mercy**—forgiveness of those wrongs and a new beginning to the relationship
- **Justice**—the establishment of new rights and programs for the oppressed
- **Peace**—the security of all, and the harmony and respect that come with it

States and international organizations have played a role in this regard. However, NGOs have generally been more effective than states, because they have been "on the ground" longer, have better local contacts, and are therefore better able to work with the parties to a conflict. There is considerable disagreement about the form reconciliation takes, apart from the acknowledgement that it will vary considerably from case to case and that it will take time. Some observers stress democratization, others social and economic equality. Some praise efforts like South Africa's Truth and Reconciliation Commission, others find it too forgiving of an old, repressive regime.

Unfortunately, the pressures of practical politics often make it hard to maintain the political momentum needed to move a peace process forward. Understandably, there is a collective sigh of relief when the violence stops. However, ending the combat almost always leaves the two sides far from a lasting agreement, because the issues that gave rise to the conflict in the first place have not been settled. In democratic countries, politicians also rarely have the luxury of making plans for the long periods needed to build a stable peace. Prudent politicians cannot realistically pursue policies that are going to harm their chances at the polls in at most a few years' time. Moreover, in these days of the spin doctor and focus group, politicians are always paying attention to their poll numbers, as well as (and perhaps more than) the demands of a conflict occurring thousands of miles away.

This is not only true of mainstream politicians. Thus, the American peace movement peaked during the Vietnam War, and again during the renewed Cold War tensions and arms build-up of the early 1980s. As soon as those immediate crises eased, the movement all but disappeared. Even hard-core activists are reluctant to take on tasks that may require a generation or more to complete. Along these lines, John Paul Lederach is by no means alone when he notes that he was nearly thrown out of a conference on reconciliation in Northern Ireland in the early 1990s, when he remarked that it might take as long to end that conflict as it did to create it in the first place.

9. The first students of conflict resolution were properly criticized for not devoting enough attention to the social, economic and environmental issues that originally give rise to conflict. In the simplest terms, if the international community and/or the parties to the dispute do not address the root causes of the conflict, it is likely to reappear. While most students of conflict resolution now have broadened their agendas to include these other types of social change, doing so makes us all the more aware of how difficult it is to achieve stable peace.

Ironically, the best example we can point to is one that has developed largely without conscious planning by political leaders. In the forty years since the Troubles began in Northern Ireland, the social status and economic conditions of the Catholic minority in Northern Ireland has improved dramatically. While the causal connections in such developments are always hard to determine, polling data suggests that those improvements helped convince many Catholics that they could adopt tactics inside the system, rather than pursuing revolutionary strategies to achieve their long-term goals.

10. There is no single approach to international conflict resolution that "works," however you define that term. That will be clearest in Chapters 7 and 8, in which we will see two very different kinds of third-party mediation. There is little doubt that George Mitchell's low-key, bridge-building work as chair of the negotiations was needed to help reach the Good Friday Agreement in 1998. So, too, was the more forceful (and some would say bullying) efforts of Richard Holbrooke in forging the Dayton Agreement that ended the war in Bosnia in 1995. Mitchell would not have been as effective in Bosnia, nor would Holbrooke have been in Northern Ireland.

The Two Theories Contrasted

At first glance, the two sets of theories introduced in this chapter are quite different from each other (See Table 4.3.) Both start with the assumption that resources are scarce, but after that their world views diverge dramatically. Realism and pluralism focus more on why conflict resolution has occurred so rarely throughout human history. Systems and conflict resolution theories seek to identify the factors that make win-win conflict resolution and stable peace possible in our globalizing world.

The theories, however, are not wholly incompatible. Each purports to analyze one segment of an international system to which the respective theory can apply.

Until recently, these theories would have been seen as mutually incompatible. But, the sea-change since 11/9 and 9/11 has led many of us to see that both sets of theories have merit, and that their feasibility depends on particular circumstances.

The end of the Cold War symbolized by 11/9 removed the roadblock that made thinking in terms of the right-hand column of Table 4.3 difficult, if not impossible. As we saw

Table 4.3 Traditional and New Theory Contrasted

Area of concern	Realism	Globalization
Availability of resources	Scarce	Scarce
Nature of relationships	Independent	Interdependent
Motivations	Self-interest	Good of whole
Time perspective	Short-term	Long-term
Nature of conflict	We *vs* them	We *with* them
Nature of power	Power *over*	Power *with*
Interpretation of conflict	Bad	Potentially good

in Chapter 3, we have begun to look at conflicts in a new light, both in terms of what caused them and the potential for cooperative mechanisms for solving them. At the same time, the tragedies of Somalia, Rwanda and the former Yugoslavia led at least some people (including this author) who had always been sceptical about the logic leading to violence, shown in the first column, to be more receptive to the limited use of force if it is part of an overall strategy for ending a conflict and moving toward stable peace.

The reaction by academics and practitioners alike to the 9/11 terrorist attacks and the wars in Afghanistan and Iraq have further blurred the line between the two theoretical camps. There is no better example of that than the growing cooperation between NGOs and the military, discussed in the last chapter. Almost all of my life as a conflict-resolution practitioner has been devoted to this work. When I came into this field in the early 1980s, I was squarely in the right-hand column. My current and former military colleagues assumed realism had to be the norm. Today, if you attended the meetings I do, you would find it difficult to differentiate between representatives of the NGOs, and those of the military and intelligence communities. We agonize over what to do in Iraq and Afghanistan (and the Middle East, Darfur and Mozambique) while the leaders of those states have come to realize that these conflicts, and the war on terrorism, cannot be won by military means alone.

We will keep shifting between the issues raised in the two columns of Table 4.3. Our challenge is to try to blend them, a point I will return to in the final two chapters.

References

Avruch, Kevin (1998). *Culture and Conflict Resolution.* Washington, DC: United States Institute for Peace.

Boulding, Kenneth (1978). *Stable Peace.* Austin, TX: University of Texas Press.

—(1988). "Moving from Unstable to Stable Peace." In *Breakthrough: Emerging New Thinking: Soviet and American Scholars Issue a Challenge to Build a World beyond War,* ed. Martin Hellman and Anatoly Gromyko, 157–67. New York: Walker.

Boutros-Ghali, Boutros (1992). *An Agenda for Peace.* New York: United Nations.

Buzan, Barry (1991). *People, States, and Fear: An Agenda for International Security Studies in the Post-Cold War Era.* London: Harvester Wheatsheaf.

Cohen, Raymond (1997). *Negotiating across Cultures: International Communication in an Interdependent World*. Rev. edn. Washington, DC: United States Institute for Peace.

Coogan, Tim Pat (1996). *The Troubles: Ireland's Ordeal 1966–1996 and the Search for Peace*. Boulder, CO: Roberts Rinehart.

Durfee, Mary, and James Rosenau (2000). *Thinking Theory Thoroughly: Coherent Approaches in an Incoherent World*, 2nd edn. Boulder, CO: Westview.

Fisher, Roger, and William Ury (1981). *Getting to Yes*. New York: Penguin.

Frank, Jerome, and Andrei Melville (1988). "The Image of the Enemy and the Process of Change." In *Breakthrough/Proriv*, edited by Anatoly Gromyko and Martin Hellman, 199–208. New York: Walker.

Friedman, Thomas L. (2007). *The World is Flat*. New York: Farrar, Strauss and Giroux.

Fromkin, David (1999). *Kosovo Crossing: American Ideals Meet Reality on the Balkan Battlefields*. New York: Free Press.

George, Alexander L., and William E. Simons, eds. (1994). *The Limits of Coercive Diplomacy*. Boulder, CO: Westview, 1994.

Gleick, James (1987). *Chaos: Making a New Science*. New York: Viking.

Goodman, David (1999). *Fault Lines: Journeys into the New South Africa*. Berkeley, CA: University of California Press.

Gore, Albert (2007). *An Inconvenient Truth*. New York: Rodale Press.

Gowa, Joanne (1999). *Between Ballots and Bullets*. Princeton, NJ: Princeton University Press.

Hampson, Fen Osler (1996). *Nurturing Peace: Why Peace Settlements Succeed or Fail*. Washington, DC: United States Institute for Peace.

Holbrooke, Richard (1998). *To End a War*. New York: Random House.

Janis, Irving (1983). *Groupthink*. Boston, MA: Houghton Mifflin.

Jervis, Robert. "Hypotheses on Misperception." *World Politics* 20 (1968): 454–79.

Keen, Sam (1986). *Faces of the Enemy: Reflections on the Hostile Imagination*. New York: Harper and Row, 1986.

Kegley, Charles, and Gregory Raymond (1999). *How Nations Make Peace*. New York: Worth, 1999.

Kolodziej, Edward (1998). "Modeling International Security." In *Resolving Regional Conflicts*, ed. Roger E. Kanet, 11–42. Urbana, IL: University of Illinois Press.

Lederach, John Paul. *Building Peace: Sustainable Reconciliation in Divided Societies*. Washington, DC: United States Institute of Peace, 1998.

Mathews, Jessica Tuchman (1997). "Power Shift." *Foreign Affairs* 76 (January/ February): 50–67.

Mayer, Bernard (2009). *Staying with Conflict*. San Francisco: Jossey Bass.

Mearsheimer, John (1990). "Why We Will Soon Miss the Cold War." *Atlantic Monthly* 266: 35–50.

Miall, Hugh, Oliver Ramsbotham, and Tom Woodhouse (1999). *Contemporary Conflict Resolution*. Oxford: Polity.

Moravcsik, Andrew (1997). "Taking Preferences Seriously: A Liberal Theory of International Politics." *International Organization* 51 (Autumn): 513–44.

Muravchik, Joshua (1996). "Promoting Peace through Democracy." In *Managing Global Chaos: Sources of and Responses to International Conflict*, ed. Chester Crocker et al., 573–86. Washington, DC: United States Institute for Peace.

Nye, Joseph (2008). *Understanding International Conflict: An Introduction to Theory and History*. 7th edn. New York: Longman.

Power, Samantha (2002). *A Problem From Hell*. New York: Basic Books.

Ricks, Thomas (2007). *Fiasco*. New York: Penguin.

Rose, William (2000). "The Security Dilemma and Ethnic Conflict." *Security Studies* 9, no. 4 (Autumn): 1–55.

Russett, Bruce (1993). *Grasping the Democratic Peace: Principles for a Post-Cold War World*. Princeton, NJ: Princeton University Press, 1993.

Senge, Peter (1990). *The Fifth Discipline: The Art and Practice of the Learning Organization*. New York: Doubleday Currency.

—(1999). *The Dance of Change: The Challenges to Sustaining Momentum in Learning Organizations*. New York: Doubleday Currency.

Singer, Max, and Aaron Wildavsky (1996). *The Real World Order*. 2nd edn. Chatham, NJ: Chatham House.

Strobel, Warren P. (1997). *Late-Breaking Foreign Policy: The News Media's Influence on Peace Operations*. Washington, DC: United States Institute for Peace.

Toolis, Kevin (1995). *Rebel Hearts: Journeys Within the IRA's Soul*. New York: St Martin's.

Waltz, Kenneth (1959). *Man, the State, and War*. New York: Columbia University Press.

Weart, Spencer R. (1998). *Never at War: Why Democracies Will Not Fight One Another*. New Haven, CT: Yale University Press.

White, Ralph (1984). *Fearful Warrior: A Psychological Profile of U.S.-Soviet Relations*. New York: Free Press.

Wilson, James Q. (1993). *The Moral Sense*. New York: Free Press.

Yankelovich, Daniel (1999). *The Magic of Dialogue: Transforming Conflict into Cooperation*. New York: Simon and Schuster.

Zartman, I. William. *Ripe for Resolution* (1989). 2nd edn. New York: Oxford University Press.

PART 3

Case Studies

CHAPTER FIVE

South Africa

This easy talk about a "rainbow nation," reconciliation, and nation- building—I think one must be very realistic about it. Given the inequalities, it's a lifelong process of trying to get a situation where we can live peacefully together—not necessarily be big friends—but somehow not use violence as a way of dealing with our conflicts. Perhaps that's what reconciliation is about at a national level—peaceful coexistence.
—Wilhelm Verwoerd

On July 18, 2008, Nelson Mandela celebrated his ninetieth birthday. The first president of the democratic South Africa governed by a multi-racial democracy spent almost a third of his life in prison because of his opposition to the dictatorial white rule known as apartheid.

It is fitting that we begin the case study section of this book with South Africa because when I was a student and later began my teaching career, my colleagues and I never assumed that Mandela would be released from prison, let alone become head of the wealthiest and most powerful country in Africa. More importantly for our purposes, with El Salvador, Cambodia, and a handful of other examples South Africa can be used to illustrate the conditions under which the new theories of conflict resolution are the most accurate empirically.

South Africa definitely deserves to be considered first. As recently as 1990, it was ruled by a tiny white minority, which cruelly oppressed the black majority. Almost twenty years later after a largely non-violent transition, it is now governed by a Black-dominated political party, whose elder statesman is one of the most respected leaders in the world.

The transition to peaceful, democratic rule is by no means complete. South Africa has one of the highest rape and murder rates in the world. Much of the violence has political overtones, especially in the inter-tribal black on black attacks that have been a central feature of political life there. Also, there is still plenty of tension between blacks and whites, which seems certain to continue as long as the economic chasm between the two communities is not closed (for a fictional account of its turmoils, see Kunzmann 2006).

Nonetheless, South Africa has done what most observers thought was unthinkable a generation ago. Its leaders reached a sweeping agreement to end a struggle that antedated the arrival of the National Party to power in 1948 and the formal adoption of apartheid. Even more important for our purposes, the new regime led by the ANC (African National

Congress) has gone further than any other covered in this book to try to forge reconciliation between racial groups that had been in conflict since the whites first arrived in 1652. Most notable here is the work of the TRC (Truth and Reconciliation Commission), which has tried to do what its name implies—discover what really happened under apartheid and use that information to build bridges across racial and political lines.

The hopes and fears regarding the South African transition are encapsulated in the statement that begins this chapter. Wilhelm Verwoerd is undoubtedly right. Reconciliation does not mean we have to become best friends with those we disagree with. Rather, stable peace requires finding ways of non-violently settling the disputes that will inevitably arise in our lives. And, he is no doubt right that it will take time and may not, in the end, work out.

At Verwoerd's level, there is nothing unusual about his statement. Just about every prominent leader in the new South Africa has said more or less the same thing.

What makes it remarkable is the fact that Verwoerd is the grandson of H. F. Verwoerd, the National Party prime minister who was the main architect of apartheid. The fact that Wilhelm joined the ANC and worked on the staff of the TRC is a symbol of how far some whites have travelled. But, as Verwoerd's family shows us, that political journey is by no means over. His father, also Wilhelm Verwoerd, no longer speaks to him. So, the younger Verwoerd knows from first-hand experience that reconciliation will be a long, difficult, and not purely political process. Indeed, full reconciliation may never be achieved. But, more than other political leaders around the world, Verwoerd and his colleagues have taken important first steps in that direction both as apartheid collapsed in the first half of the 1990s and since then under the governments of Presidents Nelson Mandela and Thabo Mbeki, at least until the latter's forced resignation in 2008.

Theoretical Focus

The South African case provides our most clear-cut support for the theories that stress win-win conflict resolution. However, for the reasons noted in the box about the case study method below, I will not emphasize theoretical concerns at the beginning of this chapter and the five that follow. Instead, I will offer a brief list of issues to guide your reading, which we will return to at the conclusion of each chapter:

- the degree to which the changing nature of international relations contributed to the transition in South Africa
- the emergence of a "hurting stalemate" in which the major parties to the conflict concluded both that they could not win, and that they could not afford to continue the struggle in its current form
- the role leaders on both sides of the dispute played from the start of the negotiations onward
- the way the post-apartheid government in general, and the TRC in particular, have tried to weaken the image of the enemy, and other psychological barriers to reconciliation
- the attempt to address the social and economic inequalities that could imperil the entire transition.

Reading a Case

To move from the facts to theory, you need to know how to "read" a case so that you can go through something like the interactive experience you would have in a class-room with an instructor who uses the technique. Therefore, as you read, consider the following set of questions and guidelines.

- Get the story right. Be sure you can answer the journalist's five key questions: Who did what, where, when, and how?
- Put the case in its historical context, which is not the one we live in today. See how the events leading up to the case helped predispose people to act and think as they did at the time.
- Don't focus too much on the details. Concentrate instead on the general questions about conflict resolution and international relations that are addressed in the case.
- Ask why the case turned out as it did. Obviously, we cannot invent a time machine and "rerun history." Nonetheless, consider how decisions made as events unfolded narrowed the options available to the people involved. And, try to figure out what it would have taken for the case to have had a different outcome, including those you would have preferred and those you think would have been worse than what actually happened.
- Ask Rosenau and Durfee's question: "Of what is this case an instance?" In other words, what general conclusions does it lead you to? How might they apply to other examples of conflict?

South Africa: The Basics

South Africa is a large country by African standards. More than twice the size of Texas, it has nearly 44 million people.

It is also one of the most diverse countries in the world. It has 11 official languages: English and Afrikaans, along with nine indigenous African languages. More than two-thirds of its population is Christian. Most of the rest follow one of the traditional African religions, though there is a sprinkling of Muslims, Hindus, and Jews.

The most important characteristic of the South African population is race. Most South Africans still use the racial categories developed by the apartheid authorities (see Table 5.1.). About three-quarters of the population is black. Blacks, however, as the table also shows, earned only about a third of the country's total income during the latter years of apartheid. Whites, by contrast, make up 10 percent of the population but account for more than half of the income. About 60 percent of the whites are Afrikaners, descendents of Dutch, German and French immigrants, and speak Afrikaans. The rest are either of English origin or have assimilated into that culture. Less than 3 percent of the population are Asians from the Indian subcontinent, who were brought to work in South Africa in the late nineteenth century. The rest are coloreds, who are the mixed-race descendants of settlers and the *khoi* people, who lived near today's Cape Town on the south coast.

Table 5.1 The Racial Composition of South Africa

Race	Percentage of income (2001)	Percentage of population (1988)
Blacks/African	79	34
Colored	9	9
Indian/Asian	2	4
White	10	54

Although Indians and coloreds have done reasonably well economically, they were almost as severely discriminated against in other areas of life as blacks.

Roots of the Conflict

The roots of the conflict stretch all the way back to 1652, when a handful of Dutch settlers arrived at what is now Cape Town to set up a refueling station for ships sailing from Europe to Asia (Thompson 1995). The area was sparsely populated. The few Dutch settlers, however, established a harsh regime, which included the enslavement of the natives. They also gradually expanded their control outward into today's Western Cape province (see Table 5.1).

The Afrikaners lost control when the British seized the Cape from the Dutch during the Napoleonic wars. Shortly thereafter, English settlers began to arrive, and London soon abolished slavery (see Table 5.2).

These actions infuriated the conservative Dutch (or Boers as they became known). To make a long story short, most of them left the Cape region in 1835 and set off on what they today call the Great Trek. As they moved to the north-east, they fought pitched battles with the Africans they encountered, the most important of which occurred at Bloemfontein in 1838. What they took to be a miraculous victory reinforced the Afrikaners' sense of their own superiority and black inferiority to the point that Bloemfontein remains the most important symbol of Afrikaner identity to this day.

Although the Afrikaners settled on land far removed from the British, the peace between them did not last. Following the discovery of diamonds (1867) and gold (1886) in the republics the Boers had created, the British set their sights on the rest of what is now South Africa. Tensions reached a peak in the mid-1890s when Cecil Rhodes (whose estate funds the Rhodes scholarships) called on the English settlers in the Afrikaner republics to rebel. Finally, in 1899, the Boer republic declared war on the British, setting off one of the fiercest struggles the world had seen up to that point.

The two sides signed a peace treaty in 1902. In 1906 and 1907, the Transvaal and the Orange Free State came under British control. In 1910 the various South African colonies merged, becoming the Union of South Africa, which was a largely self-governing entity inside the British Empire and, later, the Commonwealth of Nations.

Although the apartheid laws, per se, were not put on the books until the late 1940s, the Union was always run by the tiny white minority. Only a handful of blacks and coloreds had the right to vote. Successive governments enacted laws limiting the political and

Figure 1 Map of South Africa

Table 5.2 The Evolution of South Africa

Date	Event
1652	Dutch arrive
1806	Final British takeover of the Cape
1835–40	The Great Trek
1867	Diamond mining begins
1886	Gold mining begins
1899–1902	Boer War
1910	Union of South Africa created
1912	ANC formed
1948	National Party elected; formal apartheid begins

economic freedoms of Africans, such as one passed in 1913 that restricted their right to buy land outside of "reserves," which were not very different from Indian reservations in the United States.

Opposition to those racist policies began as soon as the Union was created. In 1912 a largely middle-class, multiracial group formed the ANC, which was modeled on its

Indian equivalent, the Indian National Congress, and was thus committed to non-violent change. The ANC and other opposition groups, however, had little impact before the 1950s.

At the time, the more serious tensions were between the English and the Afrikaners. The latter were particularly frustrated by their lack of economic and political power, even though they outnumbered the English. Frustrated Afrikaners turned to the National Party and the even more militant Broederbond (literally, band of brothers) to maintain the purity and power of what they, like the Germans, called the *volk*.

World War Two proved to be the major turning point for the Afrikaners. Many refused to support South African participation on the Allied (British) side. A minority actively supported the Nazis, whose racist and anti-Semitic policies they found appealing. After the war, the Afrikaner community came together as never before and the National Party won the 1948 election, as it did every subsequent election until 1994. Immediately, it began introducing apartheid legislation.

Apartheid

Apartheid produced the all but total separation of the races as part of a regime in which the minority White population brutalized everyone else. Among other things, apartheid

- denied the few blacks, Asians and coloreds who were still on the rolls the right to vote
- banned mixed marriages and sexual relations across racial lines
- limited where Africans could live outside the "homelands," and required them to carry "passbooks" or internal passports
- segregated all public facilities.

Especially under the third National Party prime minister, H. F. Verwoerd, an elaborate justification for apartheid was developed. In it, the Afrikaners drew on their belief that they were God's chosen people and were thus superior to the Africans. That led them to the "need" to develop their culture and society separately from "inferior" groups. Also in keeping with world politics at the time, the National Party presented itself as anti-communist.

Most scholars, however, also emphasize the fear that Afrikaners felt toward the blacks and even the English. After all, they were a tiny minority and had, themselves, lived under British domination for the better part of a century (Sparks 1990).

Apartheid was enforced by one of the most repressive regimes of the second half of the twentieth century. The best estimates are that over 40,000 people were killed by a police force that used everything from random arrests to torture in attempting to keep Africans and other opponents "in their place."

We should also note something that was to prove critical in the negotiations in the early 1990s. The National Party used its forty years in power to modernize the South African economy. Before World War Two, most Afrikaners were poor. Most lived on small, inefficient farms or lacked the skills to get good jobs in the English-dominated urban, industrial economy. The National Party used the patronage powers of the state to shift contracts to Afrikaner-led firms, give a disproportionate number of jobs to their own people, create state-owned enterprises run by Afrikaners, and create living conditions for the white population that were nearly equal to those in Europe or North America.

Resistance

Opposition to apartheid began before the first laws were enacted. A handful of white liberals (mostly English) openly opposed apartheid. So, too, did the South African Communist Party, but its influence was limited because it was banned as early as 1950 (see Table 5.3).

The most effective internal resistance came from the ANC. For its first forty years, it emulated the non-violent and non-confrontational tactics of its Indian namesake. Under the influence of its Youth League (including Mandela, Walter Sisulu, Oliver Tambo and Govan Mbeki, father of the former president), the ANC moved leftward in the 1950s. Most notably, it adopted a more militant Freedom Charter (1955) and launched a Defiance Campaign reminiscent of the US civil rights movement of the same period.

The government refused to yield. As a result, many younger leaders began to question non-violence, especially following the 1960 Sharpeville Massacre in which at least 69 peaceful demonstrators were killed. That caused Mandela and many of his colleagues to endorse violent resistance against the regime and led to the creation of its armed wing, Umkhonto we Sizwe, or MK (Spear of the Nation), two years later.

Over the next quarter-century, MK launched attacks from bases outside South Africa. To say the least, it was not very effective. It never had many members, and most of the guerrillas it sent into the country were captured; many were killed.

The regime was also able to neutralize the ANC leadership. One group of leaders, including Mandela, was arrested on treason charges and sentenced to long terms, including life, in prison. Most ended up on the infamous Robben Island off the coast of Cape Town, where they lived under grueling conditions. The leaders who were able to escape arrest, including Tambo and Joe Slovo, fled the country and ran the ANC and MK from exile in Britain and, later, friendly African countries.

The National Party's repressive apparatus and propaganda machine were relentless. As noted earlier, 40,000 blacks and other opponents were killed and perhaps ten times that number were arrested. Even more remarkable in this media age, the regime was able to keep all pictures and any mention of Mandela and his fellow prisoners out of the press from the time of their imprisonment until the eve of their release.

Nonetheless, from the mid-1970s on, protest against the regime stiffened. The ANC continued to organize and orchestrate much of the domestic opposition from underground. However, other groups that shared goals and had some organizational ties with the ANC, but had not been banned, took center stage. In particular, the churches and, later, the black trade unions helped build opposition against the regime at home and abroad.

In 1976 Soweto and other townships erupted with protests by young people whose anger was sparked by a government decision to require teaching in Afrikaans in black schools. The Black Consciousness Movement was able to focus much of that anger until its leader, Steve Biko, was arrested, tortured and executed by the police in 1977.

In the 1980s the state cracked down ever harder. Despite the repression, protestors effectively disrupted the educational, township and industrial systems in an attempt to make the country ungovernable. There were also developments on the more conventional

Table 5.3 Resistance to Apartheid in South Africa

Date	Event
1955	ANC issues the Freedom Charter
1960	Sharpeville massacre
1962	*Umkhonto we Sizwe*, "armed struggle," begins
1964	Mandela arrested and imprisoned
1976	Soweto uprising
1977	UN arms embargo imposed
1977	Death of Steve Biko
1984	UN declares apartheid a crime against humanity
1986	EC and United States impose sanctions

political front. Most notably, the ANC was the driving force behind the United Democratic Front (UDF) in 1983. It eventually numbered 600 groups and went a long way toward solidifying the ANC's grassroots organization, especially among the young people who knew little or nothing about Mandela or the ANC because of the continued censorship.

There was also mounting opposition from abroad. As early as the 1940s, foreign activists such as Britain's Father Trevor Huddleston had opposed South Africa's racist policies and helped organize resistance inside the country. The first General Assembly of the United Nations took note of the South African situation when India objected to the way people from the subcontinent were treated there.

By the 1960s and 1970s, apartheid sparked an extensive and, eventually, effective series of sanctions and other diplomatic efforts. The Soviet Union and its allies gave the ANC substantial money and training (remember, the South African Communist Party was an ANC ally). However, because the Soviet Union was about to collapse at the same time as apartheid did, it had little to do with resolving the conflict, and we will therefore focus our attention on the West and the rest of Africa here. Although the impact and enforcement of the policies discussed below was always limited, the opposition to apartheid did mark the first time that so many states, international organizations and non-governmental organizations (NGOs) made a concerted effort to end a domestic dispute.

The United Nations was often the focus of the anti-apartheid movement, though its actions were stymied by the British and/or American desire to continue working with the South African regime, which they saw as a Cold War ally. The UN General Assembly had begun criticizing South Africa in the late 1940s. However, the General Assembly has no real power, and its resolutions therefore had next to no impact. Attention therefore shifted to the Security Council, where British and American reticence was more important because of their ability to cast a veto and thereby block any action. Still, the Security Council passed a mandatory embargo (Resolution 418) on all sales of arms and related technologies to South Africa in 1977. Later it banned the sale of spare parts and police equipment to South Africa, and the purchase of arms made in South Africa.

Meanwhile, the General Assembly continued taking symbolic steps that helped crystallize public opinion against apartheid. South Africa was expelled from the General Assembly, and then from the UN's affiliated organizations whenever a simple majority of the member states was enough. In 1984 the General Assembly declared apartheid a crime against humanity.

The UN was often criticized for its failure to take tougher stands on South Africa. Nonetheless, it channeled hundreds of millions of dollars in humanitarian aid into the country, and consistently kept the opposition and Mandela on center stage internationally.

The UN was not the only international organization involved. Because it had been a British colony, South Africa was a member of the Commonwealth of Nations. As more and more former British colonies gained their independence, apartheid became an important and divisive issue within the Commonwealth. Despite the regular opposition of the British government, the Commonwealth took ever stronger stands against South Africa and the breakaway white-dominated government of Rhodesia (now Zimbabwe). The Commonwealth passed sanctions against South Africa and sent an Eminent Persons Group, which met Mandela and found the ANC open to a dialog with the regime.

The final significant international organization was the Organization of African States (now the African Union), many of whose members also belonged to the Commonwealth. It, too, took stands against apartheid but lacked the economic clout to pass sanctions that would have much of an impact on Pretoria. Instead, its member states did what they could to raise global awareness about apartheid. South Africa's neighbors tried to reduce their economic dependency on South Africa. Most, too, became frontline states, which were willing to house and otherwise support the ANC and other guerrilla forces.

Individual states were far less consistent in their opposition to apartheid. None was more disappointing than Britain, whose less than constructive involvement in the region before 1912 has already been discussed.

Britain had major cultural and economic ties to South Africa. On the one hand, that sparked opposition to apartheid, especially from the unions, left-wing political parties, and liberal interest groups. On the other hand, the anti-apartheid movement was not able to build strong enough bridges to its British counterpart for any noticeable shift toward racial equality. It also failed to get a place near the top of the Labour Party's foreign policy agenda, which meant that Labour did little for South Africa when in office from 1964 to 1970 and 1974 to 1979. The Conservatives under Margaret Thatcher (in office 1979–90) opposed any strong steps against the South African regime. They rationalized their position as an attempt to save jobs in Britain, stop the spread of communism, and keep the situation in South Africa from getting any worse. As we saw earlier, the British government resisted proposals for more sweeping action from the Commonwealth in the end by turning the issue over to the European Community (now the European Union). When that body enacted partial sanctions in 1986, London had no choice but to go along, although recently revealed scandals suggest it often paid only lip-service.

The United States played a similar, though in the end slightly more assertive, role in opposing apartheid. The United States did not have as extensive cultural or economic ties to South Africa as Britain did. Nonetheless, the two countries were major trading partners, and successive American administrations saw South Africa as a bulwark against the spread of communism in an otherwise volatile region. That said, given its own civil rights problems, South Africa was bound to become an issue in US domestic politics. Indeed, as early as 1960, the Rev. Martin Luther King, Jr took a strong stand, denouncing apartheid as worse than segregation in the United States.

Momentum against apartheid grew during the Carter administration, which made human rights in general an important foreign policy priority. Unlike in Britain, American activists were able to bring the civil rights community and the traditional left on board in its anti-apartheid activities, which included educational efforts, sit-ins, and other protests.

The 1980s also saw the start of the disinvestment movement that probably did the most to change American policy. American activists, universities and interest groups led the pressure for disinvestment and application of the Sullivan principles, which banned American companies from discriminating if they continued doing business in South Africa. In 1985, for example, Chase Manhattan led a consortium of banks that denied a cash-strapped South Africa $24 billion in short-term loans. These moves were not just American initiatives. Corporations around the world either pulled out of South Africa altogether or, along Sullivan lines, ended the racist policies practiced by their subsidiaries in South Africa. Indeed, the most important blow came when the British-based Barclay's Bank stopped dealing with South Africa as a result of business losses there and pressure from its customers at home.

Some international NGOs were able to establish conflict resolution, and educational and development operations, in the black community. Events ranging from Desmond Tutu's winning the Nobel Peace Prize, to the release of the popular film *Cry Freedom* which popularized the late Steve Biko, all added to the opposition to apartheid. Though it might seem trivial to outsiders, South Africa's expulsion from international athletic competition was actually a tough blow for the sports-mad country.

Still, the 1980s did not start out auspiciously. The new Reagan administration adopted constructive engagement, or a policy of staying involved in South Africa while pressuring its government to reform. Critics were incensed by the administration's failure to move all levers possible against Pretoria, and by the president's frequent misstatements (for example, praising National Party leaders for their role as World War Two allies, when many of them spent time in prison as Nazi collaborators).

By the middle of the decade, liberals and moderate Republicans had come to reject constructive engagement as ineffective. And, whether as a matter of principle or from a desire to get more votes from blacks, a broad coalition of most Democrats and Republicans passed the Anti-Apartheid Act. It was vetoed by President Reagan, but Congress overrode the veto. The act called for Mandela's release, imposed restrictions on most areas of trade between the two countries, and required American firms to use a version of the Sullivan principles.

Anatomy of a Miracle

Most South Africans first heard about the momentous changes that were about to sweep their country when President F. W. de Klerk made his surprise announcement to the National Assembly on February 2, 1990:

> The prohibition of the African National Congress, the Pan Africanist Congress, the South African Communist Party, and a number of subsidiary organizations is being rescinded. The government has taken a firm decision to release Mr Nelson Mandela unconditionally. (Waldmeier 1997: 142)

The negotiations that led to that statement had occurred on two tracks.

The first was between the still-imprisoned Mandela and the top leadership in South Africa. The second involved informal discussions between the ANC and white private citizens who sometimes acted with, and sometimes without, the approval of the government.

Useful Websites

The most obvious and important website for our purposes is run by the Truth and Reconciliation Commission. It documents all the Commission's activities and has a link to the government site that has all five volumes of the report which users can download: <www.truth.org.za>.

There are also many sites dedicated to South African politics. The South African Political Information Exchange is one of the best, though not one of the most active: <sapolitics.co.za>.

SANGONet is a clearing house for the leading NGOs working in the country: <www.ngopulse.org>.

In his meetings with foreign visitors and the white authorities, Mandela consistently demanded that any agreement had to include three main points:

- elections in which everyone could vote
- a government determined on the basis of one person, one vote
- whites belonged in South Africa, since they were Africans, too.

The second half of the 1980s were not easy for the South African government, and the regime's difficulties undoubtedly contributed to its willingness to find a negotiated solution. The ungovernability campaign had forced President P. W. Botha to impose a state of emergency. Meanwhile, as sanctions began to take hold, economic conditions deteriorated to the point that the white standard of living was threatened.

In response, Botha offered limited reform. Some of the more noxious symbols of apartheid, such as segregated beaches, were eliminated. Botha also privately offered to release Mandela if the ANC renounced the armed struggle. Mandela refused. Nonetheless, Botha had Mandela moved from Robben Island to a less austere prison and allowed him to have regular contact with the ANC leaders in exile.

The available evidence suggests that the government thought these moves would outsmart Mandela and split the ANC. In fact, the opposite occurred.

Between 1988 and 1990, Mandela held 47 meetings with the authorities. Few of his colleagues knew the details of what was happening, prompting some tensions within both the prison community and the ANC as a whole.

In those meetings, Mandela routinely spoke Afrikaans and, in many cases, charmed his adversaries with his dignity and graciousness. Some of the stories from that period are truly remarkable. Mandela was once taken for a drive by a prison warden who went into a store to buy a soda, leaving the keys in the car. Mandela made no attempt to escape. Mandela liked one of his guards, James Gregory, so much that he invited him to his presidential inauguration. Gregory had voted for the ANC in the election. Most remarkable of all, Mandela built an exact replica of his final prison house to serve as his retirement home.

Then, on July 5, 1989, Botha invited Mandela to his office outside Cape Town for tea and an informal meeting. They surprised each other by how well they got along, although no progress was made on either Mandela's release or on broader issues.

At that point, the situation seemed to take a step backward. Botha was too uncompromising and too worried about appearing weak to find a way to release Mandela and deal with the wider matters raised in the negotiations. Then, in one of those "accidents of history" that play a vital role in political life, Botha resigned. He had suffered a stroke in January, yet tried to hold onto power. However, once word of the meeting with Mandela leaked out, pressure on him to resign intensified. Six weeks later, he did so and was replaced by F. W. de Klerk, who was widely viewed as a hard-liner.

Track-two discussions began at about the same time as those between Mandela and his captors. In September 1985, Gavin Relly, chair of the immensely influential Anglo-American Corporation, met (illegally, given South African law) with Oliver Tambo and other ANC leaders in Zambia. The fact that it was a business leader of English origin who began this set of contacts was not surprising. English speakers had always been somewhat more liberal than most Afrikaners. More important, the business community was deeply worried about the state of the economy, which they were convinced would continue to deteriorate as long as apartheid was in force.

There were rumblings of change within the Afrikaner community as well. In 1986 Pieter de Lange, the new head of the Broederbond, met Thabo Mbeki at a Ford Foundation-sponsored meeting on Long Island. De Lange stated flatly that South Africa would have to change; Mbeki was skeptical. Groups of Afrikaner clergymen violated South African law by meeting ANC and other opposition figures in neighboring countries. A British politician who was also an executive of Consolidated Goldfields facilitated 12 meetings in which middle-level ANC and Afrikaner leaders met at country homes in the United Kingdom.

As was the case in the secret negotiations that led to the Oslo agreement between Israel and the Palestine Liberation Organization, the informal aspect of these meetings may have accomplished more than the negotiations themselves. Thus, at one of the first meetings, ANC and Afrikaner representatives alike watched a cricket match and bemoaned the fact that apartheid deprived them of the opportunity to see their mutually beloved cricket, soccer and rugby teams play in international competition.

Many key Afrikaners emerged from those meetings convinced of the need for fundamental reform. Included among them was de Klerk's younger brother. Though the two de Klerks did not agree politically, Wilhelm joined the other well-connected Afrikaner participants in reporting what they were doing to the South African security forces. In an ironic twist of fate, the political leaders of the security apparatus—who of course understood how bleak the situation was—ended up spearheading support for a negotiated settlement in the National Party and the Broederbond.

Everything came to a head in the six months following Botha's resignation. Before taking office, de Klerk had not been informed of the secret discussions. At his first State Security Council meeting, he routinely approved one of those initiatives without fully understanding the importance of his actions. When informed that two of his top intelligence officials had met with Thabo Mbeki and others in Switzerland, de Klerk was furious. When he was fully briefed, he realized how badly the situation had deteriorated at home and how far negotiations with the ANC had proceeded. As one of the government participants in those meetings put it, "from that moment on, he took the ball and ran with it" (Sparks 1995: 114).

De Klerk then allowed the first legal ANC demonstration in nearly thirty years. In December 1989 he met with Mandela. Though the two did not hit it off well personally, it was clear to both of them that they could work together. So, on February 2, 1990 he made his famous speech. Mandela was informed he would be released on the 11th. Later that day, he spoke to a crowd of over 100,000, most of whom had not even seen a picture of a man who had not been mentioned in the South African media for more than a quarter-century.

Transition to Democratic Rule

Freeing Mandela and unbanning outlawed organizations by no means ended the conflict. In fact, it seems that de Klerk acted quickly so that he might catch the ANC unprepared and regain the political initiative, thereby limiting the concessions the whites would have to make. As was the case throughout the transition, that is not what happened (see Table 5.4). For example, it took weeks simply to arrange the legal indemnifications that allowed ANC exiles to return home without facing prosecution. More important, it was well over a year before the Conference on a Democratic South Africa (CODESA) was appointed, and another two years passed before it reached an agreement on an interim constitution. Eighteen parties were represented, but in the end, the differences separating the ANC, the National Party and the Inkatha Freedom Party proved to be the biggest obstacles.

The transition took so long because the differences between the ANC and the government were still vast, and because the overall situation remained tense and often violent. Not surprisingly, the ANC wanted a system of one person, one vote that would all but certainly bring black (and ANC) rule. The National Party insisted on provisions that would guarantee minority representation in the cabinet, and limit the redistribution of income and wealth.

Table 5.4 Transition to Majority Rule

Date	Event
1985	Mandela meets with Commonwealth Eminent Persons Group
1987	Mandela begins meeting with government officials
1989	Botha and Mandela meet, de Klerk replaces Botha
1990	Mandela released, ANC and other groups unbanned
1991	CODESA formed
1993	Interim constitution adopted
1994	First all-race elections, Mandela and ANC elected
1996	Permanent constitution adopted
1999	Second election, Mbeki and ANC elected
2008	Mbeki resigns as president

In August 1990 the ANC called off the armed struggle, though it maintained a small underground organization just in case it was ever needed again; and called on the international community to maintain sanctions. The government realized it would have to accept black participation, but hoped to find ways to limit it so that the National Party could stay in power at least for the short term. De Klerk also wanted to avoid an election to choose an assembly that would draft a new constitution, something that Mandela at first demanded. To make matters more complicated, the personal relationship between the two leaders deteriorated.

The difficulties were not only at the bargaining table. Violence swept the black townships. Although the evidence is still incomplete, there is good reason to believe that a shadowy "third force," operating through the security services, helped to organize and fund the more conservative Inkatha to try to blunt the strength of the ANC.

The security services also probably instigated fighting that pitted Inkatha-supporting Zulus against ANC-supporting Xhosas, which threatened to add a second ethnic dimension to South Africa's conflict. In the worst single incident, Zulus hacked 37 workers to death in a hostel in Boipatong, outside Johannesburg, on June 16, 1992. Indeed, the violence continued until the eve of the first election, when a group of right-wing fanatics tried to seize power and set up a new apartheid state in rural Bophuthatswana, one of the apartheid-era sham homelands.

Finally, the ANC agreed to an all-party constituent assembly as long as elections would be held shortly after it concluded its deliberations. On December 21, 228 delegates from 18 parties assembled for the first meeting of CODESA. The parties agreed that they would move forward once the chair decided they had reached "sufficient consensus" (a term also used in Northern Ireland).

The desire for consensus masked a game of political hardball played by the ANC and the National Party. Both took more intransigent positions on such issues as minority representation. After Boipatong, Mandela issued a list of 14 demands the government would have to meet for negotiations to resume, including an end to violence against ANC organizers and increasing security in the townships.

Mandela began to back down as the violence escalated. In September 1992 police in the homeland of Ciskei killed 28 demonstrators at a rally held by the ANC. Indeed, the possibility that violence could derail the entire transition seems to have jolted both sides, especially the people one level below Mandela and de Klerk in their respective hierarchies. Roelf Meyer led a group of younger National Party officials who argued that holding out would even further jeopardize the political and economic status of whites. To the surprise of many the communist leader, Joe Slovo, convinced the ANC that it needed whites not just to run the economy but the state as well, because the government in waiting did not have anywhere near enough qualified people to staff the state apparatus. Slovo also convinced Mandela to go along with some form of power- sharing with the National Party for a limited period.

Negotiations began again after Mandela and de Klerk signed a memorandum of understanding in late September 1993. Ironically, their task was aided by the obstructionist tactics followed by the Inkatha leader, Mangosuthu Buthelezi, which drove the ANC and National Party closer together. However, in yet another tragic irony, it may have taken two more bursts of violence—the attempted coup in Bophuthatswana mentioned earlier and the assassination of Chris Hani, secretary-general of the Communist Party— to convince the negotiators to close the deal.

In the pre-dawn hours of November 18, 1993, the negotiators agreed to the final clause of a 142-page interim constitution. Much of the document was written to reassure whites by:

- institutionalizing minority representation in the cabinet for five years
- guaranteeing property rights, although also holding open the possibility of reparations for people whose property had been illegally seized
- providing for a degree of decentralization and an upper house that would represent the provinces.

The country's attention then turned to what many expected to be a tumultuous election campaign. While there was some violence, and Buthelezi did what he could to disrupt the election until he decided to run a slate of candidates at the last moment, the voting took place amazingly smoothly.

As expected, the ANC won handily, with 62 percent of the vote. The National Party, Inkatha, and a number of minor parties trailed far behind. On May 10, 1994 Mandela was sworn in as president with, in perhaps the most remarkable irony of all, de Klerk as his first deputy president.

The impossible had happened.

Tomorrow is Another Country

As we will see in the next section and the rest of the book, there are many reasons why conflict resolution in South Africa has been smoother than in most other countries. At the top of any such list is the fact that parties to the negotiations paid more attention to what happened after the beginning of majority rule. Though we will see here what South Africa has done on this score, the importance of those efforts may not be clear until you read about the "orphaned" agreements in Northern Ireland and the Middle East in the chapters that follow.

The Truth and Reconciliation Commission has received the lion's share of the publicity in respect of conflict resolution (Tutu 1999). However, the Commission's work is but part of a larger effort to heal the wounds caused by 45 years of apartheid, and centuries of other racist policies before that.

The new government, however, took three broad initiatives that sought to heal the rifts that had built up over the decades. All these measures were controversial, especially among some of the ANC's supporters at home and abroad, because they flew in the face of what most "winners" expect to do when they prevail after an intense conflict.

First, the ANC sought to govern with members of the old regime as far as possible. That process started with the inclusion of de Klerk and the National Party in the cabinet after the transition. No one expected this power-sharing to last indefinitely, and de Klerk and his colleagues resigned in 1996, once the permanent constitution was adopted without provisions guaranteeing minority representation. Perhaps more important for the long term, the government has taken Joe Slovo's concerns to heart and kept on most of the white civil servants, only firing those who had been most deeply implicated in defining and enforcing apartheid policies. The federal component of the constitution also allowed the National Party to stay in power for some time in its regional bastion around Cape Town, and for Inkatha to do the same in KwaZulu Natal.

Secondly, the ANC has pursued surprisingly market-oriented economic policies. Before taking office, the ANC was committed to democratic socialism and was affiliated with the South African Communist Party. That past led many observers to assume that it would expropriate white-owned resources that remained in private hands, and pass laws that would redistribute income and wealth to the poor.

The pressures to do so were overwhelming. Some 40 percent of blacks were unemployed. Only 2 percent of all whites, but over half of the blacks, lived in poverty, earning less than $200 a month. Mandela's government started out with policies in keeping with its socialist past. It did not have to nationalize many industries, since the National Party had set up state-owned companies in most key industrial sectors. It did, however, commit itself to fulfilling the "basic needs of the people" by adding new jobs, building a million houses by 2000, expanding access to running water and electricity, improving health care in the townships and rural areas, and more. At first, it seemed as if the strategy might work. With the lifting of the last sanctions in 1994 and the general goodwill shown the government, growth bounded up to 3 percent a year in 1994 and 1995.

But the government changed course for two main reasons. First, the economy as a whole was in a tailspin largely because of sanctions and other costs of apartheid. Second, the global economic powers-that-be had turned their backs on socialism and were increasingly concentrating aid, loans and investment in Third World countries that did the same.

Most notably, in 1996 the South African government realized it would need a growth rate of at least 6 or 7 percent a year to reach its ambitious social goals. Indeed, at current rates of growth, unemployment among blacks would actually increase by 5 percent by the end of the decade. And, it could only hike its growth rate by accommodating itself to capitalism at home and abroad. In 1996, therefore, it adopted its Growth, Employment and Redistribution Plan (GEAR), which is typical of the structural adjustment policies that are now followed in most of the Third World. This plan calls on the government to:

- reduce government debt to 3 percent of GNP
- bring inflation under control by keeping wage and price increases below the rate of growth in productivity
- establish stable exchange rates
- privatize many of the companies nationalized or created by the National Party (for example, Swissair bought much of the South African airline in 1999)
- increase labor market flexibility.

All of these policies were designed to improve the chances of luring back the foreign investment that had left during the final years of apartheid.

Despite what many critics on the left—including many in the ANC's own coalition—claimed, GEAR and related policies did not simply signal a capitulation to international capitalism and the South African white community. Within this pro-capitalist framework, the government has added programs that it expects to benefit its core constituents in the 2000s:

- Encouraging the small group of young black entrepreneurs, and participants in other public-private joint ventures, to succeed and then plow back some of their profits into the community.

- Using government investment funds to create industrial development zones and other regional projects, especially in rural areas. These funds are not only to be used to expand employment, but also to be concentrated in black-owned firms. Thus, millions of rands have already been invested in projects to encourage tourism and agricultural exports on the coast near the border with Mozambique, and in building a world-class port near Port Elizabeth.
- Expanding the use of microcredit to create small businesses in poor black, Asian and colored communities as a vehicle for helping people pull themselves out of poverty. (On microcredit in general, see Yunus 1999; Bornstein 1997.) For instance, the Small Enterprise Foundation in the Northern Province (where two-thirds of the population is unemployed) has made nearly 20,000 loans of about $700 each, primarily to women for dressmaking, small grocery stores, and other businesses that employ an average of 2.5 full-time workers each.

As with most structural adjustment programs, it is too early to tell if these policies will do much to improve the conditions of the half of the population that currently lives in poverty. For now, it is enough to note that these programs were adopted to encourage economic as well as political healing. Along those lines, leftist critics correctly point out that this was a political and not a social or economic revolution. The jury is still out, however, on whether or not the necessary steps toward social and economic equality can be made in this way.

Thirdly, the best-known example of the efforts at lasting conflict resolution in post-apartheid South Africa is the Truth and Reconciliation Commission. It started as a compromise between the ANC, which wanted to reveal the crimes of the apartheid era, and the National Party, which hoped to limit the legal retribution that could be taken against its own supporters.

Quickly, however, the idea of truth *and reconciliation* became something bigger than, and different from, what either party had anticipated. The 1993 interim constitution ended with a call for a commitment to human rights and peaceful coexistence among all South Africans. To that end, on July 19, 1995 the parliament passed a law creating the Truth and Reconciliation Commission, to be headed by Archbishop Desmond Tutu.

The Commission was by no means the only institution of its type. In recent years, more than 15 other countries have created similar bodies to uncover the truth about the human rights violations under a previous, authoritarian regime. The TRC was different in that it also explicitly sought reconciliation between black people and their former oppressors.

The TRC was thus based on a different vision of justice than one normally finds in political life, which revolve around retribution and punishment for wrongdoers. Instead, the TRC has had two main goals: first, to learn as much of the truth as possible in order, secondly, to speed up the healing across racial lines in what Martha Minow has called "restorative justice" (Minow 1998: ch. 4; also see Tutu 1999). Countries that have endured genocide and mass violence suffer from a society-wide equivalent of post-traumatic stress disorder, for which a kind of collective therapy is needed. Indeed, if the perpetrators cooperate, a truth and reconciliation commission can both elicit more information in public, and help old enemies put at least some of the past to rest. The traumatic story can be "transformed through testimony about shame and humiliation to a portrayal of dignity and virtue, regaining lost selves and lost worlds" (Minow 1998: 66). Prosecutions, confiscatory economic policies and the like, by contrast, tend to reinforce the anger of the former rulers but rarely provide many tangible benefits for the people they oppressed.

The TRC was actually three separate bodies. The best known of them held hearings around the country (most of which were televised) in which victims and perpetrators alike were encouraged to tell their stories. A second and separate committee determined if amnesty would be granted to violators of human rights who requested it. The third determined how much, if any, reparation would be paid to the victims.

The hearings in many cases marked the first time that people were able to talk about what they and other family members had suffered, or what crimes they had perpetrated. The results were mind-numbing; even Tutu and the other commissioners were often seen weeping.

In three years the commission heard from 20,000 witnesses. In October 1998 it published a 3,500-page document that minced no words about crimes committed by the apartheid state. It also criticized the more limited violations of human rights perpetrated by the opposition, including those orchestrated by Mandela's former wife, Winnie Madikizela-Mandela.

There is one common misperception about the TRC. It could not grant amnesty unconditionally. Rather, someone who was accused had to formally ask for it, their crime had to be explicitly political, and the applicant had to demonstrate contrition. When the initial report was released, the TRC had dealt with almost 5,000 of the 7,000 pending applications. To the surprise of many, it had granted amnesty to only about 125 people. It is not clear how many of the others will ever be prosecuted. Nonetheless, the low rate at which amnesty was given suggests that the TRC was not simply freeing abusers of human rights.

In the short term, the TRC had a tremendous impact. No other country has gone so far, so fast, to heal divisions that were three-and-a-half centuries in the making.

Consider two brief examples from the documentary film *A Long Night's Journey Into Day*. The first involved the parents of Amy Biehl. She was a Fullbright student helping with the transition. One day, she drove some friends back to one of the townships and was pulled from her car and killed by some teenage activists. The film charts how her parents coped, most notably by supporting the killers' amnesty request and then hiring two of them on the staff of the Amy Biehl Foundation (www.amybiehl.org).

The other example showed two policemen who had "set up" seven teenagers and killed them, planting guns next to their bodies. One of the officers was white and showed no remorse. He was denied amnesty. The other was black. The TRC insisted that he spend time with the boys' mothers. As you can imagine, that was not an easy session. After hours of anger and tears, one of the mothers asked him: "Doesn't your first name mean 'mercy' in Xhosa?" He nodded yes. Then she said she now realized that as a Christian she had to forgive the policeman, though she would never forget what he did to her family.

The TRC's shortcomings, however, were also obvious from the beginning. Some people—including Steve Biko's family—denounced it for not obtaining justice in the traditional sense of the term. Botha, de Klerk, and some other prominent National Party leaders either refused to cooperate or did so half-heartedly. Similarly, one of the first public opinion polls suggests that in such circumstances a desire for revenge may be as common as a hope for reconciliation, though this evidence is sketchy at best (Gibson 2004).

Still, there are signs that many of the victims who testified regained some of their lost dignity. And there is some evidence that the TRC's procedures allowed many of the perpetrators of those crimes who did feel remorse to come forward and become partners in the building of the new South Africa.

There were other attempts at reconciliation outside of the formal political world. For example, during the violence that marked the transition between Mandela's release and the first elections, a Dutch Reformed minister, Theuns Eloff, who had begun meeting with the ANC in the late 1980s, organized the National Business Institute. His assumption was that the "space" where blacks and whites came together had to be expanded if South Africa were to avoid catastrophe. And since South Africa would have to be peaceful in order to be prosperous, the business community had a powerful incentive to bring the communities closer together. In the early 2000s Eloff became the head of the most prestigious Dutch Reformed seminary, which he then led into a merger with a poorly funded black university to form the University of the Northern Cape.

A similarly positive move was the lifting of sporting sanctions, which allowed South African teams to participate in international competitions again. The World Rugby Federation decided to hold its 1995 World Cup match in South Africa. Rugby had long been the favorite sport of most Afrikaners, and consequently was detested by most blacks. In fact, ANC activists put considerable pressure on Mandela to outlaw the sport. However, the president not only attended the 1995 final, but handed the victorious South African team its trophy while he was wearing a copy of the shirt worn by its Afrikaner captain, François Pienaar. Twelve years later, South Africa won the World Cup again. This time its starting 15 players included two blacks, and about 20 percent of the squad as a whole came from minority groups.

No one would argue that reconciliation alone will solve all of South Africa's problems, let alone do so quickly. Nonetheless, it is an increasingly widely used strategy that states and the international community have turned to, which Desmond Tutu perhaps summed up best in his introduction to the 1998 TRC report:

Reconciliation is not about being cosy; it is not about pretending that things were other than they were. Reconciliation based on falsehood, on not facing up to reality, is not reconciliation at all. We believe we have provided enough of the truth about our past for there to be a consensus about it. We should accept that truth has emerged even though it has initially alienated people from one another. The truth can be, and often is, divisive. However, it is only on the basis of truth that true reconciliation can take place. True reconciliation is not easy; it is not cheap. (Accessed at <http://www.truth.org.za> on August 1, 2000)

What Happens Next?

In every other chapter in Part 3, I will focus on the most recent events in the country or region it covers.

Not here.

As should be clear from the last few paragraphs, the "miracle" and the emergence of a "new country" by no means solved all of South Africa's problems. Nonetheless, the country has made strides in race relations which none of us could have imagined a quarter-century ago.

To illustrate that, consider this statement from a typical, recent article by a respected journalist:

It feels light years away from the era of apartheid, when the bizarre, brutal apparatus of race classification, separation, and enforcement would stun the visitor on arrival to South Africa as though he had landed on a strange planet.

These days in Melville, once a dowdy Afrikaner suburb of Johannesburg but now a fashionably cosmopolitan village of bars, bookshops, and internet cafes, young blacks and whites laugh and josh together on Friday nights—more noticeably than in most American cities. In the shopping malls, some of the 25,000 odd dollar millionaires said to have been created since 1994, buy trendy clothes from solicitous white shop assistants. In the nearby better state schools, black children play happily with white ones. (The *Economist* 2005)

Or, consider the fact that one of the most popular television programs on the national network is Isidingo (www.isidingo.co.za), which is a multiracial soap opera. It has all the sex and scandal that Americans expect from General Hospital, or British viewers know will happen in EastEnders. But what is important here is that in Isidingo the cast and the plots are truly inter-racial. One should not read too much into soap opera plots, but they have been used in a number of countries to raise issues involving identity-based conflict in an indirect and apparently successful manner.

Soap Operas for Peace

It may seem odd, but a number of NGOs have specialized in producing soap operas and other radio and television programs designed to build peace and reconciliation. The "industry leader" is Search for Common Ground, which has produced stories that include an apartment house that springs to life to help Macedonian teenagers solve their problems, and a fictional 24/7 news television station in Nigeria.

www.sfcg.org/programmes/cgp/programmes_cgp.html

There is little doubt that South Africans have made tremendous strides toward peace and reconciliation. Nonetheless, several problems remain on the horizon, any or all of which could seriously harm—if not destroy—the South African miracle in ways that would reverse the events at the heart of this chapter (for more detail, see Hauss 2008). The most important of these include:

- The wrenching poverty that most black South Africans endure. The economic policies described above may work in the long term, especially if more direct foreign investment and aid are forthcoming. However, the results so far are not encouraging. Meanwhile, new social problems loom on the horizon, such as an HIV infection rate that tops 25 percent among young people.
- There is still no evidence that the government can dramatically improve the living conditions of its black constituents without eroding those of the white population. Meanwhile "white flight" continues, with as many as 250,000 whites leaving the country each year.

- Especially if these social and economic problems are not effectively addressed, there is serious danger of what Steven Friedman of Johannesburg's Centre for Policy Studies calls the "re-racialization of South African politics" (1999). Now, the issues are not about apartheid or overt racism. Rather, crime is center-stage. Whites who can afford to do so live in gated communities. All new cars come with built-in GPS devices, since so many are stolen. In this decade, South Africa has ranked in the "top" five nations for rates of rape, robbery and murder. Much of the crime is black on black, but whites are often victims, too.
- There is no viable alternative to ANC rule. Democratization theorists stress the importance of regular and routine alternation between incumbent and opposition parties as evidence of a stable and successful democracy. That is simply not on the horizon in South Africa. The ANC fell just short of the two-thirds majority it would have needed to amend the constitution on its own in the 1999, 2004, and 2009 elections. However, no other party has given any indication that it will pose a serious threat to the ANC. Inkatha has only done well in a single province. White-based potential successors to the National Party have disintegrated. In late 2008, Mbeki was forced to resign the presidency as part of an internal power struggle within the ANC. After the 2009 election Joseph Zuma took over the office. A small splinter group left the ANC but did very poorly in those parliamentary elections. The ANC remains firmly in charge.
- Racial tensions remain. They are nowhere near as intense as they were while Mandela and his colleagues were still in prison a generation ago. However, as the mystery novels of Richard Kurnmann (2006) and others show, the hatreds built up over centuries lie just below the surface.

Lessons Learned

Since this is the first of six cases we will consider comparatively, it is hard to draw any firm conclusions at this point. Nonetheless, six of the factors discussed in Part 1 had a major impact on the South African transition. In particular, the first two—shifts in the international balance of power and the emergence of a "hurting stalemate," which play a central role in the academic literature—seem less vital here. There probably could not have been a transition to majority rule without them. Nonetheless, they are, as the cliché puts it, necessary but by no means sufficient factors. They set the political stage that made accommodation possible, but the other four factors were needed to make the shift away from apartheid possible.

1. *The international environment.* This came into play in two ways. First, sanctions undoubtedly took a toll on the white population. Although it is hard to reach definitive conclusions about these and most other sanctions, they almost certainly indirectly led to an erosion of support for hard-line apartheid policies. As Tutu likes to put it, if the sanctions weren't having an impact, why did the South African government lobby so hard for their removal? Second, the end of the Cold War stripped the ANC of a major source of funds for its armed insurrection, and the National Party of what it called the communist threat that it used to rationalize the maintenance of apartheid.

2. *The hurting stalemate.* There is little doubt, too, that leaders on both sides of the racial divide understood that the country had reached a hurting stalemate by the late 1980s, in two senses of the term. First, each understood it could not win a definitive and

decisive victory. Second, they both also realized that the continued conflict was imposing unacceptable costs on their own supporters, something that was magnified by the changing geopolitical and economic conditions that accompanied the end of the Cold War. No one put it better than Mandela:

> It was clear to me that a military victory was a distant if not impossible dream. It simply did not make sense for both sides to lose thousands if not millions of lives in a conflict that was unnecessary. It was time to talk. (Waldmeier 1997: 94)

3. *Domestic leadership.* The compromise reached between the government and the ANC held open the possibility of real benefits for both sides. But that, too, would not have been possible without amazing leadership in both the ANC and the National Party. Mandela truly was a remarkable leader for shunning the revenge he might well have sought, and pushing instead for a multiracial democracy. Perhaps even more surprising is de Klerk, whose family and whose own career until 1989 offered no signs that he was willing to even question apartheid. Nonetheless, he too overcame his past and helped forge the agreement that led to the transition of 1994 and the Nobel Peace Prize he shared with Mandela. There were other visible leaders, including Archbishop Tutu, who helped spearhead opposition to apartheid, and Joe Slovo who, to the surprise of many, pushed his comrades toward reconciliation rather than revenge.

4. *The image of the enemy.* The same, too, is true of the commitment to getting beyond the image of the enemy, and overcoming other debilitating values and assumptions. Such stereotypes abounded, as in the Afrikaners' use of the term *kaffir* (roughly equivalent to the word "nigger" in America) to describe black Africans. This is not just a question of language. Post-apartheid South Africa saw two major efforts: ending apartheid, and promoting reconciliation. It is in the latter area that the TRC, along with other attempts at reconciliation, are most important and, so far, succeeding.

5. *Social and economic change.* As noted in the preceding section, social and economic difficulties could well be the Achilles heel of the transition in the first years of the twenty-first century. Despite that fact, one cannot help but be impressed by the seriousness of the government's plans to integrate social and economic change into its broader strategies for achieving reconciliation and stable peace. At first glance, that might seem an obvious conclusion for the ANC and other leaders to have reached. But as we will see in later chapters, domestic leaders as well as the international community have rarely done so, even when the conflicts caused far more physical damage than in South Africa.

6. *Third parties.* The one thing missing to make South Africa a "classic" example of win-win conflict resolution is the extensive use of outside third parties. To be sure, the Commonwealth Eminent Persons Group gave the antiapartheid movement new momentum when it was allowed to meet with Mandela in 1985. Similarly, British business leaders and others helped bring ANC officials and whites together in the track-two diplomacy of the late 1980s and early 1990s. Nonetheless, the agreement that led to the ANC's election in 1994 was for all practical purposes achieved by South Africans acting on their own. As such, this may be the "exception that proves the rule." None of the other cases we will consider (or any others not included in this book) benefited from the kind of leadership we saw in South Africa.

Select Bibliography

Bornstein, David (1997). *The Price of a Dream: The Story of the Grameen Bank*. Chicago: University of Chicago Press.

The *Economist* (2005). "If Only the Adults Would Behave Like the Children." April 23.

Friedman, Steven (1999). "South Africa: Entering the Post-Mandela Era." *Journal of Democracy* 10: 4, 3–18.

Gibson, James (2004). "Truth, Reconciliation, and the Creation of a Human Rights Culture in South Africa." *Law and Society Review* 38: 5–40.

Hauss, Charles (2008). "South Africa." In *Comparative Politics: Domestic Responses to Global Challenges*. www.cengage.com/cengage/instructor.do?codeid=5FDA&sortby=copy&type=all_radio&courseid=PO01&product_isbn=9780495501091&disciplinenumber=20&codeFlag=true.

Kunzmann, Richard (2006). *Salamander Cotton*. New York: Thomas Dunne.

Lieberfeld, Daniel (1999). "Post-Handshake Politics: Israel/Palestine and South Africa Compared." *Middle East Policy* 9: 131–40.

Mandela, Nelson (1994). *Long Walk to Freedom*. Boston, MA: Little, Brown.

Marks, Susan Collin (2000). *Inherit the Wind*. Washington: United States Institute for Peace.

Meredith, Martin (1997). *Nelson Mandela: A Biography*. London: Hamish Hamilton.

Minow, Martha (1998). *Between Vengeance and Forgiveness: Facing History after Genocide and Mass Violence*. Boston, MA: Beacon Press.

O'Flaherty, J. Daniel, and Constance J. Freeman (1998). "Stability in South Africa: Will It Hold?" *The Washington Quarterly* 22: 151–60.

Sparks, Allister (1990). *The Mind of South Africa*. New York: Ballantine.

—(1997). *Tomorrow is Another Country: The Inside Story of South Africa's Negotiated Revolution*. London: Arrow Books.

Thompson, Leonard (1995). *A History of South Africa*. Rev. edn. New Haven, CT: Yale University Press.

—(1999). "Mbeki's Uphill Challenge." *Foreign Affairs* 78: 83–9.

Tutu, Desmond (1999). *No Future without Forgiveness*. New York: Doubleday.

Waldmeier, Patti (1997). *Anatomy of a Miracle*. New York: Penguin.

Yunus, Muhammad (1999). *Banker to the Poor: Micro-Lending and the Battle Against World Poverty*. New York: Public Affairs Press.

CHAPTER SIX

Northern Ireland

Up until the 26 March this year, Ian Paisley and I never had a conversation about anything—not even about the weather—and now we have worked very closely together over the last seven months and there's been no angry words between us. This shows we are set for a new course.
—Martin McGuinness

On Good Friday 1998, the British and Irish governments made a momentous announcement. A team of international mediators led by former US senator George Mitchell had

Figure 2 Map of Ireland

succeeded in brokering an agreement between themselves and the leading political parties in Northern Ireland (or Ulster as it is called, mostly by Protestants) to end the thirty years of the "Troubles" between Catholics and Protestants in that disturbed province.

There were many issues still to be resolved when the Good Friday Agreement was reached. No one wanted matters such as the destruction of weapons to take a decade, but they did.

Once these issues were dealt with, perhaps the most important transition in the troubled province occurred. Almost nine years later to the day, The Rev. Ian Paisley and his long-time enemy Martin McGuinness took office as First Minister and Deputy First Minister of Northern Ireland respectively, thereby bringing the peace process to a legal and symbolic end. Paisley and McGuinness had represented the extremes in Northern Irish political life for decades—and Paisley made the decision to move forward on the day of his fiftieth wedding anniversary.

This is all the more remarkable since the Catholics and Protestants have not even been able to agree on a name for the province. For the Protestants it is Ulster, despite the fact that the term itself has Gaelic, and thus Catholic, roots. To the Catholics, the term Ulster is taboo because it is a symbol of British domination of Ireland for centuries. Even city names became political flashpoints. To Protestants, the second largest city in the province is Londonderry. To Catholics it is simply Derry, because they cringe at the notion of having the United Kingdom's capital attached to its name.[1] I will use the terms Ulster and Northern Ireland interchangeably.

At the start of this decade, no one expected the Good Friday Agreement to be anywhere near as effective as the transition to a multiracial democracy in South Africa. Like the Oslo Accord that marked the first breakthrough between Israelis and Palestinians (see Chapter 8), it seemed like a classic example of a partial agreement that marked a major step toward peace but left many issues still to be addressed.

On the one hand, the agreement ushered in "a level of peace, a promise of prosperity, and a climate of cross-community cooperation [Northern Ireland] has not known for most of [the twentieth] century" (Hoge 1999: 7). The agreement laid out plans to hand control over many of the province's internal affairs to a new parliament and cabinet in which all the major parties, Catholic and Protestant alike, would share power. It would also create "cross-border" institutions through which the British and Irish governments could help assure peace. And most important of all, the paramilitary groups all but completely stopped the violence that had wreaked havoc both in Northern Ireland and on the British "mainland" since the late 1960s.

On the other hand, the deal seemed to be what Fen Osler Hampson calls an "orphaned" agreement (Hampson 1997). While it certainly was a major breakthrough, it failed to address many critical issues. It did little, in particular, to promote reconciliation, which was so vital in the South Africa settlement. Even more important for the short term, it postponed the critical question (especially to Protestants) about how the IRA (Irish Republican Army) and other paramilitaries would hand in their weapons.

The problems surged to the surface almost immediately. The IRA made it clear that it would not start decommissioning its weapons before the new government

---

[1]   Emigrés from the region solved the problem two centuries ago in New Hampshire, where Derry and Londonderry are neighboring towns divided only by Interstate 93.

was formed. In response, the leading Protestant or unionist Party, through its leader, David Trimble, refused to serve in a cabinet with Sinn Fein, which is commonly viewed as the political wing of the IRA, until the paramilitaries started handing in their bombs and guns.

After months of haggling, the British and Irish governments gave the parties a deadline: June 30, 1999. It came and went without any progress toward forming the new government.

The British and Irish governments then tried to impose a take-it-or-leave-it plan in which a new government would be formed on July 15 and decommissioning would begin within a matter of days. However, Trimble stuck to his position, linking unionist participation in the cabinet with decommissioning.

Pessimists were convinced that the bombing, shooting and rioting would soon begin anew. Instead, London and Dublin called Mitchell back in, and in mid-November the parties agreed to a plan whereby the IRA promised to turn over the first portion of its weapons as soon as the new cabinet was created, which duly happened on December 2.

The peace process was dealt another serious blow in February 2000. Jean de Chastelain, a retired Canadian general who was part of the team of international mediators, issued a report that confirmed that the IRA had not begun to hand in its weapons. The IRA then issued an announcement that it would not do so on either the British or the unionists' terms. On February 6, a splinter republican group that rejected the peace process out of hand exploded the first bomb in nearly two years. The unionists threatened to quit the new government. Instead, the British government suspended the new institutions on February 12.

Once the IRA agreed to "completely and verifiably" put its arms beyond use and the international team inspected the first two arms caches, the British put the provincial institutions back in operation. Nonetheless, the rest of the year 2000 went anything but smoothly. Both sides were dissatisfied with the decommissioning process, and Catholics were upset at the failure of London to implement recommendations for sweeping change in the police force. In short, Northern Ireland remained far from anything like stable peace.

Nonetheless, the momentum began to shift after 9/11. The terrorist attacks in New York and Washington had the indirect effect of convincing the IRA and the Protestant paramilitary leaders that the violence they had engaged in for decades was no longer an option. And over the next six years, leaders on both sides of the sectarian divide worked doggedly to find a solution. The provincial government teetered on the brink of collapse several times, until the IRA made a momentous decision on July 28, 2005:

The leadership of Óglaigh na hÉireann has formally ordered an end to the armed campaign. This will take effect from 4 p.m. this afternoon. All IRA units have been ordered to dump arms. All Volunteers have been instructed to assist the development of purely political and democratic programmes through exclusively peaceful means. Volunteers must not engage in any other activities whatsoever. The IRA leadership has also authorized our representative to engage with the IICD to complete the process to verifiably put its arms beyond use in a way which will further enhance public confidence and to conclude this as quickly as possible. We have invited two independent witnesses, from the Protestant and Catholic churches, to testify to this.

In sum, this chapter focuses on a longer and stormier peace process than the one in South Africa. That said, it may be more typical of what countries emerging from decades of violence have to go through. To that end, consider these words by Fintan O'Toole, a columnist for the *Irish Times*, written during one of the crises following the Good Friday Agreement:

> In the resolution of bloody conflicts, the difficult can be achieved quickly but the impossible takes a little longer. It is well to remember how recently any kind of deal on the future of Northern Ireland seemed a pipe dream.
>
> The very frustration of the recent inconclusive talks at Stormont is a mark of the astonishing success of the peace process. We are frustrated not because there is no solution to the Northern Ireland problem, but because a settlement that once seemed like a madly optimistic fantasy is now so tantalizingly close to becoming reality. (O'Toole 1999: B4)

Theoretical Focus

Northern Ireland may not have taken spectacular steps forward like those instigated by the Truth and Reconciliation Commission in South Africa. However, the parties have made enough, admittedly gradual, progress that it is all but impossible to see them returning to the bloodshed of earlier years—something we will not be able to claim for any of the other countries to be considered in Part 3.

In the pages that follow, we will be concentrating on six theoretical issues.

* The Northern Ireland conflict is more complicated than the one in South Africa. It is much more than a dispute over religion: it is one with strong cultural and economic roots as well. What's more, unlike South Africa, it has greater and wider international implications for politics in Great Britain and the Republic of Ireland, as well as within Northern Ireland itself.
* We will not, however, see that changes in the international system surrounding the end of the Cold War had much impact in Northern Ireland.
* As in South Africa, this is a conflict with a base in differences of identity; it also reflects the asymmetrical nature of the power relations between Protestants and Catholics over the years.
* This is the first case in which we will clearly see the indispensable role a third party can play as a mediator facilitating a peace process.
* As was also the case in the Middle East, the Good Friday Agreement and the November 1999 creation of the new government in Ulster produced only incremental change. Nonetheless, such a less-than-total agreement can have a lasting impact, as O'Toole's comment and the 2007 agreement between Paisley and McGuinness suggest.
* The negotiations and institutions created by the Good Friday Agreement may offer a model that can be used in settling other disputes that cross national borders. This involved what Jonathan Stevenson (1998) calls "the partial dilution of sovereignty," given the growing power of the European Union, which made the creation of the cross-border institutions in 1998 and 1999 easier than it would have been earlier.

The Troubles

English political domination of Ireland began when the Pope granted King Henry II the right to take control of the island, shortly after his coronation in 1154. After nearly a quarter-century, the English established formal rule over all of Ireland.

English influence ebbed and flowed over the next several centuries. For most of the time, England dominated only the so-called English Pale along the coast near Dublin. Despite the English influence, and Henry VIII's imposition of Anglicanism during the Reformation, Ireland remained overwhelmingly Catholic.

A rebellion broke out in the early 1640s, but it was resolved when most of its leaders agreed to support the Royalists during England's civil war. They were defeated in 1651 by the forces of Cromwell, who then gave more than two-thirds of the island to the Protestants, pushing the Catholics to the south and west (O'Leary and McGarry 1996).

The fighting continued after the monarchy was restored. On July 12, 1690, Protestant troops under King William III crushed Catholic resistance at the Battle of the Boyne (see Table 6.1). It was at that time that Protestants came to be known as Orangemen because of their support for William, who had come to England from the Dutch state of Orange. It was another year before the English took Limerick and, with it, control over the entire island. At that point, the king negotiated reasonably generous terms, which would have granted the Catholics a degree of religious freedom and returned most of their land to them. However, the parliament rejected the plan and imposed a regime that virtually banned Catholicism and the Irish language.

Most Catholics worked the land as virtual slaves of English-based landlords. The small urban economy was dominated by Protestant immigrants from Scotland and England. The Scottish Presbyterians, however, were not allowed to vote, and most of them ended up supporting the American and French revolutions. To quell the budding rebellion, British prime minister William Pitt had the Act of Union passed in 1801, which joined the two islands politically. He also had planned to emancipate all Catholics, but that initiative was blocked by King George III.

Table 6.1 The Evolution of the Conflict in Northern Ireland

Date	Event
1690	The Battle of the Boyne
1801	The Act of Union
1840s	The potato famine
1916	The "Easter Rising"
1921	Partition
1969	Start of the "Troubles"
1972	"Bloody Sunday"
	Imposition of direct rule
	Large-scale deployment of British troops

The nineteenth century made a bad situation worse for most Catholics. Economic conditions deteriorated, especially during the potato famine of the 1840s, which killed hundreds of thousands of Irish people, and forced an even larger number to emigrate. Political uprisings broke out early in the century and again toward its end, as more and more people demanded either home rule or outright independence.

In the late 1890s, the journalist Arthur Griffith founded Sinn Fein to support moves for independence. It, and other groups, fomented the Easter Rising of 1916, which took Dublin but was soon brutally crushed by the British. In 1919 the revolutionaries regrouped, formed a parliament, declared Irish independence, and formed a guerrilla army, which later became known as the IRA.

In 1921 the British agreed to partition Ireland. The 26 counties in the south became the Irish Free State, with dominion status equivalent to that of Canada. (Ireland became a fully independent country in 1949.) The six counties in the north remained part of the United Kingdom. Partition also split Sinn Fein: a small faction demanding a fully united and independent Ireland continued to fight. Though the IRA was defeated before the end of the 1920s, support for unification never disappeared either in the south or in the north.

Britain gave Ulster its own provincial government based at Stormont. Like every other institution in the province, it was dominated by the Protestant unionists.

The Players

Because this case is complicated, it is useful to lay out who the main players have been:

- Most unionists are Protestants who want to remain a part of Great Britain. The main unionist parties operate through the constitutional system.
- Loyalists claim they are loyal to Great Britain, but through their paramilitary wings they have been as willing as the IRA to attack the British.
- Most nationalists are Catholics who favor the unification of Ireland, but only by constitutional means.
- Republicans have been willing to resort to violence in the pursuit of unification.
- The British government has, until recently, viewed Northern Ireland through a largely unionist lens. In the 1980s, however, it acknowledged that the Republic of Ireland had to be involved, and began to act in a more even-handed way toward both Catholics and Protestants in Ulster.
- Until 1999 Articles 2 and 3 of the Irish constitution called for unification. And the two main parties have their roots in the civil war of the 1920s that was fought in large part over the fate of the north. In most of the period covered here, however, Irish priorities lay elsewhere, and the Republic did not have much of an impact on the north until quite late in the peace process. If anything, southerners of almost all political stripes found the Troubles in general, and the IRA in particular, objectionable.

From Civil Rights to Civil War

Protestants have been fiercely attached to the union with Britain, because they see it as the only way to protect their religion and culture. A good deal of statistical data could be provided on that score, but just as revealing is the chorus from one of the loyalists' most popular songs, sung to the tune of "Home on the Range":

> No, no Pope of Rome,
> No chapels to sadden my eyes.
> No nuns and no priests and no rosary beads,
> And every day is the Twelfth of July. (McKittrick 1996: 39)

Protestant domination in Ulster approached the former domination of whites in the segregated American South. To be sure, there were no "Jim Crow" laws that denied the Catholics basic human rights. Nonetheless, the Protestants succeeded in gerrymandering local councils, the provincial assembly at Stormont, and its seats in the House of Commons in London, which reduced Catholic representation to a minimum. To cite only the most glaring example, the overwhelmingly Catholic city of Derry (Londonderry to the Protestants) was always run by a Protestant unionist administration. Protestants ran the economy, preventing Catholics from getting good jobs to the point that unemployment among Catholics frequently topped 40 percent. Perhaps most galling of all to the Catholics, Protestants dominated the police force (the Royal Ulster Constabulary), which was often accused of treating Catholics brutally and arbitrarily.

The IRA reconstituted itself in the 1950s and carried out a series of attacks. However, by the 1960s it had lost most of its support and had degenerated into little more than a sect that spent most of its time trying to blend Marxism with Irish nationalism.

Then, inspired in part by protests sweeping the rest of the Western world, a Catholic civil rights movement emerged in the late 1960s. Unlike in most other countries, it quickly turned violent, though much of the early fighting was instigated by Protestants. For instance, several hundred Catholic families had their homes in mixed neighborhoods burned; the same thing happened to a far smaller number of Protestants. Not surprisingly, the IRA reconstituted itself again.

The situation worsened in 1971 when the British introduced a policy of internment. Suspected terrorists could be arrested and held without trial, and without the usual judicial provisions regarding the rights of the accused. Hundreds of IRA activists were interned, or imprisoned without trial. No Protestants were.

The violence culminated in Bloody Sunday on January 30, 1972, when British paratroopers opened fire on a demonstration, killing at least 14 people. Subsequently, young militants led by the likes of Gerry Adams and Martin McGuinness took over from the older generation and created the new, Provisional IRA.

The British government had already sent troops to Northern Ireland in 1969 at Stormont's (that is, the unionists') request. The authorities in London hoped to bolster the moderate unionists with what they expected would be a brief military mission. The soldiers were initially welcomed by many Catholics, who hoped that their presence would reduce Protestant violence and aid them in their struggle for civil rights.

In practice, the British bias in favor of the unionists made them anything but an ideal third party or peacekeeper. For example, the British troops largely turned a blind eye as Protestant mobs forced Catholics to flee their homes.

After Bloody Sunday, British presence and power both grew dramatically. The government of Prime Minister Edward Heath dissolved Stormont and imposed direct rule by London. British authority was buttressed by the deployment of thousands of British troops, making Northern Ireland the only example covered in this book in which a government had to send peacekeeping forces to control its own citizens. The army has remained in Northern Ireland ever since, although the presence there today is very small. Almost 1,000 soldiers died, 100 of them in 1972 alone.

The army's role has always been controversial. In the early years, it was widely—and probably accurately—perceived as supporting the Protestants. Even as it became more impartial, the best that could be said was that it was partially effective in keeping the peace, since there were neighborhoods in which the soldiers had next to no impact.

To their credit, the British soldiers and British political leaders did at least try to stop the fighting. They were not, however, terribly effective in doing so. Indeed, one of their most lasting achievements is also one of the most powerful metaphors for the high level of hatred and violence in the province. They built a 30-mile-long "Peace Line" to separate Catholic and Protestant areas in the Belfast metropolitan area that reminded everyone of the infamous Berlin Wall.

Northern Ireland became a very violent place indeed. More than 3,300 people were killed in wave after wave of shootings and bombings that stretched beyond Ulster to the Irish Republic, the British "mainland," and as far as Gibraltar. Bombings in English train stations were so frequent that the government removed all trash cans. A bomb planted at the Grand Hotel in Brighton during the Conservative Party conference in 1984 nearly killed Prime Minister Margaret Thatcher and most of her cabinet colleagues. Sometimes, British soldiers and Irish paramilitary members were targeted. At other times, the victims were civilians who were in the wrong place at the wrong time when a bomb exploded.

The conventional wisdom is that the IRA was largely responsible for the violence. It did carry out the most spectacular attacks, especially in England. In later years, however, loyalist paramilitaries were responsible for as many deaths. Indeed, they killed more people than the IRA from the mid-1980s onward.

By 1995 there were more than 120,000 legally held firearms in the province, or more than one for every ten adults. No one knows how many more illegal weapons there were.

When the Berlin Wall fell in 1989, there was little hope that the Belfast Peace Line would follow in its wake. Indeed, the area was as divided and as violent as ever. Typical of the sentiment at the time was this statement by an IRA member given in an interview with David McKittrick, who is by most accounts the best journalist writing about politics in Ulster:

We can state absolutely, on the record, that there will be no ceasefire, no truce, no "cessation of violence," short of a British withdrawal. That, as blunt as that, is our position. (McKittrick 1996: 5)

Toward Good Friday

As is almost always the case with international conflict resolution, it is hard to define the exact date when the peace process began. In Northern Ireland, the first steps to end the fighting were taken shortly after the start of the Troubles. From the beginning, they included what would prove to be the components of the Good Friday Agreement reached nearly thirty years later—relations between Catholics and Protestants, and cooperation between the British and Irish governments and, occasionally, outsiders (Tonge 1997).

Between 1969 and the mid-1990s, none of those steps seemed to get anywhere, though in retrospect some of them did have an impact. But little of the anger subsided, and none of the parties backed away from their long-term goals. Nonetheless, more and more of the participants in the Troubles saw both the need for, and the possibility of, taking steps that would make the province more peaceful.

Under Conservative and Labour governments alike, the British supported direct rule and a hard line toward the IRA. They were anything but neutral, because all institutions, from the Royal Ulster Constabulary to the leading private businesses, were in Protestant hands. Thus, the British tended to deepen both the Catholics' sense of injustice, and the divide between themselves and the Catholics.

To its credit, the Conservative government of Prime Minister Edward Heath did try to find a solution to the Troubles. However, for most of the last quarter-century, the British focused on what David Bloomfield (1997, 1998) calls a "structural outcome" negotiated by governments and party leaders, and did not address the cultural divisions between the two communities on the ground. In 1973 the Secretary of State for Northern Ireland, William Whitelaw, brokered the Sunningdale Agreement, which created a new government in which constitutional parties (excluding terrorist organizations) would share power. The agreement also created a Council of Ireland in which representatives of the new assembly would meet regularly with their counterparts in the southern Dail (the all-important lower house of the Irish Parliament). Grassroots unionists rejected the cross-border arrangements and launched a series of crippling strikes that destroyed the new institutions within a matter of weeks (see Table 6.2).

Table 6.2 The Irish Peace Process

Date	Event
1974	Sunningdale Agreement collapses
1985	Anglo-Irish Agreement
1993	Downing Street Declaration
1994	IRA cease-fire
1995	Initial appointment of George Mitchell and other mediators
1996	Canary Wharf bombing
1997	Elections in Britain and the Republic of Ireland
1998	Good Friday Agreement
1999	Northern Ireland government takes office
2007	Joint government of Sinn Fein and DUP

Useful Websites

The BBC (British Broadcasting Corporation) has a vast site that includes the text of its stories, and it now 'streams' many of its television and radio broadcasts: <http://news.bbc.co.uk>.

The *Independent* has the best coverage of Northern Ireland in the mainstream British press: <http://www.independent.co.uk>.

The Northern Ireland Office of the British government can provide many official documents, including the Good Friday Agreement: <http://www.nio.gov.uk>.

CAIN (Conflict Archive on the Net) is a project on the Troubles, based at the University of Ulster: <http://cain.ulst.ac.uk/index.html>.

INCORE (Initiative on Conflict Resolution and Ethnicity), also based at the University of Ulster, is one of the world's best sources of information on ethnic conflict in general, and in Northern Ireland in particular: <http://www.incore.ulst.ac.uk>.

The main Northern Ireland political groups include Sinn Fein, http://sinnfein.ie/index.html, and the Ulster Unionist Party: <http://www.uup.org>. The Democratic Unionist Party website is at www.dup.org.uk.

Corrymeela has an extensive site explaining its activities and philosophy: <http://www.corrymeela.org.uk>.

Little progress was made in the next decade. Some observers cite Pope John Paul's criticism of violence during his 1979 visit as an important first step toward convincing the IRA and Sinn Fein to seek peace. However, the first truly significant events occurred in the 1980s.

The Irish Taoiseach (prime minister), Garrett Fitzgerald, once again proposed a Council of Ireland in another effort to unravel the North–South strand of the problem. Publicly, that initiative collapsed before it got off the ground when Prime Minister Margaret Thatcher rejected it out of hand, shortly before the Brighton bombing mentioned earlier, when an IRA bomb almost killed her and her cabinet colleagues. Behind the scenes, however, the British and Irish governments were inching toward the 1985 Anglo-Irish Agreement. This made the Dublin government a permanent participant in the peace process in exchange for its *de facto* acceptance that Ulster would remain in the United Kingdom as long as a majority of its population wished it to do so. The unionists reacted against the agreement far more vehemently than Thatcher had expected. Nonetheless, it marked the beginning of what has been reasonably successful cooperation between London and Dublin ever since.

Between 1987 and 1991, London initiated a series of pre-negotiations with the various constitutional parties that became known as the "talks about talks." They accomplished little, largely because the parties representing the paramilitaries were excluded. Meanwhile, John Hume of the Social Democratic and Labour Party (SDLP) began a series of unsuccessful (at the time) negotiations with Gerry Adams following Sinn Fein's decision to end its policy of abstention from elections in the Republic. Many observers took that move as a first sign that the IRA was prepared to accept some sort of "two-Ireland" solution.

In the end, it took new leadership in Dublin, London and Washington to drive the negotiations toward a successful conclusion. In 1990, Thatcher's Conservative colleagues forced her into retirement and replaced her with John Major. Though he was Thatcher's protégé, Major was more flexible and a better negotiator than the "Iron Lady." Two years later, Albert Reynolds became Taoiseach. He moved his formerly pro-unification Fianna Fail Party toward acceptance of a permanent partition of the island. He also began a series of meetings with the SDLP and Sinn Fein leaders, who were also meeting secretly with British civil servants.

Those discussions produced the Downing Street Declaration of December 15, 1993. It reiterated the two governments' commitment to a British Ulster as long as a majority of its people wished to stay in the United Kingdom. Moreover, it anticipated that political parties that represented the Catholic and Protestant paramilitaries could join negotiations toward a permanent settlement if they rejected violence and started decommissioning their weapons. Significantly, the British cabinet declared that it had "no selfish strategic or economic interest in Northern Ireland," while the Irish government stated that "it would be wrong to impose a united Ireland, in the absence of the freely given consent of a majority of the people of Northern Ireland."

Although it is hard to document this with any precision, most average citizens had begun to tire of the violence. It wasn't just the fear of death: everyday life was filled with difficulties. Simple trips to the store were delayed by searches by security officers looking for weapons. The ever-present armed patrols and the euphemistically named Peace Line were among the many constant reminders of just how troubling the Troubles were.

While the details still are not clear, it seems that a growing number of the "hard men" in the paramilitary groups were also moving toward the conclusion that they had to put down the gun. We may never know exactly why that happened. To some degree, it reflected a genuine rejection of violence by men and women who had spent years in the Maze and other prisons, and had seen dozens of their friends and relatives killed. To some degree, too, it was the result of pragmatic decisions by politicians who realized that they were highly unlikely to get what they wanted through violence. The IRA, in particular, came to see that it could turn to the ballot box and the negotiating table because Sinn Fein was building a strong base of support in the Catholic community.

Whatever the mix of causes, in 1993 and early 1994 leaders from both communities began issuing more hopeful statements, such as the following one by David Ervine, who had been a member of the Ulster Volunteer Force and a prisoner in the Maze:

> The politics of division has seen thousands of people dead, most of them working class, and headstones on the graves of young men. We have been fools: let's not be fools any longer. All elements must be comfortable within Northern Ireland. We have got to extend the hand of friendship, we have to take the peace lines down brick by brick, and somehow or other we have got to introduce class politics. You can't eat a flag. (McKittrick 1996: 39–40)

Similarly, instead of referring to the unionists as little more than pawns of British colonial rule, Adams and his colleagues started talking about the need for both communities to coexist with dignity. As this was happening the political wing of the IRA was moving ever closer to the leadership in the South, and to David Hume and the SDLP, the one northern politician and party that had worked steadfastly for a peaceful resolution to the conflict from the onset of the Troubles.

At about this time, the IRA and Sinn Fein apparently decided that talking was not tantamount to defeat. Their supporters in the United States, as well as the new Clinton administration, had convinced them that considerable economic development funds would stream into Ulster if peace were to break out.

Then the most dramatic and, to some, unexpected event in this long saga occurred. On August 30, 1994 the IRA announced "a complete cessation of all military activity." The main Protestant paramilitaries followed suit within a week. While people outside Ulster saw the IRA decision as the key, in some ways the Protestant one was at least as important, because their paramilitaries had been far less disciplined and were responsible for more killings in the 1980s and 1990s.

For the first time, there was real hope that the Troubles could end. In the short term, the British were able to scale back their military involvement, and life in Northern Ireland returned to something approaching normal.

Still, there were three major obstacles to overcome, which made the situation in Ireland quite different from that in South Africa:

- The IRA and other republicans were still unwilling to give up their weapons until major political steps had been taken, because they remained convinced that the authorities were still biased toward the Protestants, and that they would leave themselves defenseless by disarming.
- The unionists left themselves with very little room for maneuver in the negotiations. Even the moderate unionists feared that any significant change in any of the strands of the talks would erode the union and thus endanger their position on the social, economic, political and security fronts.
- Progress toward peace was hampered by politics in the United Kingdom and, to a lesser degree, in Ireland. In London, John Major's majority all but disappeared, and he needed the support of the nine unionist MPs to stay in office and get legislation passed. Moreover, by mid-1995 almost all attention was focused on the upcoming 1997 parliamentary elections. Consequently, Prime Minister Major was unable to take any major risks as far as Northern Ireland was concerned. Meanwhile, the Republic of Ireland careened through a number of scandals that had nothing to do with policy toward Ulster, but which did lead to three different Taoiseachs in one three-year period.

In the meantime, Sinn Fein gained considerable credibility. Adams, McGuinness and its other leaders were frequent visitors to London and Dublin, and seemed always to be on radio and television. Sinn Fein now regularly won about a third of the Catholic vote in provincial elections (over 10 percent of the total), and its leadership insisted that it had become a conventional political party that had no formal ties to the IRA.

Still, Sinn Fein did not get what it wanted—entry into the negotiations. The unionists refused to participate in talks with Sinn Fein as long as the IRA refused to decommission its weapons. The frustration of Adams and McGuinness mounted.

On February 22, 1995 the British and Irish governments threw a political monkey-wrench in the works when they issued a new document, *Frameworks for the Future*, which was designed to be the basis for all-party talks. It anticipates much of the Good Friday Agreement, including the creation of North-South bodies and a new parliament in which all parties in Northern Ireland would share power. The Framework document was seen as a step forward by many Catholics. However, it confirmed the worst fears of many unionists and loyalists, that Britain was prepared to "sell them out" and had already started the province on the slippery slope toward unification with the South.

In early 1995 the British finally decided to ask for outside help. Until then, the British government had viewed Northern Ireland as a domestic political issue and rejected any outside intervention as a violation of its sovereignty.

That year, Major's government reversed that long-standing position, in large part because the United States was willing to weigh into the negotiations. In January, George Mitchell, who had recently retired from the US Senate, agreed to serve as a special adviser in the State Department on Irish issues for a brief period, primarily to organize the White House Conference on Trade and Investment in Northern Ireland. After that conference, Mitchell agreed to stay on until the end of the year to do some follow-up work and assist with President Clinton's planned trip to Belfast. During Clinton's visit on November 30, 1995. The British and Irish governments agreed to appoint an international team to head negotiations, including George Mitchell, former Finnish prime minister Harri Holkeri, and retired Canadian general Jean de Chastelain. Mitchell agreed to London and Dublin's offer to chair the negotiations. Because he coordinated the political talks and has written on the process, I will focus on Mitchell here.

George Mitchell

George Mitchell provides us with the best example in this book of a "third party" mediator.

Mitchell was born in 1932 in Waterville, Maine. He was the adopted son of a Lebanese-American family, and that was the cultural and religious tradition that most shaped him as a young man. Mitchell graduated from Bowdoin College and Boston University law school, and after a number of political false starts was appointed to the Senate when Edmund Muskie joined the Carter administration. Mitchell quickly developed a reputation as one of the most effective coalition-builders in the Senate, which propelled him to the post of majority leader. Mitchell prides himself on his skills as a listener and for his ability to "leave his ego at the door." And by the time he left the Senate, he was no longer particularly ambitious, having turned down an appointment to the Supreme Court and the job of Commissioner of Baseball.

In the end, it is probably that set of skills—of listening to all sides, respecting all participants, and building bridges between them—that makes a Mitchell, a Jimmy Carter, or a Terje Larsen (see Chapter 8) so effective in facilitating this kind of tense and difficult negotiation.

On the second day of the Obama administration Mitchell was named Special Envoy to the Middle East, to see if he could help end the conflict between Israel and Palestine which we will discuss in the next chapter.

The negotiators' initial task only dealt with decommissioning, which was then holding up the negotiations. In early 1995 the British Secretary of State for Northern Ireland, Sir Patrick Mayhew, had made decommissioning a precondition for entry into the talks, a position Sinn Fein rejected.

Mitchell and his colleagues understood that decommissioning before the start of all-party negotiations was a non-starter. Gradually, the mediators convinced themselves and then the British government that the parties should be allowed to participate in the talks if they:

- openly accepted non-violence and democracy
- made a commitment to hand over weapons as part of any agreement.

The Mitchell team presented their report on January 23, 1996, and assumed their work was over. The next day the British government threw the process off track by seizing on a minor portion of the report and calling for elections in Northern Ireland that would yield a new governing body for the province. This proved to be the last straw for the IRA and Sinn Fein. On February 9, a huge explosion ripped through the new, upscale Canary Wharf neighborhood in London, where many of the newspapers and financial corporations are located. The IRA cease-fire was over. There was no return to the widespread violence of earlier decades, but still a number of bombs went off in England and Ulster, while more numerous bomb threats periodically disrupted road and rail traffic.

The British went ahead with elections to a new assembly. Parties that accepted the Mitchell principles and won seats would then be eligible to take part in talks to begin on June 10. Although the elections threw the negotiations off even further, they did provide the unionists with one of their key demands, and Sinn Fein gained more credibility when it came in a strong fourth with almost 16 percent of the vote.

Mitchell and his colleagues returned for what he expected to be a few more months of talks. In fact, they took almost two years. The negotiations started poorly. Sinn Fein was not present, because the IRA had not yet reinstated its cease-fire. Ian Paisley's Democratic Unionists and another small loyalist party rejected Mitchell as chair and walked out.

The two governments and the seven Northern Irish parties that were left did agree to the Mitchell principles committing themselves to democracy and nonviolence. Despite that one step forward, the prospects for peace did not look bright.

The following Monday, the IRA set off a bomb that destroyed a new shopping mall in downtown Manchester, England. Rioting broke out when the RUC banned the Protestant Orange Order from taking its annual march through a Catholic neighborhood in Drumcree. The head of the RUC then drew the wrath of the Catholics as well when he changed his mind and let the march go ahead.

Mitchell and his colleagues persevered. By early fall, they had reached agreement on sufficient consensus. A proposal would be considered adopted if it gained the support of a majority of the representatives of each community. That meant, in particular, that Paisley and his supporters could not block an agreement on their own.

The election of Tony Blair and his Labour Party gave the peace process some much-needed new momentum. The Conservatives, who had been in power for eighteen years, had made their share of contributions toward peace in Northern Ireland. However, they were also seen as too pro-unionist and risk-averse. Labour brought more energy and a more positive attitude to the talks. Like Prime Minister Tony Blair, the new Secretary of State for Northern Ireland, Mo Mowlam, was young and enthusiastic, by contrast with the most recent Conservative ministers. Also, with its massive majority Labour had the freedom to maneuver in Northern Ireland that John Major never had and Margaret Thatcher never wanted. Shortly after taking office, Blair began talking of a May 1998 deadline for the talks, since the elected forum, which did little other than provide the personnel for the talks, would cease to exist after that.

Meanwhile, the Irish Republic also held an election. While the victory by Bertie Ahern at the head of a coalition led by his Fianna Fail party did not mark such a major change as the one across the Irish Sea, the new Taoiseach was more willing to try new approaches to the negotiations than his predecessor, John Bruton, had been.

Then, on July 20, the IRA declared another cease-fire. This second end to the hostilities marked a truly dramatic transformation for the likes of Adams and McGuinness, who had begun their careers as IRA soldiers, spent time in jail, and been treated as ruthless terrorists by their opponents. And this cease-fire brought Sinn Fein into the negotiations for the first time.

Not everyone approved of the cease-fire and Sinn Fein's participation in the talks. Paisley's Democratic Unionist Party, and the tiny United Kingdom Unionist Party, quit the negotiations.

The violence did not end. Some republican splinter groups continued the "armed campaign," and a bomb in Markethill almost derailed the talks. The murder of the loyalist Billy Wright (better known as "King Rat") inside the infamous Maze prison touched off a series of sectarian killings.

At this juncture, the mainstream unionists in general and their leader, David Trimble, in particular, became the focus of attention. Throughout his career, Trimble had been a loyal and intransigent member of the Orange Order. Like most politically active Protestants, he doubted everything Sinn Fein said and did. Moreover, he agreed with the unionists, who understandably felt they had the most to lose in any agreement, since whatever happened, they were not likely to retain their all but total control of the province.

At about the same time, the final push toward an agreement began, during which Mitchell's skills as a negotiator came to the fore. He gradually got the participants to stop—in his words—demonizing each other, because you cannot make peace while thinking the worst about your opponent. Despite his rather deadpan manner, Mitchell could effectively play on people's emotions. For instance, his wife gave birth to a son at a particularly tense point in the negotiations. Mitchell had his staff find out how many children were born in Northern Ireland that day, and asked the participants why those babies shouldn't have the same opportunity to live in peace as his son Andrew.

Gradually, the momentum began to shift toward an agreement. Political prisoners play an important role in Northern Ireland. Many of them began to support an agreement, especially following an unprecedented visit by Mo Mowlam to the loyalists in the Maze prison.

Ironically, the growing violence increased the pressure for an agreement. Sinn Fein and one of the small loyalist parties were suspended from the talks when their paramilitaries were shown to have participated in the ongoing violence. Both left, but made it abundantly clear that they were committed to returning as soon as the details could be worked out for doing so.

Finally, Mitchell set Thursday, April 9, as the deadline for an agreement. That date was chosen so that there would be enough time to hold elections to the new assembly before the always-contentious marching season began in July. Privately, Mitchell warned the participants that "they could not fail, because the alternative was unthinkable" (Mitchell 1999: 127). Publicly, the three independent commissioners issued a statement:

> The participants know what needs to be done. It's now up to them to do it. We are totally committed to this effort. We are not considering any alternative plan in the event of failure because we believe that failure is unacceptable. These next few weeks will be decisive. Those who are determined to wreck the process cannot be allowed to prevail. The success of these negotiations will require steady nerves and courageous leadership by the men and women in whose hands rests the future of Northern Ireland. (Mitchell 1999: 145)

The two weeks before the deadline were hectic. Draft agreements flew from fax machine to fax machine, meeting to meeting. Blair and Ahern spent the last days in the non-stop discussions that almost always occur in the hours before a deadline. This was particularly difficult in Ahern's case, since his mother had just died and he had to fly to Dublin for her funeral at a particularly tense moment in the talks.

The negotiations continued past the deadline into Good Friday itself. Finally, that afternoon, Trimble phoned Mitchell to say that the unionists had accepted the agreement. Fifteen minutes later, Blair and Ahern announced it to the waiting world. The agreement included the following provisions:

- an elected assembly and cabinet in which all parties that received at least 20 percent of the vote and accepted the Mitchell principles would participate
- decommissioning of weapons by May 2000
- new cross-border consultative bodies that would bring Northern Ireland and Republic of Ireland leaders together on questions of joint interest
- reinforcement of the British policy that Ulster would stay in the United Kingdom unless a majority of its people voted otherwise
- removal of clauses in the Republic of Ireland's constitution that call for the unification of the country

As most observers expected, the Good Friday Agreement was not implemented quickly or easily (Lloyd 1998). In particular, the unionists refused to take their seats in a government that included Sinn Fein until the IRA agreed to at least begin decommissioning its weapons. Sinn Fein countered that the agreement did not require them to hand over any weapons as a precondition for forming a government.

Decommissioning, therefore, held up progress for the rest of 1998 and most of 1999. As noted at the beginning of the chapter, it was the primary cause of the July 1999 breakdown in the negotiations that led to Mitchell's return the following September.

Just before he came back to the province in 1999, Senator Mitchell ended an interview on the Public Broadcasting System's *NewsHour* by stating that people in Northern Ireland now agreed on two, contradictory, things:

- Almost all of them want peace and cannot face the possibility of a return to the Troubles.
- All groups want to see the peace made on their own terms.

Eleven more weeks of tough talks followed. On November 12, it seemed as if the negotiations were about to collapse once and for all when the unionists refused to accept a new plan put forth by Mitchell. The senator adjourned the talks for the weekend. As he had done in the days and hours before Good Friday, he asked the parties to give serious thought to what would happen should they fail to reach an agreement.

Over the weekend, the IRA reached an agreement with de Chastelain, who still headed the decommissioning negotiations. This would begin the process of turning in weapons the day a government was formed, and the organization committed itself to meeting the May 2000 deadline for complete disarmament. On November 16 the unionists agreed to the new deal.

It took another two weeks for the details to be worked out. Nonetheless, on December 2, 1999 the British and Irish parliaments enacted the legislation that put the Good Friday Agreement into effect. On December 3, the new cabinet met for the first time, though the two members from Paisley's Democratic Unionist Party refused to attend. On December 4, an unnamed official of the IRA began meeting with de Chastelain's commission, and all sides reported that substantial progress had been made at that first encounter.

To see how far Northern Irish politicians had come, contrast the statements from three of the leading participants in the 1999 talks with the remark from the anonymous IRA member quoted near the beginning of the chapter (unless otherwise noted, all are from Hoge 1999b):

Gerry Adams:

[Violence] is now a thing of the past, over, done with and gone.
[Sinn Fein] wishes to work with, not against, the unionists.

David Trimble:

It is our belief that the establishment of new political institutions and the disarmament of all paramilitary organizations will herald a new beginning for all sections of our people—a new peaceful, democratic society where political objectives are pursued solely through democratic means, free from the use or threat of force. (<http://cnn.com>, accessed November 16, 1999).

For too long, much of the unrest in our community has been caused by a failure to accept the differing expressions of cultural identity. [We need] mutual respect and tolerance rather than division and alienation.

Monica McWilliams of the small Women's Coalition, which played an active role both before and after Good Friday:

These are the kinds of statements we thought were never possible in Northern Ireland.

Reconciliation and Social Change

At the time, the 1998 and 1999 agreements seemed like many recent pacts. They marked a major step forward, made violence less likely, and opened the door to further negotiations.

However, there were still dozens of issues that divided Catholics and Protestants, and therefore long-term peace-building was anything but a certainty.

In fact, when I wrote almost a decade ago, I worried that the compromise would turn into what Fen Osler Hampsen calls an "orphaned agreement." Because few provisions were in place for either further agreements or steps toward reconciliation, I felt the accord was fragile and could easily collapse, something that has happened in as many as half of the cases where the parties reached a cease-fire, or even went further.

So far, at least, I seem to have been wrong. Thankfully so. Northern Ireland has not had anything as public and popular as the South African Truth and Reconciliation Commission. Yet it is arguable that the province has made at least as much progress, though we do not have the analytical tools to measure or compare how far each has really come.

Four reasons for success in Northern Ireland stand out, none of which were easily predictable a decade ago:

- Gradual and often tension-filled negotiations which ended up bringing both the DUP and Sinn Fein into the provincial government.
- Efforts at the grassroots level, often small and quiet, in many cases involving faith-based organizations.
- A dramatic increase in foreign investment from European and American sources that especially helped improve the standard of living of Catholics.
- Surprisingly, a new and more constructive role played by the British military, and even some former inmates of the Maze and other prisons.

To achieve reconciliation and stable peace, the province's politicians and citizens have addressed the South African-style popular divisions that Bloomfield calls the "cultural" side of conflict resolution. But far more than in South Africa, the peace process continued because of conscious efforts by political elites in the province and beyond.

Negotiations

Before the talks leading to the Good Friday Agreement, the unionist and Sinn Fein leaders had never met. They sat together in occasional official meetings after that, but as far as I know, Gerry Adams and David Trimble never exchanged a civil word before the eve of the 1999 agreement. As George Mitchell put it when he returned to the negotiations in July 1999, "each side works on the assumption that the other side won't keep its promises" (PBS *NewsHour*, July 29, 1999).

Indeed, negotiations after the provincial government was created were never easy. On two occasions, the British government suspended it largely because of disputes about the nature and pace of decommissioning weapons.

Oddly, events that occurred 3,000 miles away may have given the political leaders the impetus they needed to move forward. The 9/11 attacks on New York and Washington undercut almost all remaining popular support for the IRA and other terrorist groups in Northern Ireland. It should also be pointed out that Blair and Ahern stayed in office until 2007 and 2008 respectively, and never wavered in their commitment to the peace process.

Even so, it wasn't easy. Sinn Fein came close to reaching a comprehensive agreement in 2004, but those talks collapsed. The IRA was accused of spying on others at Stormont and supporting the FARC rebels in Colombia. The next year, a young man was killed in a pub by IRA members. The IRA acknowledged what had happened and offered to kill the perpetrators; the man's sister turned them down.

But then in 2005, Gerry Adams said that the IRA should pursue its goals only through peaceful means. Later that year, the IRA declared that the armed campaign was over. In 2008, the IRA (but not Sinn Fein) was disbanded.

The most important turning point came in late 2006, when British and Irish governments and all the political parties in Northern Ireland signed the St Andrews agreement that, among other things, committed all of them to supporting the new police service of Northern Ireland. Following elections in March 2007, a new Northern Ireland executive was formed with Ian Paisley as First Minister and Martin McGuinness as his deputy. In spring 2008, the 82-year-old Paisley retired and was replaced by Peter Robinson.

During a visit the leadership team paid to the White House in 2007, McGuinness summed up the magnitude of the changes of the previous decade. Shortly thereafter, he flew to Baghdad to extend his newfound peace-builder role to the conflict there.

Reconciliation

There have also been many reconciliation projects, most of which have fallen below the media's radar screen. Many began before the Good Friday Agreement itself (see Bloomfield 1997 and Love 1995). While they pale in comparison with those in South Africa, they are now more extensive than similar initiatives involving Israelis and Palestinians.

The two communities in Northern Ireland remain amazingly isolated from each other. Housing is more segregated than it was before the Troubles began, because thousands of people were forced to move into now-homogeneous neighborhoods in the 1960s and 1970s. Nonetheless, Protestants and Catholics do work with each other more, and more often as peers. More and more of them attend higher education together. However, the all-important elementary and secondary education, social organizations, and, of course, the churches are still almost always exclusively Catholic or Protestant.

Two political parties—Alliance, and the Women's Coalition—have explicitly tried to reach voters from both communities. Together, they have never won even 10 percent of the vote, although the Alliance's Lord John Alderdyce was the speaker of the first assembly. The Women's Coalition disbanded after it lost all of its seats in the legislative assembly in 2005.

The key to continued success has been the work of dozens of small, mostly grassroots organizations. One of the most interesting of these is Belfast United, a program that continued for most the 1990s. It was jointly run by the Institute for International Sports (www.internationalsport.com) in Rhode Island, and sports coaches in Northern Ireland. The program initially assembled teams of Catholic and Protestant teenagers, who spent several months in the United States practicing and playing together while also learning more about each other, including how they could get along. The project was highly successful, and helped to launch similar efforts to use sports in conflict resolution by the Institute and other NGOs during the last fifteen years.

The most famous of these is Corrymeela. The retreat center opened in 1965 as a place for reconciliation between Christians. As such, it was driven by theological rather than political goals. But once the Troubles began in earnest, Corrymeela became a focal point enabling people on both sides of the sectarian divide to come together.

Corrymeela itself is not a big organization. Not even 200 people formally belong to it, and its full-time staff numbers no more than thirty officers. It has a house and office in Belfast and a retreat center in rural Ballycastle, which can accommodate 120 people. However, it has a broader reach and impact than these numbers might suggest. In the 1970s it started by hosting rather formal conferences that brought together academics, members of the clergy, and others from the two sides. Since the early 1980s, it has broadened its efforts to bring people from all walks of life to Belfast and Ballycastle. Ballycastle typically hosts 8,000 people a year for week-long seminars for families, single parents, victims of violence, families of prisoners, and the like. Corrymeela also has programs in most cities that try to bring young Catholics and Protestants together.

It's not just Corrymeela.

Another influential and innovative organization is the Northern Ireland Memorial Fund. Like Corrymeela it promotes cross-community understanding and cooperation. In some ways it even goes farther, having sponsored joint trips to other troubled countries in the world such as Sri Lanka and Romania.

Although we have no way of demonstrating it, small local groups may have had an even greater impact. The Peace and Reconciliation Group works almost exclusively in Derry/Londonderry (remember that even the name of the city is controversial). The PRG has a staff of six and conducts training workshops about most of the issues that gave rise to the Troubles. Like many NGOs in the region, its training programs focus on life and career skills as well as political reconciliation.

Perhaps the most surprising change has been the efforts of a number of former republican and loyalist paramilitary group members to reach out to each other. Organizations such as the Glencree Centre (www.glencree.ie) have taken a lead. Glencree has held residential workshops with ex-combatants once every two months since 2002 (Shirlow and McEvoy 2008).

Finally, the European Union has funneled well over a billion dollars into the province. Some of the funding has been designed to spur economic growth (see the next section). Almost all of it includes schemes to bring together Protestant and Catholics, and residents of the province and border regions in the Irish Republic. The Special European Union Programmes Body (www.seupb.org) is best known for funding the development of new restaurants, folk music festivals, and other non-political events. However, it also has committed over fifty million dollars to programs that help people acknowledge and deal with the past. Indeed, in its self-description SEUPB heads its list of goals as: "To reinforce progress towards a peaceful and stable society and to promote reconciliation."

Nonetheless, when Protestants and Catholics do come together, mistrust often gets in the way of making progress. Consider an example from earlier in this decade. Queen's University in Belfast now has almost as many Catholic as Protestant students. Catholics objected to the playing of "God Save the Queen" at graduation ceremonies. Since the national anthem is rarely played at British graduation events, university officials agreed and proposed Beethoven's "Ode to Joy" as an alternative. Protestants objected, saying that "God Save the Queen" is a symbol of Northern Ireland's status as an integral part of the United Kingdom. Debates over anthems themselves do not spark violence, but such disputes are a sign of the still-deep mistrust and, therefore, of how far away the province is from stable peace.

Economic Growth

As noted earlier, all the conflicts covered in this book are asymmetrical in nature. One side has a lot more power than the other, an imbalance that is not just political. In Northern Ireland, almost all members of the Royal Ulster Constabulary were Protestants. Almost all of the major business and, therefore, almost all of the top jobs were controlled by Protestants. The Protestants enjoyed a noticeably better standard of living.

The situation had begun to change even before the Good Friday Agreement was signed. For reasons that go beyond the scope of this book, the Republic of Ireland underwent an economic boom in the 1990s which spilled over to the north.

But, there is little doubt that Northern Ireland benefited from a "peace dividend" as a result of the peace. Obviously, a combat zone is not going to be attractive to investors, domestic or foreign. With the stability of the last decade, however, Belfast has trailed only London as the site of long-term economic investment in the UK, and the province's GDP per capita exceeds that of Scotland and Wales.

The changes are most obvious in Belfast—most of the rest of the province remains bucolic and rural, which also makes it a tourist attraction now that the political situation has calmed. Tourism has, in fact, grown by about 4 percent per year since the turn of the century. The Belfast waterfront has seen most investment, with at least $5 billion pledged for long-term projects. The waterfront is politically significant because it was home to one of the world's largest ports and shipbuilding facilities a century ago, jobs that went mainly to Protestants and have mostly disappeared. In other words, refurbishing the Titanic Quarter (where the infamous ship was built) with jobs for both Catholics and Protestants is politically, economically, and symbolically significant.

Much of the growth has come in high-tech industries, which also bodes well for the economic future of all the province's residents. Bombardier—the Canadian-based jet plane manufacturer—added 15 percent to its workforce in the years after 1998. Many of the other companies that added jobs were also foreign-based, including Caterpillar, DuPont, Nortel and Seagate.

Although it is hard to document in detail, one cannot underestimate the role of the Irish diaspora in this investment boom. Many Irish Catholics in the United States at least tacitly supported the IRA; many donated money they almost certainly knew would be used to buy weapons. The engagement by the Clinton administration and by politicians such as George Mitchell (who has close ties to the Kennedy family) meant that many Irish-Americans shifted their commitment. It wasn't just the private companies they owned, but institutions such as the New York City employee pension fund, which invested $150 million in the province in 2008 alone.

The Military and the Police

By almost all accounts the police, and the British military after the United Kingdom took control in 1972, were obstacles to anything approaching a peace process until the 1990s or even later (Clark 2008). As we have already seen, the Royal Ulster Constabulary was properly seen as a bastion of the Protestant cause. When the British army arrived, it saw its role in classic law-and-order terms, meaning that its main focus was on the IRA and its allies who, at the time, were committing the majority of terrorist attacks.

However, as the 1980s and 1990s wore on, the British military, in particular, paid more and more attention to new versions of counter-insurgency strategy, something we will see again in the chapters on Iraq and terrorism. To be sure, the military has to provide physical security, as in the American "surge" under General Petraeus in Iraq. But as Petraeus and many of his colleagues have argued, effective counter-insurgency campaigns also require seemingly non-military efforts involving amnesty, reconciliation and reintegration ("AR2" in military-speak).

Although the British military had been reasonably successful in earlier AR2 efforts in countries such as Malaya and Kenya, it took a long time for the lessons learned there to sink in. As Mari Fitzduff, a leader in the peace process, put it after years of heavy-handed law enforcement, "the security forces increasingly realized that their own occasionally hostile interface with the communities and the tactics they sometimes employed became a problematic of the conflict itself" (Clark 2008: 39).

But as the peace process began in earnest, the military played a hard-to-quantify role in bringing all the parties into the negotiations. Along with the British government, the military agreed to the amnesty of many republican and loyalist prisoners who would have to play a key role in any negotiations. More importantly, the amnesties encouraged many of the former prisoners to work increasingly through democratic political institutions. Despite the fact that everyone knew that these (mostly) men were perpetrators of heinous crimes, the fact that they were working "inside the system" gave new momentum to the search for peace. With the withdrawal of the last British troops in 2007, responsibility for security and AR2 has fallen more than ever on the new police service, which encourages citizens to report hate crimes against all people, including gays and immigrants.

Lessons Learned

Our last task for this chapter is to tease the theoretical implications from the history of the peace process. Because this is the second case we have considered, the points that follow are more detailed and nuanced than those of Chapter 5, and that will continue to be the case with the four remaining case studies.

1. *The international system.* This is the one case we will consider in which the momentous changes in the international political system since the end of the Cold War have not mattered much. It is still the case that the international community has not been actively involved whenever the vital interests of one of the major powers are at stake. Thus, as in the two wars in Chechnya, there has never been any real possibility that the UN or any other international organization could intervene in Northern Ireland. That said, international forces have come into play here. There is no more obvious example of that than the impact of the Clinton administration in supporting the talks after 1995. Still, the impact of global forces has largely been on the margins—with but one exception.

2. *Third parties.* That one exception is the role of third parties. As we saw above, Senator Mitchell and his colleagues deftly gained the trust of the leading politicians, which allowed them to gradually build bridges between the previously antagonistic parties. Indeed, it seems highly unlikely that the parties could have reached an agreement without outside help.

As will be clearer after the next chapter, having a third party does not guarantee success. Much depends on two factors: the size of the chasm between the two sides, and how effectively the third party uses the combination of political "carrots" and "sticks" at their disposal. Mitchell had few levers to use in forcing the parties in Northern Ireland to accede to his wishes. Instead, he drew on all the skills he had developed in his years in the US Senate as a coalition-builder.

And, though we lack the tools to measure this with any precision, his task was probably made somewhat easier by the fact that the violence in Northern Ireland did not claim as many lives or cause as much destruction as the fighting in any of the other countries covered in this book. If nothing else, that probably made it possible for him to gradually build trust as envisioned in the general literature on conflict resolution, international or otherwise.

3. *Asymmetry.* This case reinforces the mainstream international relations conclusion that a negotiated settlement is hard to reach when there is a sharp disparity in the resources which the different parties bring to the conflict. Individuals and groups on the weaker side feel particularly aggrieved, and worry that negotiating from a position of weakness could only undermine their position. The stronger side, by contrast, sees no particular need to talk, because successful negotiations could well lead to compromises that would "unnecessarily" erode their advantages.

During the course of the late 1980s and 1990s, the relationship between Catholics and Protestants became much more balanced. In part, that reflected the higher birth rate among Catholics and the emigration rate among Protestants, which has left the latter with a much smaller majority among the province's population. More important, as the example of the national anthem at Queen's University suggests, Catholics are obtaining a somewhat "fairer share" of most resources, including professional and other lucrative jobs.

The more neutral attitude of the British government toward the two communities has also produced a more even distribution of political, if not economic, resources. In particular, the authorities now treat the two groups in a more even-handed way. This trend seems bound to continue, especially as plans come to fruition to replace the RUC with a new police force that explicitly tries to recruit Catholics.

Finally, there has been a distinct change in public opinion. In the 1970s and 1980s, most people in Britain, the Irish Republic, and Northern Ireland blamed the IRA for the Troubles. As the bombings and fighting dragged on, and the Protestant paramilitaries began to do more killing than the IRA and other nationalist splinter groups, a growing number of people turned against all the perpetrators of the violence, whatever their religion or their goals. That was especially true of residents of Omagh, site of the last (August 1998) and most deadly bombing in the history of the Troubles. Journalists have repeatedly returned to the town as the negotiations progressed, and have consistently found that family members of the victims, in particular, think there is next to no difference between the Catholic splinter group that carried out the attack and the Protestant paramilitaries.

4. *Hurting stalemate.* Our concrete evidence on the way political leaders think is never complete. Nonetheless, the limited interviews they have given and the analytical work that has been done on Northern Ireland both strongly suggest that leaders of the key political groups all came to the conclusion that the province had reached a "hurting stalemate."

The conclusion was reached at various times and in various ways. John Hume and his colleagues in the SDLP reached it first. They always rejected the use of force in reaching nationalist goals. In the early and mid-1990s, most of the IRA leadership seems to have reached the same conclusion. Critics point out that the IRA only dropped their "Armalite and the ballot-box" strategy because they knew they could not win a "military" victory.

That may well be true, but even if their decision to seek peace only occurred because they realized they could not win the war, it does little to undermine empirical support for the argument about the importance of a hurting stalemate. The last (and most important from a theoretical perspective) group to renounce violence—and then only at the final moments of the negotiations—were the unionists. Mainstream unionists were never willing to resort to violence, other than the fisticuffs that often followed Orange Order and other marches. However, they were convinced well into 1997 and 1998 that they dare not give up violence, and that they need not make concessions on such critical issues as direct negotiations with Sinn Fein, let alone participating in a government with its representatives. In fact, as we are about to see, Trimble and his colleagues had a very hard time selling the idea of negotiation and power-sharing to a large minority of their fellow Protestants, for both tactical and ideological reasons. The sell was even harder for the DUP. But as its vote soared at the expense of the UUP, its leadership realized it would have to participate in provincial government, something made possible after the IRA "ended" the war.

5. *Political leadership and domestic politics.* Here, the difference between Northern Ireland and South Africa is easiest to see. As we saw in the last chapter, South Africa was blessed with a number of remarkable leaders who forsook vengeance and sought reconciliation instead. While Nelson Mandela gets most of the public credit for this, there were dozens of prominent leaders in all political camps working for peace and reconciliation. Northern Ireland has also had its share of advocates for reconciliation. John Hume of the SDLP, the Northern Ireland Women's Committee, and the Alliance Party all worked long and hard for a non-violent solution to the Troubles. However, with the exception of John Hume, none of them had a significant following in either the Protestant or Catholic community.

Perhaps more important in the long run is the fact that little opposition exists to the Good Friday Agreement today. Some paramilitary groups have announced their plans to continue the armed struggle, but at the time of writing there have been no new attacks like the one at Omagh. However, if one of these small groups does launch a major bombing campaign, it could do irreparable damage to the gains made so far.

6. *An international dimension.* The Troubles have largely occurred inside the borders of a single country. In addition, as we saw above, Britain's power, and the all but universal recognition of its state sovereignty, made outside intervention impossible. Nonetheless, there are important international aspects to the way the Good Friday Agreement was reached and implemented that could conceivably be adapted to some other long-standing religious and ethnic conflicts.

The Irish and (because of the large Irish-American population) the American governments had ties to the Catholic community in the north. Therefore, they could persuade the SDLP, and later Sinn Fein and the IRA, to take a more moderate and conciliatory line. The prospect of more foreign investment in a peaceful Northern Ireland also no doubt had an impact on the willingness of the parties to negotiate.

Perhaps more important in general terms is the way that the Good Friday Agreement, to use Jonathan Stevenson's term, "dilutes" British sovereignty in Northern Ireland (Stevenson 1998). The cross-border institutions, in particular, will make the Republic of Ireland an active participant in Northern Ireland's political affairs. Furthermore, if Stevenson is right, the growing power of the European Union made this agreement possible precisely because the EU provides more opportunities for one member state to engage itself constructively in the internal affairs of another.

7. *Slow and incremental progress.* More than South Africa, Northern Ireland supports a pair of overlapping conclusions rarely found in the literature on win-win conflict resolution. It typically takes a long time to reach an agreement, and the deal that is eventually concluded invariably addresses only some of the issues at stake in the conflict.

South Africa's transition to democracy occurred relatively quickly. Still, nearly a decade elapsed from the start of negotiations between Mandela and his jailers to the election of the African National Congress as ruling party. In Northern Ireland, we have seen that the informal exploration of a peaceful settlement began almost as soon as the Troubles did, and nearly thirty years elapsed before the Good Friday Agreement was reached.

That conflict resolution takes time should not be surprising. After all, the conflicts under consideration here are deep indeed. The years of violence and tension have driven crippling psychological wedges between the participants in all of them. In fact, as the Irish case shows, just getting the leaders of the parties to the table can by itself take years.

Under those circumstances, it should also not come as a surprise that negotiators have to settle for incremental progress. We academics may well be able to envision more sweeping changes, but it may not be practically possible to implement them, especially in a case like this one in which most of the participants in the talks faced opposition from within their own communities—a point we will return to in the next chapter.

8. *Reconciliation.* The preceding point should not be read as suggesting that participants in peace processes should settle for any agreement. Rather, it is important that an incremental agreement do at least two things above and beyond putting an end to the fighting.

First, a resolution should be like the confidence-building measures in arms control, whereby an initial agreement establishes procedures that will make it easier to reach more sweeping ones later on. There is reason to believe that the implementation of the Good Friday Agreement in late 1999 made that start. As Britain's then Secretary of State for Northern Ireland, Peter Mandelson, put it during a visit to the United States shortly after the new Northern Ireland government was formed, "trust is creeping in" among the politicians who are part of the new institutions.

Secondly, moving from the tension that characterizes Northern Ireland today to anything approaching stable peace requires a concentrated effort at reconciliation. On that front, the Irish have done far less than the South Africans, or even the Israelis and the Palestinians. As noted earlier in the chapter, there have been few formal attempts to bring the Catholic and Protestant communities together. If anything, they probably meet informally in their jobs or their neighborhoods less than they did before the Troubles began. And, as John Lloyd (1999) put it in one of the first extended essays on the state of Northern Ireland after the government was formed, there is still a very volatile mix of violence and hatred throughout the province. Lloyd cites the work of John Scott, who has led a team of unemployed young people to cover over some of the most hateful and offensive graffiti in Dublin. But, as Lloyd concludes:

> John Scott's story might show that the vast damage that civil society has suffered over the past three decades can be pushed back by courage and reassertion of what people really want. Yet it is not ordained: this is no happy ending. The Union Jacks and the tricolors [Republic of Ireland flags] still flutter on lampposts, and the gray walls of the estates scream hate and pride at each other. Peace has been proclaimed, but as attested to by the bitter experience of South Africa, Kosovo, Nicaragua, and many others in the last decade or so, it takes far more than a political pact and good intentions to root out the pathologies of war and build a healthy society. (Lloyd 1999: 93)

Select Bibliography

Bloomfield, David (1997). *Peacemaking Strategies in Northern Ireland*. Basingstoke: Macmillan.

—(1998). *Political Dialogue in Northern Ireland*. Basingstoke: Macmillan.

Clark, John (2008). "Northern Ireland: A Balanced Approach to Amnesty, Reconciliation, and Reintegration." *Military Review*. January–February, 37–49.

Coogan, Tim Pat (1996). *The Troubles: Ireland's Ordeal 1966–1996 and the Search for Peace*. Boulder, CO: Roberts Rinehart.

Hoge, Warren (1996). "Pledges by Ulster Rivals Break the Deadlock at Talks." The *New York Times*, Washington Edition, November 17, A3.

—(1999). "Roadblock to a Peace Pact: Irish Mostly Say 'No.'" *New York Times*, Washington Edition, July 3, 1999, 7.

Holland, Jack (1999). *Hope against History: The Course of Conflict in Northern Ireland*. New York: Henry Holt.

Lloyd, John (1999). "Ireland's Uncertain Peace." *Foreign Affairs* (September/October): 109–23.

—(1999). "The Troubles That Won't Go Away." The *New York Times Magazine*, December 12, 89–93.

McKittrick, David (1996). *The Nervous Peace*. London: Blackstaff.

Mitchell, George (1999). *Making Peace*. New York: Knopf.

O'Toole, Fintan (1999). "The Ulster Conundrum: The Words Used to Broker Peace Have Become Stumbling Blocks." The *Washington Post*, July 11, B4.

Shirlow, Peter and Kieran McEvoy (2008). *Beyond the Wire: Former Prisoners and Conflict Transformation in Northern Ireland*. London: Pluto.

Stevenson, Jonathan (1998). "Peace in Northern Ireland: Why Now?" *Foreign Policy* (Fall): 41–54.

Toolis, Kevin (1995). *Rebel Hearts: Journeys within the IRA's Soul*. New York: St Martin's.

CHAPTER SEVEN

Israel and the Palestinians

*The Pope, according to a no doubt apocryphal story, maintained that there were two
possible solutions to the Arab-Israeli conflict: the realistic and the miraculous.
The realistic solution involves divine intervention; the miraculous solution, a voluntary
agreement among the parties themselves.*
—Avi Shlaim

Late-breaking News

I finished this chapter in late November 2008.

In late December a tense cease-fire between Israel and the Hamas leadership in the Gaza Strip came to an end. Fighting broke out. Hamas launched primitive missiles that could not be targeted in any meaningful way. Israel responded with precision air attacks and then an invasion that lasted until the day President Obama was inaugurated. At last count more than 1,300 Palestinians were killed, but only 13 Israelis.

On the second day of the Obama administration, George Mitchell was named Special Envoy to help find a solution between the Israelis and the Palestinians.

It is too early to judge the long-term significance of either event, and too late to include them other than with this brief mention here.

On September 13, 1993 Israeli prime minister Yitzhak Rabin and Palestinian leader Yasser Arafat signed the historic Oslo agreement on the lawn of the White House in Washington DC. It was dubbed the Oslo Accord, because the negotiations that produced it had been held in secret under the leadership of a team of Norwegian academics and diplomats. At the ceremony, Rabin spoke for many when he said:

Let me say to you, the Palestinians: We are destined to live together on the same soil in the same land. We, the soldiers who have returned from the battle stained with blood; we, who have seen our relatives and friends killed before our eyes; we, who have attended their funerals and cannot look into the eyes of parents and orphans; we, who have come from a land where parents bury their children; we, who have fought against you, the Palestinians; we say to you in a loud and a clear voice—enough of blood and tears. Enough.

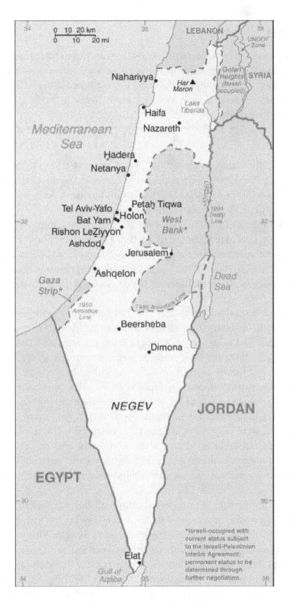

Figure 3 Map of Israel

It was a remarkable day, filled with hope. Three weeks earlier, no more than 100 people in the world knew that the negotiations were in progress, let alone near fruition. Many of us who watched the ceremony shared Rabin's hopes, which were similar to those we saw expressed in South Africa and Northern Ireland.

Arabic Terms

There are many ways of transliterating Arabic words and names. I have chosen to use the same transliterations one finds in the leading American news media such as the *New York Times* or the *Washington Post*. They are not necessarily the best. They are, however, the ones readers of this book are most likely to be familiar with and/or encounter in further reading.

Unfortunately, the Israeli–Palestinian peace process did not fulfill those hopes during the rest of the 1990s. The signs were already visible that sunny afternoon. Coincidentally, my wife was in Israel and Jordan on business. As is my wont, I asked her to get me some T-shirts. There weren't any. Not a good sign.

Negotiations continued for the rest of the decade but accomplished little, especially after Rabin was assassinated by a right-wing Israeli, elections brought Binyamin Netanyahu to power in Israel. His conservative government was far more intransigent at the negotiating table than Rabin's had been, and little progress was made on such critical issues as the transfer of the remainder of the West Bank land to the new Palestinian Authority.

Netanyahu and his Likud Party lost the 1999 election, bringing Labor back into office. The new prime minister, Ehud Barak, committed himself to reaching a definitive peace agreement, not just with the Palestinians but with Syria and Lebanon as well. Late that year, final status talks on the future of Jerusalem began at last (even though the deadline for their resolution, set out by Oslo, had already passed). Throughout 2000, US-sponsored talks continued. Most notably, the two sides came closer than ever to an agreement on such divisive issues as the status of Jerusalem during talks held at the presidential retreat of Camp David, Maryland. In practice, too many stumbling blocks remained over what were referred to as "final status issues"—the status of Jerusalem, the right of Palestinians in exile to return, water resources, and more. President Clinton argued that the two sides had agreed on 95 percent of the outstanding issues. At that point, the remaining 5 percent represented a huge ideological chasm. Today, that chasm is even wider.

The prospects for further serious negotiations all but evaporated when the second *intifada*, or uprising, broke out among Palestinians following the unwelcome visit of conservative Israeli politician Ariel Sharon to Jerusalem's Temple Mount, the third holiest site in Islam. That unleashed a series of clashes between Palestinians and Israeli forces in Gaza and the West Bank. Dozens of suicide bombers blew themselves—and hundreds of Israeli civilians—up in markets, on buses, and in office buildings. At a number of points, Israel and the Palestinian Authority were all but at war; Israel also fought two unsuccessful wars with Hezbollah militants in southern Lebanon.

Subsequent Israeli elections moved the country even further to the right. Just as importantly, they reduced the size of the major parties to the point that forming a government which could act decisively was all but impossible. In the 2006 election (another is likely to be held in 2009) Kadima, the *largest* party, won 29 of 120 seats in the Knesset or parliament. The government was weakened as well by the stroke that paralyzed but did not kill Sharon, and the corruption scandal that forced his successor, Ehud Olmert, from office in 2008.

Meanwhile, the Palestinian community splintered as well, beginning with the lingering illness that finally claimed Arafat's life in 2004. Although many people in Palestine and abroad respected Mahmoud Abbas, his successor lacked the PLO's de facto founder's charisma or power. Matters in the Palestinian community got worse when the more militant and orthodox Hamas won elections in Gaza in 2006 and took total control of "the strip" early the next year.

The international community bears its share of responsibility. Many observers—including this author—were critical of the role the United States played before 2000. As much as the Clinton administration, in particular, worked for a two-state or similar solution, its firm support for Israel made it less than an ideal third party. That said, it is hard to avoid the conclusion that the Bush administration did not concentrate enough on the escalating crisis between Israel and the Palestinians. It did pay lip service to it as part of its efforts to combat terrorism and the regional crises that grew out of 9/11. However, despite occasional flurries of activity, it did not devote anywhere near as much effort as it could have to working as an intermediary between the two sides.

Thus, there is an obvious question. What went wrong? But there is another equally important one. What went *right* in the months and years leading up to the Oslo Accord? This chapter will try to address both questions, and in so doing tease out some more general conclusions about conflict resolution as a whole.

A Complicated Conflict—and Some Analytic Limits

This chapter will focus on relations between Israel and the Palestinians. As should already be clear, that conflict is but part of a larger cluster of disputes between Israel and all its Arab neighbors.

Unfortunately, we cannot do justice to the entire conflict here. Therefore, I will bring in material on the other Arab countries and their relations with Israel only when it is needed to see what remains the thorniest problem in the Middle East.

Some of these issues will reappear in the next two chapters on Iraq and the war on terrorism.

Theoretical Focus

As just noted, this chapter will concentrate on theoretical factors that help us understand why the Israelis and Palestinians made some progress toward peace, but also why remaining major roadblocks in the peace process have made matters worse in the first years of this century. At the end of the chapter, we will therefore return to the following issues:

- the changing structure of the international system after the end of the Cold War, the Gulf crisis of 1990–91, and the aftermath of 9/11
- the overall weakness of the international community in addressing conflicts in which one or more of the world's major parties believes it has a powerful interest
- the importance of third parties, but also the difficulty in finding an effective one
- the role of informal or track-two diplomacy and grassroots citizens' initiatives in producing steps toward peace and reconciliation even during "down" periods in formal negotiations

- how the asymmetric nature of the relationship between Israel and the Palestinians has hindered progress toward peace since the beginning of the conflict
- the ways that domestic politics in general, and leadership in particular, can be both a source of progress and an obstacle to peace both in the region and beyond
- the continued role of "rejectionist" groups, and the effect of widespread "images of the enemy" among both Israelis and Palestinians.

The Origins of the Conflict

The roots of the Israeli–Palestinian conflict are encapsulated in the titles of two books on it: *One Land, Two Peoples* (Gerner 1994), and *Sharing the Promised Land* (Hiro 1999). Both the Jewish Israelis and the mainly Muslim Palestinians have powerful claims to the same territory. To complicate things further, that land is also home to many of the sites which are most sacred sites to those two religious traditions—and to Christianity as well. Indeed, one of the most powerful symbols of how entangled the communities are is the al-Aqsa mosque, which is the third holiest place in Islam and which sits atop the ruins of the Second Temple and the Wailing Wall, the most sacred site in Judaism. It is also only a few hundred yards from the Church of the Holy Sepulchre, which many Christians believe is the point from which Jesus rose to heaven.

The fact that these peoples can trace their origins in Israel/Palestine back thousands of years has led many observers to see this as a centuries-old conflict. That is not really the case. Until quite recently, the few Jews in Palestine got along reasonably well with their Arab neighbors. In other words, the Arab–Israeli conflict is largely a product of twentieth-century political choices made by people both inside and outside the region.

Modern-day Israel began as the dream of Zionists in the 1890s. Those were tough years for Jews in Russia and the rest of eastern Europe, where they were subject to widespread discrimination and indiscriminate attacks known as pogroms. A relatively small number of Jews, led by Theodore Herzl (1860–1904), saw their future in the traditional homeland of the Jews.

The Jewish return (*aliyah*) began as a trickle. Only about 25,000 Jews lived in Palestine at the end of the nineteenth century, most of whom were descendants of people who had been allowed to move back to Jerusalem during the Crusades. A 1918 census registered 56,000 Jews, or about 8 percent of the total population of Palestine. The early Zionists were surprisingly uninterested in how they were received by the Palestinians. The few who did pay attention to the Palestinians treated them as inferior to the Jews.

By contrast, the 600,000 Palestinians had little real sense of national identity. That was not surprising, since Palestine had been under foreign rule for hundreds of years.

The political tide began to turn against the Palestinians during World War One. The British and French wanted to encourage local resistance against the Ottoman Empire, which had joined the war on the German and Austro-Hungarian side. London and Paris sent mixed signals. They told the Arabs that they would grant them independence if they supported the Allied effort. As we will see in more detail in the chapters on Iraq and terrorism, they failed to live up to those promises (see Table 7.1).

More important for our purposes here, the British issued the Balfour Declaration, which many observers on all sides took as an endorsement for an eventual Jewish state, despite its ambiguous wording:

His Majesty's government view with favour the establishment in Palestine of a National Home for the Jewish people, and will use their best endeavours to facilitate the achievement of this object, it being clearly understood that nothing shall be done which may prejudice the civil and religious rights of the existing non-Jewish communities in Palestine.

Palestine was designated a British mandate in the Treaty of Versailles, and there is nothing in Britain's administration of the region to suggest it planned to hand it over to either its Jewish or its Arab population.

Nonetheless, the Balfour Declaration was but one of many acts that convinced leading Palestinians that the Jews were a key element of British imperialism throughout the Middle East.

Meanwhile, the pace of Jewish migration stepped up, especially after Hitler came to power in Germany in 1933. By that point the British were taking a more even-handed approach toward the two communities, and they imposed stiff limits on the number of Jews who would be allowed to emigrate to Palestine.

Not surprisingly, the Palestinians resented the new settlers on "their" land. The first protests broke out in 1921. In 1929 Jews attempted to make the Wailing Wall, in the Arab-dominated Old City of Jerusalem, accessible for prayer. Riots ensued in which 133 Jews were killed. A full-scale Arab revolt disrupted the mandate from 1936 to 1938. At least 5,000 people died.

The British established the Peel Commission to investigate the situation. Its 1937 report concluded that the Jews and Palestinians were unlikely to work out their differences, and recommended partition and the creation of a small Jewish state. Most Zionists joined David Ben Gurion and other leaders in accepting the principle of partition, if not the specifics of the Peel Report.

Table 7.1 The Evolution of the
          Israeli–Palestinian Conflict

Date	Event
1897	First Zionist conference
1917	Balfour Declaration
1933	Hitler comes to power in Germany
1947	UN Resolution on partition
	Arab–Israeli War starts
1948	Israel declares its statehood
1949	First war ends
1956	War starting with invasion of Suez
1967	Six-Day War
1969	Fatah and Arafat take control of PLO
1973	October/Yom Kippur War
1982	Invasion of Lebanon
1987	Start of the first *intifada*

Most Jews were willing to put the struggle for statehood on hold during World War Two. But, as reports of the Holocaust streamed in, they became even more committed to creating the state of Israel than ever before—and more impatient with the British.

By the end of the war the Jewish army was well-armed, as were small bands of terrorists that were part of the more militant Revisionist movement, which opposed partition. The British cracked down, but the government in London had no desire to fight Jews a few short months after the appalling revelation of the Holocaust. Britain therefore announced plans to return the mandate to the United Nations.

On November 29, 1947 the UN General Assembly passed Resolution 181, which called for the creation of a Jewish state. The new state would also include 400,000 Palestinians. Needless to say, the Palestinians and other Arabs were adamantly opposed to this or any other arrangement that would take away what they saw as their land. Fighting broke out again and consumed the region for more than a year.

There is still considerable debate about who was responsible for what then occurred. In early 1948 there were intense battles between Jews and Palestinians. The Jews used both a regular army, the Israeli Defense Force (IDF), and less disciplined groups that today would be called terrorists. The latter carried out a series of attacks, the most important of which, to their critics, was at the village of Deir Yasin, where more than 200 civilians were killed.

On May 14, 1948 Prime Minister David Ben Gurion proclaimed the state of Israel. Immediately thereafter the neighboring Arab states attacked, in what would be the first of six full-scale wars. The outnumbered but better disciplined and motivated Israelis won. Although there was no formal treaty ending the fighting, a series of negotiations led to the establishment of borders that would last until the 1967 war, and could well become the frontiers of Israel again should the current peace process reach fruition.

The Iron Wall

The Zionist movement split in the 1920s. While the left-wing inheritors of the Herzl version remained dominant, the minority revisionist faction made one contribution that marked almost all Jewish Palestinians, and then Israelis, well into the 1980s.

In a 1923 essay, the revisionist leader Rabbi Ze'ev Jabotinsky wrote of an "iron wall" that should separate Jews and Palestinians. He argued that it was impossible both to force all the Palestinians to leave and to reach a *modus vivendi* with them through which they could comfortably share the land. In fact, unlike many of the left-wing Zionists, he expected a struggle. Jabotinsky wrote:

> Every indigenous people will resist alien settlers as long as they see any hope of ridding themselves of the danger of foreign settlement. That is how the Arabs will behave and go on behaving so long as they possess a gleam of hope that they can prevent "Palestine" from becoming the Land of Israel. (Shlaim 2000: 13)

The fighting intensified as the Arab states declared war on Israel. The Israelis finally won after months of intense fighting that cost over 6,000 Jewish lives. On January 13,

1949 the UN chief negotiator for Palestine, Ralph Bunche, led Israel and the various Arab states to an agreement on an armistice that ended the fighting. In some people's eyes, it marked a de facto acknowledgment by the Arab states that Israel existed, though none of them would recognize it formally for another thirty years.

The establishment of a Jewish state brought tremendous joy to Jews around the world. It brought the opposite for Palestinians and other Arabs.

The defeat was a dual tragedy for the Palestinians, in what they call *al-nakba*, or "the disaster." Not only did they lose control over most of their land but at least 800,000 people, or over 80 percent of the Palestinian population, fled, creating the refugee problem that still plagues the region to this day.

The Arab–Israeli Conflict before Oslo

For the next twenty years, the conflict was centered not on the Palestinians but on Israel's relationship with the Arab states. The status of Palestinians at home and in the diaspora was an all-important issue. However, virtually everyone—including most Palestinians—assumed that the Arab states would best represent Palestinian interests.

The Arab Focus

The failure of the other Arab states to redress Palestinian grievances set the stage for the violence of the Palestinian–Israeli conflict from the 1970s onward. From that perspective, there were five crises (many of which turned into all-out wars) that deepened the tensions. For reasons of space, we can only note them in passing here:

- In 1956 Israel, France and Britain launched a war against Egypt after it took over the Suez Canal under its new nationalist government headed by Gamal Abdel Nasser. The war was a catastrophe for the British and French, but the Israelis again demonstrated their military superiority over the Arab states.
- In 1967 Israel launched a pre-emptive attack, which became known as the Six Day War. In a matter of hours, the Israeli defense force destroyed the various Arab forces and occupied the West Bank, the Gaza Strip, the Golan Heights, and the Sinai Peninsula, initiating the territorial dispute that rages to this day.
- In 1973 Israel fought its last full-fledged war with the Arab States, known as the October War to most scholars but as the Yom Kippur War to many Israelis and Americans. This time, the Arab states gave the Israelis a stiffer fight but were eventually defeated, which meant that Israel retained control of the territories it had occupied in 1967.
- In 1982 Israel invaded Lebanon and killed thousands of Palestinians in its raids on refugee camps dominated by the Palestine Liberation Organization (PLO), some of which were in Beirut. This was the only war during this period that did not involve all the major Arab states. Israel maintained its occupation until 2000, and its withdrawal contributed to the outbreak of the second *intifada* to be discussed below.
- In late 2008 and early 2009, Israel and the Hamas-led government in Gaza fought a three-week war. As I write a week after the Israelis withdrew, it is by no means clear what will come next in this phase of the conflict, which many think has destroyed any hope of a two-state solution for the foreseeable future.

Palestinian Resistance

There had always been some resistance against Israeli rule among Palestinians. From their perspective, Israel had taken their land and made hundreds of thousands of them into what turned out to be permanent refugees.

From the late 1940s onward, small groups of *fedayin*, or rebels, launched attacks from refugee camps. Those raids only strengthened Israeli commitment to building a modern version of Zabotinsky's iron wall, even though the country was governed by men and women whose roots were in original, left-wing Zionism. Every strategy, from the development of the IDF to the creation of settlements along the borders, was designed to protect the new state's security from attack by Arab armies and Palestinian guerrillas.

As noted earlier, the Palestinians initially deferred to the leaders of the Arab states. That changed after the Six Day War for three main reasons. First, the war demonstrated that the Arab states were not likely to defeat Israel. Secondly, even more ominously for the Palestinians, it showed that the other Arabs were not very committed to their cause. Thirdly, and most importantly, nearly a million Palestinians had all of a sudden come under Israeli rule in the Occupied Territories in the West Bank and Gaza.

Until then, there had been dozens of Palestinian organizations, some demanding the immediate return of their lands, others willing to follow a more gradual strategy. Among them was *Fatah*, organized by Yasser Arafat with the encouragement of Egyptian president Nasser. In 1964 Nasser organized a meeting in Cairo that created the PLO and its military wing, the Palestine Liberation Army. That May, 422 delegates met in East Jerusalem (then still controlled by Jordan) and adopted the Palestinian Charter, which read in part:

> The partition of Palestine in 1947 and the establishment of the State of Israel, are entirely illegal regardless of the passage of time, because they were contrary to the will of the Palestinian people and to their natural right in their homeland, and inconsistent with the principles embodied in the Charter of the United Nations, particularly the right to self-determination.

Fatah was not one of the earliest or most effective guerrilla groups. In fact, its first raid was a failed attempt to destroy a canal taking water from the River Jordan to the Negev desert. But because of its financial resources and the skills of Ararat and his colleagues, Fatah was able to take control of the PLO organization in 1969, after which it became the heart of Palestinian resistance.

The PLO has never been a unified organization. Its membership has always included moderates who favored negotiation and coexistence with Israel, and radicals whose only goal was the destruction of the Jewish state and who were willing to use violence, including terrorism. For most of the 1970s, the latter group was by far the most influential within the PLO.

The PLO initially hoped to form a regular army that could win back Palestine. However, it burst onto the world's political stage in the 1970s when, with other groups, it staged a series of dramatic terrorist attacks. Planes were hijacked. Israelis and other Jews were killed. In the most dramatic act, Palestinian militants seized Israeli athletes at the 1972 Olympic Games in Munich, many of whom were killed in the shootout that ended the crisis. The PLO was not responsible for all the acts of terrorism, a fact often lost on

Yasser Arafat and the PLO

Yasser Arafat became the most visible and controversial figure in the Palestinian resistance against Israeli rule after he became leader of the PLO in 1969. Arafat was born in Gaza in 1929 and went into exile as soon as the state of Israel was formed. In the 1960s he formed *Fatah*, which became the leading guerrilla force and political movement in the Palestinian community after the Six Day War.

Arafat was an implacable opponent of most Israeli policies regarding the Occupied Territories, and he backed the use of violence for most of his long political career.

Despite his deserved radical reputation, Arafat turned into one of the more moderate PLO leaders, who always at least talked about negotiations even while leading the PLO's guerrilla campaign against Israel. In the 1980s, Arafat made the peace process possible on the Palestinian side by renouncing terrorism, accepting UN Resolution 242 as the basis for negotiation, and endorsing Israel's right to exist.

In 1989 he was named head of the Palestinian government in exile, and six years later he became president of the Palestinian National Authority, as the emerging Palestinian government is formally known.

Arafat was always seen in public with his *kaffiya* draped in a way that resembles the map of Palestine.

He died in 2004.

Americans and Israelis, who saw the group as by far the most important faction in a resistance movement they often labeled terrorist.

However, as early as 1974 Arafat sent signals that the PLO was willing to consider some sort of peaceful solution to the conflict. Thus, in his first address to the United Nations General Assembly, he stated:

Today I have come bearing an olive branch and a freedom fighter's gun. Do not let the olive branch fall from my hands.

For the next twelve years, however, the olive branch mostly "fell from his hands." The PLO continued to attack Israel, which maintained its often brutal administration of the Occupied Territories. The Israelis tried—and failed—to create Palestinian officials with whom they could work, who were not part of the PLO. Meanwhile, the PLO's relations with the rest of the Arab world deteriorated, especially following its forced departure from Jordan and then Lebanon.

The start of the *intifada* made the prospects for peace seem ever more distant. *Intifada* can best be translated as "shaking off," and for many young Palestinians who joined in the demonstrations and threw stones at Israelis, they were literally trying to shake off the yoke of Israeli rule.

On December 8, 1987 a vehicle carrying Israeli troops collided with a car in the Gaza Strip. Four Palestinians were killed. Rumors quickly spread that this was a deliberate Israeli attack. Whether it was true or not, the rumor touched off the most massive wave of protests yet seen in Israel and the Occupied Territories.

At first the Israelis tried to put the revolt down by using violence against the protesters and making wide-scale arrests, much of the response being planned by Yitzhak Rabin, who was then defense minister. In the first thirty months of the *intifada*, over 800 Palestinians were killed, more than 200 of whom were under sixteen. Israeli repression, in short, only served to stiffen the resistance. It was only in early 2000 that Israel officially acknowledged that it had used torture on many of the Palestinians it arrested.

What's more, to the degree that the *intifada* was a coordinated movement, its initial leadership was only loosely connected to the PLO. The PLO was also somewhat concerned about the *intifada*, because many of its veterans found their way to more militant groups like Hamas and Hezbollah in the 1990s.

The Road to Oslo

Even before the *intifada* reached its peak, many influential leaders in the region and beyond came to the conclusion that they needed to end the violence and take steps toward some kind of permanent settlement between Israel and the Palestinians. But, to illustrate a conclusion that is clear from the previous two chapters, such negotiations invariably take a long time, and they only reach fruition when leaders on both sides of the dispute can summon up the political will to make significant progress. And, as we will see here, even what looks like a dramatic step forward may only be temporary.

Israel and the Arabs

Israel began discussions with neighboring Arab states almost as soon as it gained its independence. However, for a variety of reasons we do not have the space to go into here, until the 1970s those talks accomplished little other than producing armistices to end the various wars.

Indeed, the most important discussions (for example, those with King Hussein of Jordan and with President Nasser shortly after he took power in Egypt) were conducted in secret because of the likely repercussions which public disclosure would have had both in Israel and in the Arab world. Although Israel at least professed interest in living at peace with the Palestinians and other Arabs, it was a long time before either side showed any serious interest in peaceful co-existence.

Israel remained convinced that the Arabs were out to destroy the Jewish state, and therefore resisted making any concessions that would put the country's security in the slightest jeopardy. The Arab states publicly reinforced those fears. At the Khartoum summit following the 1967 war, they repeated their refusal to legally recognize the existence of Israel, let alone make peace with it.

In retrospect, however, we can see that the outcome of the 1967 war moved the sides closer to a hurting stalemate, and opened the door to separate negotiations with individual Arab states as well as the Palestinians. The 1973 war truly opened the door that ultimately led to a series of agreements starting with the Camp David Accords.

After the 1967 war, the United Nations adopted a series of resolutions on the Middle East. The most important of these was Resolution 242, which called in part for "the withdrawal of Israeli armed forces from the territories occupied in the recent conflict" and asserted the right of "every state to live in peace within secure and recognized boundaries." The UN also deployed peacekeepers in Sinai to monitor the tense standoff between Israel and Egypt. But the "blue helmets" were withdrawn at the request of the Egyptians, an action that encouraged the outbreak of fighting in 1973.

Useful Websites

The University of Texas's Middle East Center maintains a list of groups supporting the peace process that have websites: http://link.lanic.utexes.edu/menic.

Neve Shalom/Wahat al-Salam, which will be described below, has an extensive site: http://www.newas.com.

PASSIA is one of the best non-governmental organizations working on Palestinian-Israeli issues, and it also trains young Palestinian university graduates in conflict resolution, diplomacy, and the development of civil society. Its website is full of data: http://www.passia.org.

An intriguing new initiative is Combatants for Peace, a group of men and women who once fought against each other and now work together to end the conflict: www.combatantsforpeace.org.

The first concerted effort by outsiders to defuse the tensions came with Henry Kissinger's shuttle-diplomacy missions during the last few days of the 1973 war and in the months that followed. Despite the fact that the United States was so closely allied with Israel, Kissinger was able to persuade the sides to stop fighting and reach an informal agreement on subsequent relations. Kissinger was spurred on by the economic consequences of the OPEC oil embargo, and the fears of many that another crisis in the region could actually bring the United States and Soviet Union to war. The United Nations did its part by passing Resolution 338, which called on all parties to start negotiations for a lasting settlement on the basis of 242. Kissinger was aided also by a real sense of war-weariness in Israel and many of the Arab states, most notably Egypt. Meanwhile Israeli and Egyptian military officers held a series of meetings, which culminated in the withdrawal of Israeli troops from Egyptian territory in early 1974.

Kissinger's initiative, however, did little to build a lasting peace. The first key steps in that direction came after two major political events occurred. In the United States, the Democratic administration of Jimmy Carter took office in 1977. That same year the Labor Party in Israel lost an election for the first time, bringing the more conservative Likud Party to power. Likud was a direct descendant of Revisionist Zionism. The new prime minister, Menachem Begin, had been the commander of the Irgun terrorist group after the war and had opposed partition, insisting that the new Israel had a legitimate claim to all of Palestine.

As has often been the case in world politics, the election of a conservative leader made new initiatives possible: someone like Begin could take risks that would have been too politically costly for a Labor prime minister. At the time, most international attention was focused on convening a Geneva conference involving all the parties. Secretly, however, aides to Begin and Egyptian president Anwar Sadat began informal discussions that would lead to bilateral, not multilateral, agreements. In a move that surprised the whole world, Sadat told the Egyptian parliament that he was prepared to go to Jerusalem and speak to the Knesset if it would help the cause of peace. Ten days later, on November 19, 1977, Sadat arrived in Israel, where he and Begin agreed on the outlines of a plan for Israeli withdrawal from Sinai.

A flurry of further meetings occurred but accomplished little, contributing to growing frustrations on both sides. Finally, President Carter invited both leaders to a summit at the presidential retreat, Camp David. After ten hard days, the two sides agreed on "A Framework for Peace in the Middle East," which was followed by a formal treaty signed at the White House on March 26, 1979.

Israel agreed to withdraw its troops and settlers from Sinai, which did not figure in Begin's hopes for a "greater Israel." Israel and Egypt also agreed to formally recognize each other and forego further wars. More important for our purposes, the treaty recognized the "legitimate rights of the Palestinian people and their just requirements" and called for negotiations, beginning with the acceptance of "Resolution 242 in all its parts." Quickly, however, it became clear that Israel, Egypt and the United States had made precious little progress in agreeing on what those terms meant, and negotiations on the status of Palestinians soon reached an impasse.

Israel and the Palestinians

The Israeli-Egyptian treaty had two contradictory effects on the Palestinians. On the one hand, it reinforced the now widespread conviction that they could not rely on the Arab states to protect their interests. On the other hand, it showed that talks could actually get somewhere.

The next decade produced little or no progress. If anything, events from the continued acts of terrorism to the construction of new settlements in the Occupied Territories made a negotiated settlement *less* likely.

The *intifada*, however, marked a major turning point for many Israelis (especially in Labor), and for the PLO. Moderate Israelis, for instance, realized that they could not negotiate the fate of Palestinians with anyone but Palestinians, and that the PLO might well be their best (or perhaps least bad) alternative.

Meanwhile, people close to Arafat worried about groups that were more militant than Fatah. As the *intifada* raged, the Palestinian National Council met in Algiers in November 1988. Despite opposition from the radicals, it voted to implicitly recognize Israel, and to agree that any peace settlement would have to begin with the acceptance of UN resolutions 242 and 338, which both Israel and the United States had made a precondition for any serious talks.

The end of the Cold War also made a peace process easier to start by removing the Soviet Union as a major player in regional politics. It no longer had the resources to fund the PLO, other Palestinian groups, or Arab states. Even more importantly, the conflict between Israel and the Palestinians could be addressed on its own, without concern about its broader implications for superpower rivalry.

Similarly, the Gulf war helped to open the door to the peace process. The PLO was weakened even further because of the reaction of other Arab states against its support for the Iraqi invasion of Kuwait. Ironically, too, the Iraqi attempt to link a proposed pullout from Kuwait in late 1990 to negotiations on the status of Israel actually built more momentum for peace once the US had defeated Baghdad in Operation Desert Storm.

The Bush administration, in particular, tried to seize the opportunity provided by the newly fluid regional relations and balance of power to hold regional peace talks. To that end, the United States and the Soviet Union officially convened the Madrid Peace Conference in 1991, at which Israeli officials openly talked with Palestinians for the first time—though they still refused to negotiate with the PLO.

The Madrid process accomplished very little, because Israel would not budge on some of the key positions it had defended for years. Various governments in the late 1960s and 1970s had proposed granting some autonomy to Palestinians in parts of the West Bank. However, these offers were made with preconditions that brought an immediate rejection. In fact, Israel (and its American allies) would not deal with Palestinians linked to the PLO, and a law passed in 1986 made it illegal for any Israeli official to even talk to a PLO member.

Although it did not seem so at the time, the 1992 Israeli election marked a momentous change. For the eight years before that, the country had been ruled by a coalition "national unity" government that included both Likud and Labor. The presence of Likud with its hard line toward the Palestinians made progress toward peace all but impossible. In 1992 Labor won, bringing the former general and prime minister Yitzhak Rabin back into office, with Shimon Peres as foreign minister.

At first no one expected a dramatic breakthrough, especially given the hard-line positions Rabin had taken against the *intifada* in the national unity government. After the 1992 election, a BBC reporter asked an Arab janitor if he thought the shift in power would make a big difference:

> Do you see my left shoe? That is Yitzhak Rabin. Do you see my right shoe? That is Yitzhak Shamir. Two Yitzhaks, two shoes, so what's the difference? (Shlaim 2000: 502)

But the new Rabin government did prove far more flexible than its predecessor in the on-again, off-again negotiations taking place in Washington: opening talks with Syria, repealing the law banning contacts with PLO members, and releasing some Palestinian prisoners. It was not, however, prepared to make major concessions in those negotiations, and it continued to take a hard line on such issues as closing the borders with the Occupied Territories in retaliation against terrorist attacks (see Table 7.2).

The breakthrough did not occur, however, as a result of any formal talks, but through a successful track-two initiative. We now know that several citizen diplomacy discussions had begun secretly in the early 1990s, despite the Israeli law banning contact with PLO members.

The one that bore fruit came as a surprise. In fact, only about 100 people in the world even knew that the Norway channel existed until hours before the agreement was announced. Even the American, Palestinian and Israeli negotiators meeting in the continuation of the Madrid talks in Washington were kept in the dark until the last possible moment.

In 1992 a Norwegian sociologist, Terje Larsen, informed the Israelis and the Palestinians that his research institute and the Norwegian government were willing to facilitate discussions between the two sides. Three days before the Israeli election, Larsen

Table 7.2 The Oslo Peace Process

Date	Event
1978–79	Camp David
1991	Madrid Conference
1992	Election of Labor
1993	Oslo Accord
1994	Israel and Jordan sign treaty
1995	Oslo II
	Assassination of Rabin
1996	Election of Netanyahu and Likud
1998	Wye River Agreement
1999	Election of Barak and Labor

met with Yossi Beilin, Shimon Peres' closest adviser in the Labor Party, and Faisal Husseini, the most powerful Palestinian leader in Jerusalem. After the election Beilin became deputy foreign minister, and two of his associates—Yair Hirschfeld and Ron Pundak—agreed to continue the discussions in their capacities as private citizens. In December Larsen helped arrange a meeting between Hirschfeld and the influential Palestinian, Abu Ala, in London. Then Hirschfeld apparently asked the Norwegians to organize a larger meeting in the guise of an academic seminar, which began on January 20, 1993, the day after Israel's parliament repealed the law banning meetings with PLO members.

The Norway channel was a virtual "how-to" manual for third-party-led track two negotiations. The Norwegians were well suited for the role. To begin with, the Norwegian academic and diplomatic elite is quite small and interconnected. For example, Larsen's wife was a diplomat specializing in Middle Eastern politics, while Johan Jorgen Holst's wife was on the staff of Larsen's institute and participated in the first session, though she did not realize that there were also negotiations going on.

Larsen, in particular, used his expertise in group dynamics to smooth the negotiations. Though he rarely participated in the talks themselves, he was prepared to step in when the parties wanted him to help clarify an issue or resolve a deadlock. Even more important, he and his colleagues created an atmosphere in which the Israelis and Palestinians got to know and like each other. It is safe to say that by August the seven negotiators had become friends, and that their personal friendship was critical to their being able to overcome many of the thorny issues they faced.

In each new session, the discussions became more specific and the deliberations more official. Thus, discussion of general issues led to agreement on more than a dozen specific points in the Declaration of Principles (DOP).

The DOP took one vital step: the two sides recognized each other. The PLO acknowledged Israel's right to exist, and Israel accepted Palestinian authority first in Gaza and Jericho, an authority that would gradually spread to more of the West Bank, although the Israelis stopped far short of accepting a formal Palestinian state.

A timetable was set (but not met) for resolving "final status" issues, including the future of Jerusalem. Side agreements called for a substantial infusion of aid and investment in

Gaza and the West Bank for social, economic and political development, which included using the CIA to help train Palestinian security officers.

Negotiations continued on a number of fronts. In February 1994 Israel and the PLO agreed to a redeployment rather than a full withdrawal of Israeli troops from Gaza and Jericho. The next year, they signed the Palestinian Interim Agreement on the West Bank and the Gaza Strip (dubbed Oslo II), which created the Palestinian National Authority (PNA) that would assume complete power in most of the urban areas in the Occupied Territories and share power with Israel in others, while Israel would retain control of sparsely settled areas it felt were vital to its interests. Oslo II and the 1997 agreement on Hebron also called for further transfers of land to "area A" status under complete Palestinian control. Final status talks on such issues as the future of Jerusalem were scheduled to start in May 1996 for completion by May 1999. In April 1996 the PLO removed the clauses about the destruction of Israel from its charter.

Oslo also established new momentum for negotiations with other Arab states. Thus, Israel and Jordan signed a peace treaty in October 1994 and came close to doing so with Syria as well (Rabinovich 1999; Feldman and Toukan 1997).

There was by no means universal support for Oslo and the subsequent agreements it spawned. Skeptics were quick to point out that it failed to address any final status issues.

Likud, many settlers in the Occupied Territories, and some Jewish fundamentalists opposed the peace process from the beginning. Israeli and Jewish-American conservatives felt that Israel had conceded too much, including its historical "right" to Judea and Samaria, as they called the West Bank. At the time, for instance, Netanyahu said of Rabin:

> You are worse than Chamberlain. He imperiled another people, but you are doing it to your own people. (Shlaim 2000: 521)

Right-wing Jews committed a number of attacks, the bloodiest of which occurred at the al-Aqsa mosque in Jerusalem and at the Tomb of the Patriarchs in Hebron. Meanwhile, fundamentalist Jews continued to establish new settlements to add to the existing ones in the Occupied Territories, in an attempt to make any "land for peace" deal more difficult.

Among the Palestinians, intellectuals such as Edward Said felt the Oslo agreement gave too little to the Palestinians (Said 1996; Guyatt 1998). Organizations like Hamas and Hezbollah took their objections to the streets in a wave of bombings and other attacks that undermined Israeli support for the peace process.

The peace process almost came to a halt after Rabin was assassinated by a right-wing Israeli on November 4, 1995. He was replaced by his long-time colleague and rival in the Labor Party, Shimon Peres, who was, if anything, even more firmly committed to peace with the Palestinians. However, Peres was not as popular a leader as Rabin had been, and in an attempt to strengthen his personal and political mandate, called for early elections on May 29, 1996. A series of bombings by Hamas undermined what started out as a huge lead for Peres in the polls. When the Israelis actually voted, Peres lost to Netanyahu in the country's first direct election of its prime minister.

Officially, Netanyahu pledged to uphold Oslo and continue the peace process. In practice, his government took a number of steps that set the peace process back. Thus in September 1996 it opened a tunnel under much of the Old City of Jerusalem which many Palestinians took to be an insult, and which violated the Rabin government's agreement to settle disputes over Jerusalem through consultation. The next year, the Netanyahu government began building 30,000 homes in Har Homa/Jabal Abu Ghneim despite protests from liberal Israelis, the Palestinians, and most foreign governments. It failed to pull its troops out of Hebron, which had a handful of Jews living in the center of the city. It also failed to open a promised safe passage linking Gaza and the West Bank. Netanyahu offered the Palestinians a settlement in which Israel would keep control of about 60 percent of the West Bank, as well as all of Jerusalem. This offer, of course, was rejected out of hand. Negotiations with Syria were stopped. The Israeli government also tried to hold the PNA responsible for instances of terrorism, and often implied that Arafat and the PLO were themselves still terrorists.

World leaders grew increasingly critical of Netanyahu. Finally, in October 1998, the United States brought the Israeli and Palestinian leaders to the Wye River Plantation in rural Maryland. President Clinton himself led one 27-hour negotiating marathon that culminated in a memorandum signed by Netanyahu and Arafat. The two sides agreed to a new schedule of Israeli withdrawals from another 13 percent of the West Bank, while the Palestinians committed themselves to tracking down terrorists. The CIA would establish training programs and communications links for the Israeli and Palestinian intelligence services.

Setbacks since Oslo

Some scholars estimate that as many as half of the conflicts that reach the equivalent of the Oslo Accords return to violence within five years of such an agreement. Other observers who use different methodologies put the figure at more like one quarter.

In any event, the number is too high. In this case it took seven years for the agreement to fail, and not all the gains made in the Oslo process have been wiped out. Nonetheless, this author is among many who thought Oslo put the region on an admittedly long and tricky, but inevitable, road toward peace.

We were wrong.

The Second Intifada

At the same time that Israeli-Palestinian negotiations were heading toward deadlock, Netanyahu's support was dwindling, largely for domestic political reasons. In late 1998 it became clear that he could not continue to govern with the existing Knesset. Therefore, new elections were called for May 17. Netanyahu and Likud were defeated by the new prime minister, Ehud Barak, who led a multi-party government in which Labor was the largest member.

Barak had been chief of staff of the Israeli army, and was initially critical of aspects of the Oslo agreement. However, during the election campaign he pledged to withdraw all Israeli troops from Lebanon within a year, negotiate a treaty with Syria, and bring the final-status talks to fruition by 2001. In his first six months in office, significant progress was made on all those fronts.

Israeli and Syrian negotiators came close to an agreement on the future of the Golan Heights, and Israelis and Palestinians feverishly tried to agree on a broad framework of final-status issues before the deadline. However, Barak was a tough negotiator who made it clear that he did not intend to back down on key points. In short, the peace process resumed, but the two sides failed to make much progress on questions of final status.

My Personal Involvement

As early as 1993, I should have known that things would not go smoothly. Coincidentally, my wife was in Tel Aviv on business the day the Oslo Accords were signed. I asked her to get me a commemorative T-shirt. She emailed me back that night saying there weren't any, and that the mood there was anything but joyous.

In 1998, I made the first of two trips to East Jerusalem to lead workshops on conflict resolution with young Palestinian professionals. Their attitudes toward a Jewish facilitator was cordial and encouraging, and a number of them were already deeply involved in the peace process. Most were angry with Israel and the slow pace of the negotiations. All were angry with Israel and the United States for their policies, ranging from the "big" policy issues to the security measures that made their movement from Gaza to the West Bank and to East Jerusalem excruciatingly difficult. But I felt safer in East Jerusalem than I did in some ultra-orthodox neighborhoods in the western part of the city.

I went back in May 2000, six weeks or so before the second *intifada* broke out. Things were much more difficult. When I was there, Israeli troops were being all but forced to pull out of South Lebanon in the wake of Hezbollah attacks on them and the official Lebanese army (which I could only watch in Arabic because the cable system at my hotel had dropped all English language stations). I was no longer encouraged to wander around even the parts of East Jerusalem that I had known so well two years earlier. I was driven the six blocks to the workshop site.

I had been invited to do a workshop in Gaza late that fall. But once the *intifada* broke out, the Palestinians had no choice but to cancel the event.

American President Bill Clinton had staked much of his reputation on finding peace in the Middle East. As his administration was drawing to a close, he invited Barak, Arafat and their teams to a last-ditch round of negotiations at Camp David. Accounts differ about what happened. There is little doubt that both sides were willing to make significant concessions, but the talks ultimately failed. Each side blamed the other for the failure. President Clinton publicly and privately laid the bulk of the responsibility on Arafat. Whoever bore most of the burden, the two sides were too divided on most of the remaining final-status issues, especially how to turn Jerusalem into the capital of both states (see Table 7.3).

Things had already deteriorated at home. Earlier that year, the militant Shiite[1] Lebanese group, Hezbollah, assassinated the head of the Lebanese army in the south and all but drove it out of the region. They then turned their attention to the Israeli troops who had been in a roughly twenty-mile strip along the border since 1982, which it euphemistically dubbed the Security Buffer Zone. At various times during the 1990s, Hezbollah

---

[1]   The distinction between Sunni and Shiite Muslims will be discussed in the chapter on Iraq.

Table 7.3   Events since the Collapse of the Oslo Peace Process

Year	Event
2000	Failure at Camp David
	Israeli withdrawal from Lebanon
	Start of second *intifada*
2001	Terrorist attacks in New York and Washington
	Election of Sharon
2002	Battles in Ramallah and Jenin
	Bush announces "road-map" for peace
2004	Death of Arafat
2005	Election of Mahmoud Abbas as President of the PA
2006	War between Israel and Hezbollah in Lebanon
	Hamas wins elections in Gaza
2007	Hamas takes total control of Gaza
2009	War between Israel and Hamas

fired rockets into northern Israel. Israel responded with even greater firepower. Very few combatants were killed, almost certainly under 20. That said, at least 150 Lebanese civilians died and upwards of 350,000 Lebanese and 20,000 Israelis were forced to flee their homes.

Late that September, two events occurred that sparked an *intifada* which, frankly, was just waiting to happen. On the twenty-seventh, an Israeli soldier was killed by Palestinians. The next day, Likud politicians visited the grounds surrounding the al-Aqsa mosque. Although the mosque is open only to Muslims, others routinely visit the rest of the site during normal tourist periods. Israelis claim that the visit had been arranged previously and that the Palestinian Authority had guaranteed it would not have negative consequences. Some Israelis also claim that Arafat had been planning a new *intifada* for months to show his dissatisfaction with the peace process after Oslo. Neither of these claims can be confirmed.

Whatever the causes were, massive riots broke out in the area around the Old City. They spread to the West Bank and Gaza within a matter of days.

At first, the second *intifada* resembled the first. Palestinians threw rocks. Israeli troops retaliated. A few people were killed and wounded, mostly Palestinians. But by the end of October things had begun to change. Israelis started throwing rocks back, and chanting slogans such as "Death to Arabs." Late that month the Israelis intercepted a ship loaded with weapons heading for Gaza, which was then under PA control.

Then things turned far more violent. Two Israeli soldiers were lynched. For the first time, the Palestinians started using guns and missiles in their attacks. The next year, a wave of suicide bombings began which targeted Israeli civilians, often children. The targets were largely random but were chosen to maximize both the shock value and the number of civilians, especially children, who would be present. For example, buses and coffee shops were often chosen. A friend of mine was coming to Washington— ironically, to help me run a conference on reconciliation. He had to go to his bank and then drop his dog at the kennel before going to the airport. If he had done these jobs in the opposite order, he would be dead.

The violence quickly escalated. While the suicide bombers inside Israel got the most attention in the Western media, the Israelis responded in kind. Their most notorious act occurred in Ramallah in 2002. After a suicide attack in the coastal city of Haifa, the Israelis refused to allow Arafat to leave his compound in Ramallah, a city of about 100,000 just outside East Jerusalem. This violated the Oslo Accords. Then, the IDF began bombing the compound in a systematic attempt to destroy it and, some thought, to kill Arafat. Estimates of the degree of destruction vary, but much of the neighborhood, if not the city as a whole, was destroyed.

After that, the level of violence ebbed and flowed. After Hamas gained control of Gaza following elections in 2005, the pace of rocket attacks on southern Israel picked up. As it has done throughout the *intifada*, Israel strengthened what it saw as its security procedures, but what its critics saw as provocative gestures. It closed the borders from the West Bank and Gaza into Israel. When I was there in 1998 and 2000, it was already very difficult for Palestinians to move to and from the two portions of their territory, let alone to visit Israeli-controlled East Jerusalem. Now, travel became all but impossible. In 2003, Israel also began building what it hoped would be an insurmountable wall on its Palestinian borders to keep suicide bombers out. Whatever the merits of the wall, it cut almost 70 Palestinian villages in two, often making it impossible for farmers to tend their fields, or members of one side of a family to see the other.

The best estimate is that by April 2008, 5,842 people had been killed. Again, contrary to what one might expect from press reports, 4,789 of them were Palestinians, more than four times the number of Israelis casualties. On both sides, civilian deaths outnumbered those of combatants, although it is often hard to determine who was a combatant and who was an innocent civilian on the Palestinian side.

Not surprisingly, the peace process all but came to a halt. In fact, most of the achievements made through the Oslo process disappeared. Rightly or wrongly, Israel reasserted most of its former control, militarily if not politically, over the Occupied Territories. American attention turned toward curbing Palestinian violence rather than preserving the peace process (see also the section on the role of the United States below).

At the time that I wrote this chapter in fall 2008, the fighting had subsided considerably. However, even liberal Israeli opinion, reflected in the newspaper *Haaretz*, was already anticipating a third *intifada* (www.haaretz.com/hasen/pages/ShArt.jhtml?itemNo=9632 97&contrassID=2&subContrassID=4v). Officially, the second *intifada* had been over for a couple of years: but Palestinian youths had started throwing stones again in Northern Israel, and more rockets were being fired into the southern part of the country.

In short, the future is far from certain.

Other Events and Their Impact on the Peace Process

Obviously, the second *intifada* was a damaging blow for the peace process, turning this into one of the dozens where the opposing sides lapsed back into violence after an initial peace agreement was signed.

However, the situation was worsened as a result of factors beyond the renewed fighting between Israelis and Palestinians. Three of them stand out.

The Impact of 9/11

The attacks on the World Trade Center and the Pentagon occurred at one of the tensest and most confusing moments of the second *intifada* (see the next two chapters). Even though no Palestinians nor Israelis were directly involved, the uncertainties following the attacks and the American-led responses in Afghanistan and Iraq made hopes of peace even harder to imagine, let alone achieve. The attacks and the reactions to them put the Israeli/Palestinian conflict into a new and broader context that further derailed cooperation between the two sides.

On the one hand, the attacks made the Israeli-Palestinian conflict more important than ever. Statements from Al Qaeda and others made it clear that an important part of their demands concerned the dispute over that small part of the Middle East.

On the other, as we will see in the next section, the attacks shifted the attention of the United States and most of the rest of the international community toward much broader regional issues, including the possibility of Iraq and Iran gaining nuclear weapons.

Many Palestinians sympathized with the plight of Iraqis, even if they did not agree with the policies pursued by Saddam Hussein. Many Israelis felt more threatened than at any time in their recent history, as the region became even more unstable. The situation did not improve from an Israeli perspective with the United States' invasion of Iraq, or the rumored nuclear weapons program in Iran.

Historically, whenever tensions mount in the region, even Israeli doves become more intransigent. This has certainly been the case since the beginning of this decade, as can be seen in evidence ranging from the support of the Israeli government for American policy to the number of flags average citizens fly from their balconies or car radio antennas.

The Diminished Role of the United States and the International Community

Most conflict resolution specialists want the third parties that mediate disputes to be neutral and impartial. In practice, that is almost never possible. In fact, most such specialists who worked on the South African transition opposed the Afrikaner government and the apartheid system. Similarly, George Mitchell is a practicing Catholic, though not, as many Ulstermen thought, of Irish descent.

Under no circumstances can the United States be considered a neutral third party regarding the Middle East. The United States recognized the state of Israel eleven minutes after it declared its independence, although there is some evidence that President Harry Truman had doubts about a Jewish state up until two days before he acted so swiftly and decisively.

More importantly, the United States has always been Israel's staunchest ally. Rarely have American political leaders criticized Israel. Israel typically receives about a third of official United States foreign aid, much of which is used to support the IDF. One estimate (foreign aid statistics are notoriously hard to fathom) has the equivalent of about $15,000 a year going from Washington to Tel Aviv for each Israeli citizen each year.

There is also no doubt that the American Jewish community keeps the pressure on the United States government to support Israel under virtually all circumstances (see the box below). Jews only make up about three percent of the American population, but they are disproportionately wealthy and influential. In the Senate whose term expired in January 2009 there were 12 Jews, almost all of whom were liberal on most political issues—but not on Israel. Even the most liberal of the group, Bernard Sanders, an independent senator and former socialist from Vermont, regularly supports legislation in favor of Israel.

The Role of AIPAC

One of the controversies regarding American Middle East policy involves the alleged role of the American Jewish lobby, especially its leading political group, AIPAC (Mearsheimer and Walt 2007; for a counter-argument, Landy 2006). As noted in the text, the American Jewish community has an influence that is far greater than its share of the population would suggest—there are probably more Muslims than Jews in the United States. And, there is no question that AIPAC is the Jewish community's most vocal and powerful lobbying group.

However, the Mearsheimer and Walt argument probably ascribes too much power to AIPAC, though Landy's critique probably underestimates what the organization can do, especially working behind the scenes.

Last but no means least, many American Jews, including this author, have deep doubts about the policies pursued both by Israel and the Palestinians. We just aren't as effective as AIPAC in getting our points of view onto the political agenda.

It is therefore no surprise that the Oslo Accord and some of the other more promising proposals in the peace process came from other countries, and especially from the Scandinavians. Nonetheless, the United States has such vested interests in the Middle East that realistically it has to be a major factor in promoting or blocking progress toward peace.

And, there is no question that the Clinton administration made peace in the region a top priority. It retained Dennis Ross from the George H. W. Bush administration as its main negotiator. In the 12 years Ross spent in that position, he and his colleagues probably did more than any other group in American political history to encourage the peace process. It did not help that Ross is both Jewish and a strong supporter of Israel. Still, he and the president worked extremely hard in the region, especially after Oslo.

One cannot say the same thing about President George W. Bush. Al Gore was apparently prepared to replace Ross (who was going to retire whoever won the presidential election) with a senior political science professor known for his commitment to finding common ground in the Middle East. Bush had far less experience in the region, and there were very few senior people in his entourage who were knowledgeable on the issue. The few who were fell into the neo-conservative camp, and were even more pro-Israeli than the advisors Clinton had relied on.

In a sign of what was to come, Bush made retired Marine General Anthony Zinni his lead negotiator for the Middle East. No one doubts Zinni's intelligence or dedication. However, he was nowhere near one of the most knowledgeable authorities on the region.

To be fair to Bush, he was the first American president to openly accept the inevitability of a two-state solution, with a new Palestine governing almost all of the Occupied Territories of the West Bank and Gaza. He promoted what he called a "road map" for peace in 2002 at the height of the second *intifada*. By contrast with the rest of his foreign policy, Bush understood that the United States could not act unilaterally. He soon brought in the United Nations, the European Union and Russia to form a "quartet" to support the "road map." But frankly, the plan did not work.

Perhaps most importantly of all, the dispute between Israel and Palestine was just not as important to Bush as it was both to Clinton and to Bush's own father. Again to be fair to Bush, his administration was preoccupied with the global war on terrorism, as well as massive and deadly combat in Iraq and Afghanistan. The point to stress here, however, is that however much politicians in Washington understand that the 60-year-old conflict between Palestinians and Israelis is a bellwether for peace or the absence of it in the entire region, they have not been able to produce much in the way of results for the eight years of the Bush presidency.

Leadership Vacuums in Israel and Palestine

There have also been important leadership vacuums in Israel and Palestine. When the Oslo negotiations occurred, both sides were blessed with strong and flexible leaders. Israel was dominated by the Labor Party, and by the leadership of Yitzhak Rabin and Shimon Peres. Both had strong records of support for Israeli security, but both also realized that some kind of accommodation with the Palestinians was necessary. Meanwhile, Arafat was at the height of his power and prestige both at home and on the world stage. As the negotiations progressed, he could cite a long record of support for peace going back to his 1973 United Nations speech. At this point, at least, many people believed him.

For the last decade or more, leaders on both sides have been far less effective and many far less committed to peace.

That is easier to see in Israel which has had six prime ministers since the 1993 accords were signed and a seventh is soon to take office as I write. The first was Yithak Rabin, who got most of the credit for the Oslo agreement (even if Peres probably had more to do with it). Unfortunately, Rabin was assassinated two years later by an ultra-orthodox Jew while speaking at a peace rally in Tel Aviv. He was immediately replaced by Peres, another senior Labor party politician (they were born in 1922 and 1923 respectively).

Early in 2006, Peres called for a new Knesset election and was narrowly defeated by Benyamin Netanyahu, beginning a period in which the right has mostly dominated Israeli politics. Netanyahu was a quarter century younger than his Labor rivals and was known as one of the fiercest critics of the peace process. It is also probably the case that he would not have been elected had public opinion not swung dramatically to the right in the months following Rabin's assassination. He was particularly known for what was often called the "three no(s)": no withdrawal from Golan Heights, no discussion of the case of Jerusalem, no negotiations under any preconditions. Although he was willing to meet with Palestinians, virtually no progress was made during his three years in office.

Netanyahu's Likud party lost the 1999 elections, and he was replaced by the new leader of the Labor Party, Ehud Barak. Barak had spent the bulk of his adult life in the military and spent the first half of the 1990s as the chief of the IDF general staff and was responsible for implementing the Oslo agreements on the military side. He retired from the army in 1995 and quickly rose through the ranks of the Labor Party in the Knesset. His victory in 1999 was by no means convincing. The Labor led slate won only 28 of the 120 seats. Barak was thus forced to form a coalition that included not only other parties on the left but three of the religious parties, which were rather far to the right on peace process related issues. Within a few months, his coalition began to fall apart when one of the religious parties quit the government to protest alleged violations of orthodox rules for the Sabbath. The government fell shortly after the *intifada* broke out the following year.

At that point, Ariel Sharon formed a new government of national unity, including both Labor and Likud and a number of the smaller parties. He did so from within the existing Knesset without recourse to new elections. Sharon was even more of a lightning rod for Palestinians than Netanyahu. As a general, he was responsible for the 1982 attacks on refugee camps outside of Beirut that left hundreds and perhaps thousands of Palestinians dead. As we saw earlier, his visit to the Temple Mount and the grounds of the al-Aqsa mosque was one of the catalysts that gave rise to the second *intifada*. Sharon was surprisingly willing to participate in peace talks. He endorsed the roadmap and announced that Israel would unilaterally withdraw from Gaza. That said, he also endorsed the plan to build a wall to separate Israel from the Occupied Territories. He also tried to shift Israeli politics to the center by leaving Likud to form Kadima, which literally means forward; Netanyahu now runs what is left of Likud.

In December 2005 and January 2006, Sharon suffered two strokes, the second of which permanently disabled him. He was succeeded by Ehud Olmert, who had been mayor of Jerusalem since 1993. Olmert never had Sharon's charisma or popularity. To make matters worse, it took months before he formally became prime minister. His position was confirmed in elections held in March 2006. However, Kadima only won 29 seats which meant that he, too, had to rely on a broad coalition of national unity that was unified in name only. In his last weeks in office, Olmert broke sharply with many of the right wing views he had held throughout his political career. However, we will never know what kind of leadership he would could have provided, because he was forced to resign as a result of corruption scandals in mid-2008. Ironically, Shimon Peres, who held the symbolic position of President, became interim prime minister until a new coalition could be put together. The ensuing elections returned the hardliner Binyamin Netanyahu to power. In his first weeks in office, he did indicate a willingness to accept a two state solution but with conditions that would not be acceptable to most Palestinians.

To sum up, Israel has faced two leadership problems in the last first fifteen years. First, it has seen a number of not very effective prime ministers come and go. Second, the "parliamentary arithmetic" has made governance difficult, since no party can hope to win much more than a quarter of the vote.

The leadership situation facing the Palestinians may be even more difficult.

The problems begin with the decline in Arafat's physical and political health in the first years of this decade. Arafat (born 1929) was not a young man. Rumors about his health began swirling after he became ill at a meeting in October 2004, was flown to Paris for treatment, and died three weeks later.

In all likelihood, his health had been deteriorating for some time and contributed to his diminished influence in the Palestinian Authority. The United States and others in the international community insisted that he play a more minor role given their concerns that he was somehow behind the *intifada*. There were rumors that he would be succeeded by Marwan Barghouti, a leader of the al-Aqsa Martyr's brigade which Tel Aviv and Washington considered a terrorist organization. Israel eliminated that possibility when it arrested Barghouti in 2002. There were also obvious signs of corruption within the Palestinian Authority that many observers stretched all the way to Arafat himself who had accumulated a massive fortune since Oslo.

Under pressure from the Bush administration, Arafat ceded the prime ministry to one of the more moderate leaders from his Fatah faction, Mahmoud Abbas, also known as Abu Mazen from his days in the underground resistance. After Arafat's death, he was elected President of the Palestinian National Party and chair of the PLO.

Abbas has continued the on again, off again negotiations with Israel and the quartet. However, his leadership has not been very strong. To begin with, he announced that he would not run for a second term and that he would resign if the negotiations begun in 2008 did not succeed.

Even more importantly, his standing in the Palestinian community deteriorated when Hamas gained all but total control in Gaza, creating what amounted to two Palestinian states waiting to be born. At first, Abbas formed a unity government with Hamas, but it soon collapsed as a result of the Gazans' refusal to recognize Israeli and its continued attacks on Israeli territory.

The very fact that Hamas has seen its popularity soar is a blow for hopes for peace. Its charter calls for the destruction of Israel and the creation of a single Palestinian state in what is now Israel and the Occupied Territories. Hamas has its roots in the Muslim Brotherhood, some of whose former members helped form al Qaeda. Hamas is also known for the quality of the social service programs it runs in Gaza. But, outside of the region, it is better known for the suicide bomber, rocket, and other attacks it has launched against Israel targets since its creation in 1987.

Hamas is considered a terrorist organization by the United States and most other major powers. Laws passed after 9/11 in the United States makes it illegal for American NGOs to have contact with Hamas, though some do through intermediaries. Former President Carter has met with Hamas leaders on at least two occasions. But hostility is so intense that Barack Obama fired the respected (and Jewish) Rob Malley from his campaign staff for proposing gradual negotiations with Hamas.

As the final year of his second term began, President Bush was optimistic that an agreement that would create an internationally recognized Palestinian state and thus reduce violence in the region appreciably before he left office. That, of course, did not happen. President Obama is more committed to peace, but it is too early to tell what might happen.

Reconciliation

The history of the Arab–Israeli conflict is primarily one of violence, hatred, and fear. However, there have also been important but ill- publicized attempts at reconciliation that mirror those in Northern Ireland. To be sure, those efforts have been sharply restricted since 2000. If nothing else, it is all but impossible for Palestinians to meet with Israelis in the region. The one exception are Palestinians who live in Israel proper (about fifteen percent of the population) and residents of East Jerusalem who usually can get into the western part of the city.

At the were enough ongoing projects that *Newsweek International* printed a magazine-length ad from Benetton on them. Each picture, of course, showed Israelis and Palestinians wearing Benetton clothes. There were graduate courses in which Israeli and Palestinian students write joint dissertations. Palestinian and Israeli intellectuals have been meeting informally for years, often at the lovely American Colony hotel just inside

East Jerusalem whose owners continue to offer their building and courtyard (and bar[2]) as a neutral oasis amid the city's turbulent political life.

In short, reconciliation efforts can be found in almost all areas of life. None are more important—or better researched—than those involving young people. According to Abu-Nimer (1999), there were at least forty such programs, some of which are funded by the Israeli government and others by private sources, including the Jewish and Palestinian diasporas, the foundation world, and various governments' development agencies.

One of the oldest and best known is Neve Shalom/Wahat al-Salam (Oasis of Peace), which was created in 1972 (Shipler 1986: 495–555). Much like Northern Ireland's Corrymeela, Neve Shalom/Wahat al-Salam began as a religious community and is located on 100 acres of land leased from a monastery. Initially established as a place where Arabs and Jews could live together, it has never had many more than thirty families living there at any one time.

Its outreach programs have had a much broader impact. Its School for Peace was founded in 1979 and runs "encounters" that are designed to "show the participants how their responses within the small group reflect the relationships and conceptions of the two national groups in the wider reality. In interpreting their responses, we attempt to pinpoint the underlying conceptions and the way these contribute to the conflict."

A full-time staff of twelve and more than twenty freelance facilitators run three-day sessions most of which are for teenagers, although some are now held for teachers and other adult groups. Each group has a Jewish and Arab facilitator. The teenagers' activities include a simulation in which they try to plan future relations between their two communities. Teachers are asked to develop new curriculum materials for their class-rooms. In recent years, Neve Shalom/Wahat al-Salam has expanded further, setting up programs for women and ongoing courses at Israel's five main universities.

In the 1998–99 academic year, the community hosted twenty-two encounters for young people, with over 1,000 participants split evenly between Arabs and Jews. It also held its first programs in territory controlled by the Palestinian Authority. Its other activities included helping prepare a group of eighteen Jewish and Arab students who would be spending the summer studying together in Norway.

To be sure, Neve Shalom/Wahat al-Salam's work has been made more difficult since 2000. That doesn't mean that it has given up. Far from it. It has shifted attention in two main directions. First, it provides humanitarian relief to Palestinians who have been victims of violence and isolation. Second, it is in the process of creating a Masters degree program in peace and conflict studies. Announced in 2008, it will probably take two years to get formal government approval; until then, with its university partners, it will conduct a one year certificate programs.

Another prominent organization is Seeds of Peace which started as a summer camp on a former llama farm in Otisfield, ME. Founded in 1993, it initially brought Israeli, Palestinian, and Egyptian teenagers to the camp. They did what one would expect of

---

[2]   There is ample if unsystematic evidence that what one United Nations official once called "Heineken diplomacy" can often smooth negotiations by helping build informal relations and trust among participants. That's not only true in Jerusalem, but there are no more charming sites than the American Colony (www.americancolony.com).

a summer camp. But they also shared cabins, discussions, and training in conflict resolution. Over time, Seeds expanded its work in the region itself, including giving a number of ex-campers video cameras so they could record how they dealt with each other and their communities after their return. Now it has programs for adults as well and includes campers from other conflict zones.

Life has not been easy for Seeds. Many of my Palestinian students who have attended the camp, now think it made the prospects for peace seem too easy to reach. Since 2001, it has been all but impossible for Palestinians from the Occupied Territories to get visas or permission to go through Israel to reach an airport. As a result, today's Palestinian campers all come from either the diaspora or the Palestinian community in pre-1967 Israel.

A more recent group is Combatants for Peace, created by a group of former fighters on both sides. There are similar groups for women, young people, parents of people killed, and even a joint Israeli-Palestinian soccer team created out of the merger of two separate teams orchestrated by veterans of the peace process.

I had the privilege of meeting with Sulaiman Khatib and Gadi Kenny who were among the founders of the organization.[3] It was moving politically and emotionally to meet these two men who had been raised as enemies yet who talk about negotiation and reconciliation as the only route to peace. It was even more moving to learn that hundreds of other veterans think the same way.

Efforts at reconciliation are also taking place between Palestinian- and Jewish-Americans. Since the mid-1980s, Len and Libby Traubman of San Mateo CA have been hosting Palestinian-Israeli dialogues in their home. With the advent of the internet, Len and Libby have maintained an online clearing house for people engaged in similar projects around the country (traubman.igc.org/global.htm). Like Khatib and Kenny, The Traubmans are not professional activists. Len is a dentist and Libby is a social worker; Len is Jewish, Libby is not. Rather, they realized that their engagement in the Beyond War movement, which focused on nuclear weapons during the Cold War, required them to explore other parts of the world where war was ripping societies in part.

I do not mean to suggest that the conflict will end as a result of summer camps or discussion over dinner in people's homes (though the Traubmans have found a group called Chefs for Peace). Ultimately, there will have to be a political resolution negotiated by political leaders who come from a very different part of their respective societies. And, as I will argue in concluding this section that there are problems with some of these programs. Nonetheless, it is important for you to see that despite the *intifada* and the other setbacks of recent years, these kinds of projects. My best friends on each side are much angrier with each other than they were in the 1990s. But to see my Israeli and Palestinian colleagues meet and embrace each other gives me some semblance of hope.

The best study on reconciliation in the region was written in a systematic and comparative assessment of six projects involving young people written by Mohammed Abu-Nimer (1999), a former facilitator in one of them who has since become a professor of conflict resolution in the United States. Note that he did not include groups that dealt with other issues or regularly included Palestinians living outside the 1967 borders. In his introduction, Abu-Nimer evokes the power this work can have:

---

[3]   Truth in advertising, my NGO, the Alliance for Peacebuilding, hosts their American fund-raising effort, which they need for tax purposes.

Words fail to describe Palestinian teenagers or teachers when they truly, and for the first time, realize that Jewish participants who are associated with dominance and power, are sincerely scared of Arabs. Or the sudden awareness of a Jewish participant who must finish his or her first personal encounter with an Arab. (Abu-Nimer 1999: xx)

But Abu-Nimer's goal was to dig beyond these initial reactions and determine just how successful these programs are. His detailed findings are not as encouraging as the statement from his introduction might lead a reader to expect. Among other things, he found:

- Considerable resistance to participating on the part of the Jewish young people even though they were typically recruited from schools where the staff was sympathetic to the idea of reconciliation.
- Ignorance of the status of Arabs among Jewish students, many of whom denied there was a problem at all.
- Different goals. Arab teachers and administrators wanted their students to learn more about their oppression and become more assertive in their dealings with Israel, while Jews were more interested in breaking down stereotypes and changing cultural values.
- Student participants often gave the encounters high marks not because of their political impact but because they got out of school, met people of the opposite gender, and had fun (most of them were, after all, between thirteen and seventeen years old).
- Language itself was often an issue. Very few Jews speak Arabic, while most Arabs speak some Hebrew, and some speak it quite well. However, many Arabs resented the fact that they had to use the oppressor's language.
- Rarely did the two sides reach the same conclusion about what the future should hold, especially regarding a Palestinian state.

His concerns would almost certainly be even more evident were his research conducted today.

Overall, Abu-Nimer reaches many of the same conclusions found in the general literature on conflict resolution. These kinds of programs can and sometimes do have a major impact on the people who participate in them, something I can attest to from my own work with recent Palestinian university graduates. However, there is no guarantee that they will "work," especially if, for instance, the facilitators are poorly trained or running the encounters because they can't find a more lucrative job.

Finally and perhaps most important, the impact of even the most successful programs diminishes the further one moves out from the experiences of the individuals involved and toward the "real world" of day-to-day politics. As noted in Part 1, it may well be that "people to people" workshops can lead to lasting political change. However, it always takes a long time, usually measured in years if not decades, and it probably requires even more widespread and better publicized efforts than are found in the Middle East today.

In short, the full accomplishments of programs like Neve Shalom/Wahat al-Salam may not be seen until the generation of young people who have passed through their encounters reach positions of influence. And there probably are still more people in both communities who reject the very idea of peace and are willing to demonstrate that rejection violently than all the reconciliation groups combined have been able to reach.

Lessons Learned

The Israeli/Palestinian example draws our attention to eight general implications. As befits an intermediary case, some help us understand why progress has been made; others shed light on the obstacles to peace.

1. There is no question that the changing nature of the international system brought on by the end of the Cold War and the Gulf crisis of 1990–91 made the peace process much easier. It may well have made it possible. As we saw in the first half of the chapter, the superpower rivalry directly and indirectly magnified the tensions between Palestinians and Jews. The changes of the late 1980s and early 1990s made it harder for the Palestinians to maintain a hard line and also made it harder for countries like the United States and the members of the European Union to play a more constructive role.

2. That said, this case drives home a more pessimistic but no less vital conclusion. The international institutions cannot do much to help end a conflict if one of the five permanent members of the Security Council believes it has a vested interest in the outcome. For good or ill, the United States has consistently used its veto to stand in the way of major international involvement on issues involving Israel.

3. Even more than Northern Ireland, this case shows us the range of ways third parties can help. It took neutral outsiders to begin most of the informal citizen-to-citizen programs in the 1970s and 1980s. More important, it is hard to imagine how the Israelis and PLO could have even begun to talk to each other without the help of an outsider. And, it is highly unlikely that an American or someone from another country that had taken a strong stand on Middle Eastern issues could have done what the Norwegian team did. However, it has increasingly become clear since Oslo that only a third party with the power and prestige of the United States can do much to bring the two sides to close the gaps that separate them today. Indeed, almost every breakdown in talks has been accompanied by a plea from both the Israelis and Palestinians for Dennis Ross or some other diplomat to return to the region with new proposals.

4. Despite the reservations raised by Oslo's critics or in the research by scholars like Abu-Nimer, there is also no doubt that track-two and citizen-based efforts have made a major difference. The Oslo track did not appear out of thin air. Progressive Israelis and moderate PLO leaders had been meeting informally for years. In her powerful insider account of the Oslo process, Jane Corbin (1994) documents how the negotiators came to better understand and sometimes even like each other despite their political and cultural differences.

5. This is also a classic example of how important a hurting stalemate can be. Statements made by Arafat and Rabin in the early 1990s indicate a clear understanding that victory (for example, the elimination of Israel or the complete annexation of the West Bank and Gaza) was not possible. That realization certainly led both of them and their key advisers to pursue a negotiated settlement more seriously than they had in the past.

It is also a classic example of some difficulties with the concept. It took the *intifada* and the end of the Cold War before mainstream leaders on both sides realized there was little chance of winning even though, objectively speaking, a mutually hurting stalemate probably existed as soon as Israel won the 1967 war. Intellectually and politically, the idea of a hurting stalemate gives us few guidelines for determining when and how the shift toward the negotiating table will actually occur.

6. Domestic politics is also vital in this—as in most—cases of conflict resolution. That is easiest to see in Israel, where the election of Labor in 1992, Likud in 1996, and Labor again in 1999 marked major turning points in the peace process. Palestinian critics

are quick to point out that the two parties share many commitments and concerns. Nonetheless, there is no question that in recent years Labor has been much more flexible in its dealings with the Palestinians.

7. As David Lieberthal (1999) has argued, there is less tying Israelis to Palestinians than there is Whites to Blacks in South Africa. In South Africa, Blacks and Whites are almost completely dependent on each other economically. That is much less true in Israel, where, if anything, Israel relies less on Palestinian labor than it did a decade ago. The two communities will have to share certain resources, especially water, and find ways of sharing parts of the entire region, since Jews live in the Occupied Territories and Arabs in pre-1967 Israel. However, unlike South Africa, there are still precious few Arabs in key positions in Israeli corporations or even on its athletic teams.

That lack of integration may also contribute to the size of the "rejectionist" groups in both communities. To be sure, organizations like Hamas and Hezbollah use violence more often than their Israeli counterparts. Nonetheless, it may well be the case that the Likud supporter, the settlers, and others who have profound objections to the peace process make up a larger proportion of the Israeli population.

8. Of the five examples covered in part 2, this case best illustrates the point that the creation of reconciliation and stable peace always takes time. Given the history of the region from the time that the first Zionists arrived, it is hardly surprising that the negotiators did not solve all their problems in a single agreement.

Select Bibliography

Abu-Nimer, Mohammed (1999). *Dialogue, Conflict Resolution, and Change: Arab-Jewish Encounters in Israel*. Albany, NY: SUNY Press.

Corbin, Jane (1994). *The Norway Channel*. New York: Atlantic Monthly Press.

Emmett, Ayala (1996). *Our Sisters' Promised Land: Women, Politics, and Israeli-Palestinian Coexistence*. Ann Arbor, MI: University of Michigan Press.

Feldman, Shai, and Abdeullah Toukan (1997). *Bridging the Gap: A Future Security Architecture for the Middle East*. Lanham, MD: Rowman and Littlefield.

Gerner, Deborah (1994). *One Land, Two Peoples*. Boulder, CO: Westview.

Hiro, Dilip (1999). *Sharing the Promised Land: A Tale of Israelis and Palestinians*. New York: Olive Branch Books.

Landy, Marc (2006). "Zealous Realism: Commentaries on Mearsheimer and Walt." *The Forum*. www.bepress.com/forum/vol4/iss1/art6/.

Lieberthal, David (1999). "Post-Handshake Politics: Israel/Palestine and South Africa Compared." *Middle East Policy* 6, no. 3: 131–40.

Mearsheimer, John and Stephen Walt (2007). *The Israel Lobby and US Foreign Policy*. New York: Farrar, Straus and Giroux.

Peters, Joel (1996). *Pathways to Peace*. London: Royal Institute for International Affairs and the European Commission.

Rabinovich, Itamar (1999). *Waging Peace: Israel and the Arabs at the End of the Century*. New York: Farrar, Straus and Giroux.

Rosenwasser, Penny (1992). *Voices from the Promised Land: Palestinian and Israeli Peace Activists Speak Their Mind*. Willimantic, CT: Curbstone.

Ross, Dennis (2004). *The Missing Peace*. New York: Farrar, Straus and Giroux.

Said, Edward (1996). *Peace and Its Discontents*. New York: Vintage.

Shipler, David (2001). *Arab and Jew: Wounded Spirits in a Promised Land*. New York: Penguin.

Shlaim, Avi (2000). *The Iron Wall*. New York: W. W. Norton.

CHAPTER EIGHT

The Global War on Terrorism

Ok, Mr Conflict Resolution Guy, what would you do about al Qaeda?
—Lawrence Wright

Prelude

I was planning to start this chapter on November 26, 2008. I woke up to find that a major terrorist attack was underway in Mumbai (Bombay). Although India had had its share of terrorist attacks and political violence in general in recent years, I had not been planning to write about the country.

As the news unfolded over the next two days, I realized that the carnage in Mumbai was a good way to begin the chapter for four reasons, even if India will not figure prominently in what follows.

First, it was a horrible act. More than ten times as many people were killed in New York and Washington on 9/11. Nonetheless, the fact that 15 men armed with nothing more than machine-guns and hand grenades could kill close to 200 people and wound more than 350 made this one of the two or three most devastating terrorist attacks in recent history.

Secondly, it was also an audacious act. It appears that the attackers came ashore in a few rubber dinghies and simply walked to their carefully cased-out targets that included two luxury hotels, a popular café, a train station, a Jewish center, and more. Moreover, the fact that they attacked sites that would be vulnerable no matter what security measures had been taken suggests that terrorists have plenty of targets no matter what we do to protect public buildings or airports (it should be noted that at the same time protesters—but not terrorists—were occupying the two airports in Bangkok).

Thirdly, even after the crisis ended it was by no means certain who was responsible. The attackers were almost certainly Muslims. But were they Indian? Kashmiri? Pakistani? What was their link—if any—to the increasingly loosely organized international terrorist movement that is now thought to be relatively independent of the weakened al Qaeda. The first guess of American, British and Indian (but not Pakistani) counter-terrorism officials is that they were part of a Pakistan-based Islamic group, *Lashkar-i-Taiba*. The organization denied any involvement in the attacks. However, it was suspect because of its radical ideology, which in some ways went beyond what al Qaeda advocates.

Fourthly, the attacks in Mumbai were unusually bloody, but otherwise they were not unique. The day the siege ended, three German intelligence officers were released a week after their arrest for allegedly bombing a European Union office in a Serbian-controlled region of Kosovo; it turned out that the attack was carried out by a previously unknown group of Kosovars of Albanian origin. There were, as usual, bombings in Iraq and Afghanistan (we will deal with the fuzzy line been insurgencies and terrorism later in the chapter).

9/11 as a Defining Moment

Each generation goes through crises that define much of its identity. As a high school junior in 1963, my much-hated history teacher gave me her car keys and asked me to listen to the radio. President Kennedy had been shot. Going back to the classroom was no fun.

On September 11, 2001, I was on my way to Jiffy Lube to change the oil on my ancient Toyota. Bob Edwards, the anchor of National Public Radio's Morning Edition, announced that an airplane had crashed into the World Trade Center. He assumed it was an accident. Just as I neared the Jiffy Lube driveway, Edwards announced the second attack. I forgot about the oil change, drove home and turned on the television, at which point my wife called to say she was being evacuated from one of the most secure buildings in the DC area. It took her two hours to get home instead of what should have been about a ten-minute drive. Meanwhile I was transfixed watching the towers come down, the Pentagon burn, and hearing rumors about other planes heading toward New York and Washington.

I know people who lost loved ones that day. I was involved in a couple of alleged anthrax attacks in the Washington subway system. My boss at the time was in a senator's office when an envelope was opened, and as a result had to take medication for six months.

The response to 9/11 was both powerful and confusing. American flag lapel pins appeared on suit coats (including mine), and red, white and blue decals showed up on the back of cars (not mine). I was among many members of the conflict resolution community who supported at least the initial stages of the war in Afghanistan against the Taliban and al Qaeda. I read what my friends wrote opposing the intervention but I was not convinced, for reasons that will become clear below. As the war evolved there was a lot I could not support, especially the detention of suspects at Guantanamo Bay who did not have prisoner-of-war status.

But, even more, as the war evolved and as it expanded to Iraq, I realized that my colleagues and I had largely been absent from the debate about what we should do. In short, this chapter builds on the last one to explore how people working in conflict resolution could and should examine the GWOT (the Bush Administration's term for the Global War on Terrorism).

This chapter will look quite a bit different from the other chapters in Part 3. Nonetheless it will include the key segments, including theoretical concerns, the history of the case, and lessons learned. But there will be more.

This is perhaps the most difficult chapter in the book. To be honest, most conflict resolution scholars have had little constructive to say about the GWOT. (At the same time, the military doesn't have a great track record on combating terrorism.)

In other words, the question Lawrence Wright asked me that begins the chapter is the most vexing one in this book, and in my field. The question could not have come from a better source. Lawrence Wright is the author of *The Looming Tower* (2006), which is arguably the best book on why 9/11 happened. A year after the book was published he performed a one-man play, *My Route to Al Qaeda*, which focused more on how the post 9/11 world had affected him personally, and our country as a whole.

My wife and I joined another couple who already knew Wright to see the play in New York. A meeting with him was planned, but we knew he only had a few minutes.

As we talked, he asked something like the question that begins this chapter. I said I had to go to the bathroom, thus gaining me the time I needed to not answer the question. A few months later I met with Wright: we had more time, and I had just come out of the bathroom. I was trapped!

I'll get to my answer at the end of this chapter. But first, we need to consider what terrorism is, how established authorities have dealt with it, and why it belongs in this book at all. In short, the question for this chapter becomes: why have we gotten this case so wrong for so long?

The chapter will also look a little different from those you have already read. The sections used above will be included here, but we will also consider some other issues, many of which are personal.

What is Terrorism?

Terrorism is one of the most difficult and controversial terms for political scientists to define. The confusion becomes obvious with a statement which most readers of this book will have already heard: "One man's terrorist is another man's freedom-fighter." We also read about "state terrorism," actions in which an established government uses unusually harsh tactics against its political enemies.

The Spectrum of Terror

By no means do I want to argue that this chapter addresses what R. Hrair Dekmejian (2007) properly calls the "spectrum" of terror. Terrorism comes in many forms. Some is ideological, some religious, some ethnic. Some borders on organized crime, and some is little else. Some is conducted by states against their own citizens. Some terrorist groups operate in many countries, some only in a single region of a single country.

By no means, either, do I want to suggest that there is any causal link between Islam and terrorism. Most obviously, almost no Muslims (or members of any other religious or ethnic group) are terrorists. More importantly, there has been terrorism in such different places as Northern Ireland and Sri Lanka, neither of which had anything to do with Islam.

However, for the purposes of this chapter, we will limit ourselves to the terrorist movements that gave rise to 9/11 and recent traumatic events, because they are the ones that have befuddled mainstream policy-makers and conflict resolution specialists alike, and are therefore squarely on the world's political agenda.

Average citizens and politicians alike react to terrorist attacks with understandable horror. Consider a few examples, the last three of which involved me personally, albeit indirectly.

- In 1984, an IRA bomb ripped through the hotel where the Conservative Party leadership was staying for its annual conference. The bomb killed one cabinet minister. Had it been placed even a little more expertly, it could have killed dozens of prominent Tories, possibly including Prime Minister Thatcher.
- In 1986, the Italian cruise ship, the Achille Lauro, was hijacked by a group of Palestinians only loosely connected to the PLO. They had hoped simply to slip into Israel, but were discovered by the ship's crew. They then took over the ship and killed a number of Jewish passengers, including an elderly disabled man whom they threw overboard along with his wheelchair.
- On February 9, 1996 I interviewed a journalist at Canary Wharf, the newly upscale London neighborhood where most UK newspapers now have their headquarters. I left in the middle of the afternoon. Four hours later a bomb went off, causing well over $100,000 worth of damage. As usual, the IRA had sent a coded message an hour and a half before the bomb exploded, and most of the area had been evacuated. Still, two innocent newspaper-sellers were killed. Nine days later, I interviewed another journalist who worked in central London. A few hours later another bomb went off prematurely in that neighborhood, though causing no injuries. There are no trash-cans in British train and subway stations, because they are convenient places to leave bombs.
- On August 7, 1998, my colleague Susan Hirsch (2006) went to cash a check at the American Embassy in Dar es Salaam, Tanzania. Susan had access to the embassy because she was a Fulbright scholar. Her Kenyan husband decided to stay outside and smoke a cigarette. While Susan was inside, a bomb shook the building. Her husband was killed. That same day, al Qaeda also bombed the American Embassy in Kenya.
- In the brief period between the 9/11 attacks and the beginning of the bombing of Afghanistan, I helped co-moderate a conference on reconciliation with an Israeli colleague and friend. We had originally planned to hold the conference in Jerusalem, but most participants would not go to Israel because of the second *intifada*, and we moved it to Washington. As mentioned previously, my colleague had two errands before he went to the airport. He had to go to the bank to get some dollars, and take his dog to the kennel. If he had done these jobs in the reverse order, my friend would be dead. His bank was blown up less than thirty minutes after he collected his cash and went to leave his beloved Muki at the kennel.

With the exception of Professor Hirsch's ordeal, none of these attacks had anything to do with al Qaeda or the issues that gave rise to the Global War on Terrorism. Hence, even more confusion.

State-sponsored Terrorism

One of the most controversial issues involves what some call state-sponsored terrorism. There is no doubt that some regimes have treated members of religious, racial, linguistic or ethnic minorities very brutally. The Armenian genocide, the Holocaust, Israeli treatment of Palestinians, and the devastation in Darfur which we will cover in the next chapter, all involved acts of terror which are at least tacitly condoned by established states.

Again, because the global war on terrorism focuses primarily on organizations that are not part of or supported by states, we have to leave out this thorny issue, too.

Theoretical Issues

Audrey Kurtz Cronin (2002/3) has been the most vocal and persistent scholar decrying the lack of theoretical understanding of terrorism especially before 9/11. The subject was rarely mentioned in textbooks written at any level. It did not fit into the dominant theories discussed in Chapter 5. To be sure, there were analysts in governments and in think-tanks who were raising concerns about terrorism, but these concerns rarely got beyond specific cases or policy responses to the broader theoretical issues scholars focused on. So, as Cronin discovered, studying terrorism before 9/11 was not a great way to build an academic career. Now, she and her colleagues are in constant demand. Some conceptual work has been done, but theoretically, terrorism remains one of the weak links in mainstream study of international relations.

Cronin did not write about the failure of conflict resolution scholars and practitioners to take terrorism seriously. She easily could have.

In the first edition of this book, for example, I did not address terrorism, per se, as an issue which conflict and peace studies had to deal with. To be sure, my colleagues and I had worked in and on places where terrorist movements had operated such as Northern Ireland, the Basque region of Spain, or Sri Lanka. However, we tended to focus on finding ways of getting all parties to a dispute to the table, rather than considering terrorism as a form of conflict in its own right, or a subject in its own terms. Thus, we too were taken by surprise and found ourselves in an intellectual and political quandary after 9/11 (Lederach 2001; Hersey and Hauss 2002).

With the exception of two edited volumes by George Mason's Institute for Conflict Analysis and Resolution (ICAR) and the Defense Threat Reduction Agency (DTRA), there have been no significant attempts by mainstream and conflict analysts to wrestle with terrorism together. A friend introduced me to Cronin the day the bombing started in Afghanistan. We have since spent hours at conferences, at informal gatherings, and on email. We rarely disagree, but we have done little to push the boundaries of terrorism theory very far.

Therefore, the questions that follow are far less conceptual than those in the other case study chapters, and are more divorced from either traditional international relations or conflict resolution theory:

- Why do people resort to terrorism or violence of any kind?
- How does the asymmetric nature of these conflicts contribute to what many call terrorism, the "weapon of the weak?"
- How does the fact that terrorists operate outside the state-centered international system affect the ability of those states to deal with terrorism?
- Can terrorism be defeated solely, largely or primarily by the use of force?
- Should we negotiate or deal with terrorists in other ways that do not involve the use of force? If so, how?

The Historical Roots of Terrorism

Most students of terrorism claim it dates back at least to biblical times (Banks, de Nevers, and Wallerstein 2008). Various groups of Jews carried out acts of political violence against their Roman occupiers. The Romans, in turn, practiced something akin to state terrorism.

A thousand years later the Federation of Assassins was formed, which killed opponents of Islam, including Crusaders.

The term "terrorism" itself is much newer. It was first used during the French revolution when Robespierre's government used brute force to restore order after the first anarchic years following the sacking of the Bastille in 1789. Since then, however, terrorism has become a tool which dissidents routinely use to attack a state.

As suggested earlier, terrorism is only one form that dissent can take. Indeed, most terrorist organizations exist alongside non-violent protest movements. Most terrorists have themselves spent time, in some cases decades, in those organization. In short, few people turn to terrorism lightly.

Modern terrorism dates only from the end of the nineteenth century. A number of anarchist groups in Russia, for instance, routinely targeted government officials. Similar movements existed in what would later become Yugoslavia. The best known of the European terrorist movements were the IRA (see Chapter 6) and the Basque ETA, which operated in both France and Spain. As we saw in the chapter on Israel and the Palestinians, the PLO and other organizations only turned to violence in the late 1960s when it became clear that the "regular" Arab armies were not going to defeat Israel.

One important change to terrorism did occur over the course of the last century or so. The late-nineteenth- and early-twentieth-century terrorists primarily tried to kill government officials, and some of them were quite effective.

Today, terrorist attacks are mostly aimed at average citizens and are designed to literally instill as much fear as possible in the population as a whole. For quite some time before airport security was strengthened, hijacking airplanes was a popular tactic. It is true that many of the planes were coming from or going to Israel. However, the people on the airplanes were taken hostage not because of their political role but because of the flight they had happened to book. When my friend's bank was blown up in Jerusalem, it was probably chosen more or less at random. The last bombing in Ireland, which occurred after the Good Friday peace agreement was signed, took place in an open-air market and took the lives of 27 people who were guilty of nothing but shopping.

In practice, terrorist targets are rarely chosen randomly. As was the case on 9/11, sometimes they are chosen because of their symbolic or economic value. Sometimes a target is chosen because it is not very well protected, as was certainly the case in Mumbai in 2008. Sometimes targets are chosen for political reasons, as is almost always the case when a high-profile leader is assassinated.

The DC Sniper

The fear which terrorism can cause hit those of us in the Washington DC area in 2002, and not because of a political incident.

That fall, two snipers carried out 15 attacks in the region. In only one incident was no one wounded. About 15 people were killed.

One of the attacks took place about two miles from our house, at a store my wife often goes to.

Even though I knew that the odds of my getting killed were almost none, I still avoided walking to the subway or taking the dog on any major streets.

Before 9/11, terrorism was not a major issue in American foreign policy. To be sure, counterterrorism experts such as Michael Scheuer and Richard Clarke were demanding that the Clinton and Bush administrations pay more attention to terrorism, especially once al Qaeda began to target American facilities. But, the attacks were all outside the United States.

As Robert Pape (2005), in particular, has argued, most people turn to terror as a last resort. His study of some 450 terrorists who committed attacks in which they also killed themselves does not meet many of our preconceptions. Pape finds that most terrorists, including the deadliest (the Tamil Tigers of Sri Lanka, who were finally and utterly defeated in spring 2009) are not Muslims. Many are well educated, including most of the 9/11 hijackers. Terrorist attacks have political goals, typically to force occupiers from areas which the terrorists see as their homeland. And most importantly of all, terrorists are almost always part of a larger, highly organized, and hierarchical organization.

If Pape is right there is a strategic logic behind terrorism, especially among suicide bombers. As the title of his book suggests, they are dying to win. They have apparently decided that their political goals are important enough and that other tactics have not worked well enough, and they have become willing to give up their lives.

Before we turn to al Qaeda, it is important to emphasize one last point that also makes the study of terrorism difficult. Almost no one refers to his or organization as "terrorist." Bin Laden has used the term, but he is one of the very few.

Some people do still claim that "one man's terrorist is another's freedom fighter." But if we define terrorism as a political act that literally tries to terrify as many people as possible by selecting civilian targets in a more or less random fashion, then it is hard to find anything noble or justifiable in their actions. International law and most systems of international ethics prohibit the killing of civilians. Of course it happens. In fact, in most recent wars, far more civilians than soldiers were killed. The point is that terrorists *intentionally* target civilians because they are trying to create as much fear as possible.

The Road to al Qaeda

Pape's argument certainly holds for Osama bin Laden and most of his supporters. It is clear from the books and articles written about him (Coll 2008 is the best) that he was not born to be a terrorist, nor was there anything in his early life to suggest he would become one.

Bin Laden is one of 54 children. He is the only terrorist. There are far more playboys among his brothers. As was already clear to those who paid attention to al Qaeda before 9/11, he is not some sort of psychotic maniac. Of course, there must be something out of the ordinary in the psychology of someone who becomes a terrorist. But, there is also a deadly political logic to the decisions that led to 9/11.

Osama bin Laden

Osama bin Laden was born on March 10, 1957 in Riyadh, Saudi Arabia, the only son of his father's tenth wife. His father, Mohamed, was born in Yemen, probably in 1905. His family was extremely poor, and Mohamed and one of his brothers decided to move to Saudi Arabia before World War One. That was before the discovery of oil turned the country into the world's largest producer of petroleum. The first concession to drill for oil was only given in 1923.

Mohamed formed a construction company before the Saudi oil boom began. He was therefore well placed to take advantage of the petro-dollars that started rolling in. He soon drew the attention of the King, who gave the elder bin Laden dozens of contracts for a range of projects from new roads to renovation and expansion of the Holy Mosque in Mecca, the site of the annual Hajj pilgrimage.

In short, the bin Ladens became amazingly rich. When Mohamed died in 1967 he left each of his sons several million dollars.

The bin Ladens were a devout Sunni family. However, most of the sons went to secular schools. The history of Osama's education is unclear. He did attend university, perhaps in engineering or public administration, both of which would have stood him in good stead in the family business. There is no evidence, however, that he ever finished a degree.

There also have been rumors that he used to party when he was studying in Lebanon, but it seems that those accounts confuse him with some of his brothers. By all accounts, Osama was one of the most devout members of this devout family, from his teenage years onward.

While he was in high school, his drift toward a more traditional and stricter version of Islam began. He began to spend time with members of the Muslim Brotherhood, including his physical education teacher. The Brotherhood was—and still is—a semi-secret organization that rejects secular leadership and has been banned in most Arab countries (www.ikhwanweb.com). Formed in Egypt in 1928, the Brotherhood spread throughout the Arab world and into some countries, such as Pakistan, that were non-Arab but Muslim. During the course of the 1950s and 1960s, the Brotherhood had turned increasingly militant as its members became convinced that non-violent methods could not bring necessary political change. Many members, in fact, were arrested, and some executed.

In Saudi Arabia, the young militants were also influenced by Wahhabism, a sect created by an eighteenth-century scholar. Wahhabis tend to take the Koran literally and believe that Islam today should be based on the values and practices developed among the first three generations of Muslim leaders. Thus, they believe in *Shari'a* or Muslim law, and think women's positions in society should be limited.

Most members of bin Laden's generation had also grown up with the specter of what now seemed like a permanent state of Israel. Bin Laden was only 16 when the 1973 war between Israel and its Arab neighbors began, but it is safe to say that he was old enough to realize that non-Muslims were likely to be in the region for a long time and that weak, overly secular Arab states were unable or unwilling to force the Jews out.

As Steve Coll puts it, during his high school years "Osama bin Laden moved freely through overlapping worlds" (2008: 198). He unquestionably became more religious. But, he also bought fancy cars, played soccer, and rode horses. He also worked in the family business during summer vacations and would go on the payroll full-time when he finished his education.

It is important to remember that most of his older brothers were not like him at all. Salem, who was the family leader following the death of their father, loved to buy airplanes and live the high life of a wheeler-dealer in the United States, Europe, and the Middle East. One brother was known to be a heavy drinker, at least when outside Saudi Arabia, which prohibits alcohol. Most of the brothers didn't mind if their wives and daughters wore jeans and make-up. One of the wives even gained her own pilot's license.

Osama's religious faith was perhaps best revealed in his relationship with his family. He married young, and his wife bore him a number of children. He banned music and photography from the home as insulting to Islam. Later he refused to allow his children to watch much television, including such shows as Sesame Street. But again, there was little out of the ordinary about that.

At first, he does not seem to have been a very enthusiastic employee of the family business. But as the 1980s wore on he became more and more interested in business administration, and apparently was quite good at it. As one of his first managers noticed, even as a teenager he had a keen attention to detail.

The Making of al Qaeda

The political turn in Osama's life began in 1979, when he was 22. That year a group of militants took over the Grand Mosque, almost certainly with the help of some members of the bin Laden family. Because their firm had done construction work at the site, they had a full set of plans and eventually helped the authorities dislodge the militants in the most brutal fighting the country had seen in years.

Late that December, the Soviet army invaded Afghanistan. The weak government in Kabul was closely allied to Moscow, and it had requested helicopters, tanks and other weapons at various points throughout 1979. By the end of the year, there was violence in 24 of the 28 provinces.

In retrospect, it was clear that the Soviet Union had been planning the invasion for some time. It feared instability on its southern flank, but also was coming to grips with the fact that Muslims were the fastest-growing religious group in their own country.

On December 27, special operations forces from the KGB entered Kabul and killed the president, hoping that would end the instability that was taking Afghanistan into war once again. They were wrong.

Bin Laden's role from then on is well enough known that we don't need to go into it in detail. In 1979, he was a typical Saudi young man. Many, like Osama, had converted to a more literal version of Islam during their teenage years, and there was no sign that he was particularly different or potentially more dangerous than any of his contemporaries. Osama bin Laden was well placed to play a political role in the aftermath of the invasion of Afghanistan. By the early 1980s, he was already well known for raising money for Islamic charities, which made him noticed and appreciated by the royal family.

Meanwhile, tremendous resentment against the invasion of Afghanistan grew among young religious Muslims throughout the Middle East. For the United States, the invasion was a dangerous and offensive move by the Soviet Union in a Cold War that seemed destined to last forever. For young men like bin Laden, it was a deeply personal affront to Islam. Yet again, white people had come in to occupy territory that was not rightfully theirs.

At this point, bin Laden still showed no sign of becoming a freedom fighter (*mujahadeen*), let alone a terrorist. That said, thousands of Arabs and other Muslims flocked to the Pakistan/Afghanistan border to join the *jihad* against the Soviets. Because the bin Ladens already had business dealings in Pakistan and Afghanistan, and because one of Osama's Muslim Brotherhood mentors had been sent by the Saudi government to open a center for religious study in Peshawar, it was natural for bin Laden to harness his fund-raising skills for the fight against the Soviets.

It was at about this time that his mentor, Abdullah Azzam, introduced the young man to "transnational jihad," or the notion that Muslims around the world had to unite to protest against the power of the "infidels." The United States was not seen as an enemy at the time, even though many of bin Laden's contemporaries did not think positively of the West. That was so because the United States was funding the Afghan rebels and foreign fighters in an attempt to force the Soviets to leave, something that would occur in 1989.

There is little direct evidence that the US government had any direct contact with bin Laden at the time. The war was run in secret by the CIA, which provided a lot of the funding for the internal resistance. Osama's older brother, Salem, did try to use some of his Pentagon contacts to persuade the United States to fund Osama's operations. That does not seem to have happened, since bin Laden's network obtained most of its weapons in the legal and not-so-legal open markets.

In 1986, at Azzam's urging, bin Laden and his family moved to Peshawar, Pakistan. The anti-Soviet forces were in disarray, and the young man's organizational skills were desperately needed. There was still no sign that he would himself become a freedom fighter.

Within a year or two he had moved across the border and taken an active part in the fighting, though it is by no means clear that he was any good at it. By 1988, the United States wanted to blend the Arab and Afghan fighters into a single force that would presumably be more effective. Bin Laden had his doubts.

At any rate, when the war ended and he returned home in 1990, he was considered one of the heroes of the struggle. That fame was not to last. First, he became openly critical of Saudi Arabia's dependence on the United States. Secondly, that summer, Iraq invaded Kuwait (see Chapter 9) and American and other foreign troops flocked to Saudi Arabia and the rest of the region. Bin Laden and his associates found the presence of foreign troops on Arab and Muslim soil unacceptable. He became more and more intransigent, and less and less acceptable to the Saudi regime. In other words, his commitment to "transnational jihad" deepened.

In 1992 he was all but forced to move to Sudan, ostensibly to work on the family's projects there. In fact, he spent far more time establishing training bases and, more generally, making a global jihadist movement possible. He went so far that the Saudi government forced him to hand in has passport. The report of the 9/11 commission suggested that the Sudanese government tried to expel him as early as 1995.

While in Sudan he developed close ties to the Egyptian Islamic Jihad, which actually supplied the core of al Qaeda forces in the early years. The EIJ also had links with the Muslim Brotherhood, and had attempted to assassinate President Hosni Mubarak. The group was led by Dr Ayman al-Zawahari, who remains bin Laden's closest colleague to this day.

The seeds of what became al Qaeda were sown by the late 1980s. However, it was during the years in Sudan that the movement came together as a powerful and dangerous force, after bin Laden cast his lot with the EIJ.

By 1995, al Qaeda were dangerous enough that the Egyptians and Saudis put sufficient pressure on the Sudanese government to force al Qaeda out of the country. They returned to Afghanistan where they became close to, and at times fought for, the Taliban, who controlled most, but not all, of the country. In return the Taliban authorities allowed al Qaeda to establish training camps, and made it relatively easy for recruits from outside the country to get in.

By that time, al Qaeda had taken on many of the features that characterize it to this day. The word literally means "the base," and bin Laden and al-Zawahari always saw it as a loose organization composed of other jihadist groups as well as their own fighters. In that sense, bin Laden should not be seen as the organizational mastermind of international Islamic-based terrorism. Or, in other words, it is not always clear how much a given terrorist attack has been inspired, organized, or funded by al Qaeda.

There is little doubt that al Qaeda was involved in a series of violent attacks in the 1990s that became ever bloodier. The first bombing associated with al Qaeda occurred at a hotel in Aden in 1992; two people were killed. The next year a group, some of whom had been trained by al Qaeda, planted a bomb in the parking garage at the World Trade Center. That incident is not always considered to be the work of al Qaeda.

In 1998, the group escalated its activity by bombing the American embassies in Kenya and Tanzania, the latter costing the life of my colleague Susan Hirsch's husband. Two years later a small boat approached the USS *Cole* as it was refueling in Aden. The men on the boat tried to act as if they were friendly members of a garbage-boat crew. As they came up against the ship, the bomb went off, ripping a huge hole in the side of the *Cole* and killing 17 sailors, most of whom were eating lunch at the time.

In the meantime, the network had experimented with the use of airplanes in attacks, but those efforts had been thwarted and few people therefore saw airplanes as potential weapons. Other plans also were blocked by authorities around the world, including a bomb that was probably designed to go off on New Year's Eve 1999 at Los Angeles International Airport. Still, it was clear to terrorism experts that al Qaeda had raised the threat by several orders of magnitude precisely because it was organized transnationally. It also had more money and other resources than previous terrorist groups, although by this time bin Laden had largely been cut off by his family.

9/11 and Beyond

The morning of September 11 was sunny and warm in Washington and New York. I had to get the oil changed in my car, prepare for class that night, and finish an overdue article on bin Laden. As I noted earlier, all that changed once the second plane hit.

Panic set in. By mid-morning it was clear that there were only four planes and no bombs on the Mall, as had been widely rumored. The fourth plane had been commandeered by passengers and crashed in Pennsylvania, killing all on board. It was almost certainly aimed at the White House.

By noon, I had recovered enough to send my editor an email asking if she was glad my article was late. We decided the next day to not publish it, because two or three pages would not be enough. That morning, Search for Common Ground had an emergency staff meeting. On the subway, you could see the hatred aimed at the people on the train who seemed to be of South Asian origin. At every corner on my ten-minute walk from the World Bank (the White House is three blocks away) to DuPont Circle, there were military police and Humvees. That would have been unimaginable the day before.

Search had scheduled a launch party for the first edition of this book on the Thursday. My initial hope was to cancel, but my boss and I decided we had to go ahead with it. This time, it took my wife two-and-a-half hours to get to Washington, which is a twenty-minute drive at rush hour. She missed the entire event and ended up having our car locked in a parking garage for the night.

Bin Laden only took responsibility for the attack in the days before the 2004 American presidential election. However, by the end of 9/11 it was clear that he and his organization were the only ones who could have committed this atrocity.

There was tremendous soul-searching, especially here in Washington and in New York. A friend, who was then on the Nightline reporting staff, wrote a story about a photographer who could not stay away from Ground Zero and ended up being its official picture-taker. As I mentioned earlier, another friend was in a senator's office when an anthrax letter was delivered.

We will discuss later the official response, and the conflict resolution community's response, to the crisis. But since some readers of this book might not have been any more than 11 or 12 years old on that dreadful day, it is important to stress just how chaotic and fearful those first days were.

I often tell a funny, or at least ironic, story to illustrate personal confusion post-9/11. The first edition of *International Conflict Resolution* was dedicated to two people whose books I received after I had finished the manuscript, and thus could not include in the bibliography. One was Susan Collin Marks, the executive vice-president of Search for Common Ground, who had written on the transition from apartheid in South Africa. The other was my former college housemate, Bernie Mayer, who had tried to pull together theories of conflict resolution largely from the experience of mediators. At the time Bernie lived in Boulder, Colorado. He happened to be in Washington on 9/11 and couldn't get out of town because all the airports were closed. So, he and yet another former house-mate came to the discussion—without telling me in advance. It was wonderful to have both Bernie and Susan there. However, it was a sign of how chaotic things were. Bernie finally rented a car and kept driving west until he found an open airport: Indianapolis.

There have been no terrorist attacks in the United States since 9/11. However, devastating bombings occurred in London, Madrid, Morocco, Turkey, Pakistan and, most recently, Mumbai. Al Qaeda became a major force in the Sunni resistance against the American occupation of Iraq, as discussed in Chapter 9.

In short, al Qaeda and the groups connected to it have not gone away.

In June 2009, Google listed more than 6 million websites that dealt with terrorism. Many of them are not very good. The two best are hosted by the United States Institute for Peace and the United States Military Academy:
www.usip.org/library/topics/terrorism.
html. www.ctc.usma.edu.

The Global War on Terror

September 11 was a confusing day for American policy-makers. They had not ignored terrorism beforehand. However, because hitherto the threat primarily lay outside the

United States it had not been a high priority, despite the embassy bombings and the attack on the USS *Cole*. The Clinton administration had used Cruise missiles to attack suspected al Qaeda targets in Sudan and Afghanistan, but had done little more.

There is still considerable debate over whether the US government should have known about, or could have prevented, the attacks that day. The intelligence community had made it clear that terrorists were planning something "big." And, at least three of the 9/11 hijackers were known to the CIA, if not to the FBI. Certainly, the fact that 20 young Arab men had come to the United States to learn to fly airplanes could and should have raised more than a few eyebrows. Nonetheless it is all but impossible to predict, let alone prevent, a terrorist attack on a particular day and in a particular place.

That said, there was no question but that the United States was going to respond to 9/11 with force. President Bush made that clear to his staff, and then to the rest of the world, within a matter of days. The president also made it clear at least to his inner circle that the war on terrorism would not just be against al Qaeda, but against everyone, everywhere who harbored and supported terrorists. Iraq was added to the list of potential targets either in the first days after 9/11 or no later than the end of 2001.

The problem was that the Bush administration had no plans to mount what soon came to be called the "Global War on Terrorism." It had no troops or bases in or near Afghanistan. It did not have overflight rights for most of the neighboring countries, which would have made the rescue of pilots who were shot down all but impossible.

As a result, it took almost a month for the war which everyone knew was going to take place to actually begin. On October 7, the United States and the United Kingdom began airstrikes on both al Qaeda and Taliban targets—although, unknown to the public at the time, there was already a small group of CIA and special forces troops on the ground in the northern part of Afghanistan. To make a long story short, the Northern Alliance of Afghan soldiers did the bulk of the fighting.

The Taliban was no match for the well-armed Northern Alliance. It abandoned Kabul during the night of November 12. By the end of the month, it had lost control of all Afghanistan's major cities.

That did not mean, by any stretch of the imagination, that the war on terrorism was over. Al Qaeda had been weakened but not destroyed. Hundreds of their fighters were killed or captured. Many of those detained were sent to special, secret prisons run by the CIA in Europe; many more were sent to the infamous prison camp set up at the American naval base at Guantanamo Bay ("Gitmo" in military slang), in Cuba. President Bush declared that the detainees were "enemy combatants" and not conventional soldiers. Therefore, the Geneva Convention regarding the treatment of prisoners of war did not apply to them. Many were treated extremely harshly, including the use of "waterboarding," an interrogation tactic that most observers believe is a form of torture.

More importantly, the United States and its allies did not capture or kill bin Laden, who escaped, probably to the mountains along the border with Pakistan. Al Qaeda was significantly weaker, having been cut off from its main sources of income and its political support from the Taliban. Nonetheless, as the post-9/11 attacks mentioned earlier attest, terrorism has not even come close to being defeated.

Once the Taliban fell, the anti-terrorism coalition expanded to include Dutch and Canadian troops. Article 5 of the treaty establishing NATO (www.nato.int) held that an attack on any member state was an attack on all of them. Therefore the Canadians,

Dutch, Danes, Australians and Estonians all sent ground troops. The French air force carried out raids. Canadian troops, in particular, have seen heavy fighting, and this is the first time they have been in combat since the Korean War of the 1950s.

The United States also modified its doctrine regarding terrorism and the broader threat to its own security. In his 2002 commencement speech at West Point Military Academy, President Bush made it clear that the United States was willing to act at any time or in any place to combat terrorism. This notion of "pre-emption" became the centerpiece of the *National Security Strategy of the United States* issued by the National Security Council that fall. The administration continued to develop its doctrine until its last days in office. Thus, in December 2008 it issued a new directive making counter-insurgency and unconventional warfare as important as traditional combat operations for the foreseeable future.

It is hard to argue that the GWOT has been a military success. Seven years after 9/11, there is still fighting in Afghanistan, some of it intense. In 2008, the Taliban regained strength. It even seemed possible that they could retake Kabul. About 30,000 NATO troops were currently in the country. The Obama administration announced that it would send two or three more combat brigades to the country by summer 2009, a build-up made possible by the draw-down of troops from Iraq.

Terrorism might pose an even more unpredictable threat with the weakening of al Qaeda, because its global participants are more able to act on their own. Al Qaeda was never a tightly knit organization, and most observers think that groups possibly inspired by it are acting increasingly unilaterally.

The United States is undoubtedly more secure internally than it was before 9/11. The creation of the Department of Homeland Security, and the introduction of the USA Patriot Act, have certainly made American citizens feel safer.

But even these developments are highly controversial. Very few analysts think that bringing dozens of agencies together in a single DHS has worked very well. Certainly in its most important challenge, Hurricane Katrina, the department failed abysmally. More often, the provisions and laws enacted after 9/11 are criticized for violating the civil liberties not only of the prisoners at Guantanamo but of ordinary American citizens as well.

Much is likely to change under the Obama administration. During the election campaign Senator Obama pledged to close Guantanamo, stop the use of torture, and adhere to international law, in addition to sending more US troops to Afghanistan. During this administration the United States will almost certainly act more internationally, and step back from the pre-emption doctrine introduced by President Bush in 2002. And, intriguingly, in its first week the Obama team never mentioned the term "Global War on Terrorism," referring only to al Qaeda in this context.

Only one thing is clear. Military means alone cannot end terrorism or the broader, asymmetric conflicts we face that Dexter Filkins (2008) calls "the forever war."

The Conflict Resolution Community

If anything, we were caught even more off our political guard than the military and the policy-makers were after 9/11. Although many conflict resolution organizations have worked in countries that had already been subject to terrorist attacks, they were not phenomena that most of us thought about. There is no simple or single explanation for this.

If nothing else, such attacks fell outside our field of expertise because it is rarely possible to sit down and negotiate with terrorists.

But still, we have to answer Lawrence Wright's question. And even though I ducked the question the first time he asked it, I have in fact been one of the few conflict resolution professionals to have worked seriously on terrorism and related policy issues since 9/11.

My engagement began on 9/13 with a discussion of the first edition of this book, joined by a childhood friend who runs a think-tank to help the Pentagon, in the cliché, "think outside the box." But I have to admit that my work and that of my colleagues probably has been no more successful than the military campaigns.

Like most of my colleagues, I tried to find a non-violent response to 9/11 and failed. Even colleagues who opposed the war a month later had to acknowledge that our country had been grievously wounded and some form of retaliation was required (Lederach 2001).

Most of us did not react quickly or coherently. I helped run a workshop on reconciliation in the week before the war started. We spent more time on terrorism than on reconciliation. Frankly, the 25 or so people in the room had little constructive to say.

The following week, the Association for Conflict Resolution (www.acresolution.org) held its first annual conference. Because the program had been planned months earlier, there were no formal sessions on 9/11 and its aftermath, and the ad hoc sessions the organization's president convened were not very well attended. One respected practitioner actually claimed that if she could sit down with Bush and bin Laden, she could settle the dispute in two hours.

Ten days later, a member of the United States Institute of Peace staff, who had been at the ACR meeting and was shocked by the lack of response to 9/11 there, convened a meeting of all the academics working on conflict resolution in the Washington area—there are a lot of us, by the way. It was one of most frustrating meetings I have ever attended. One colleague had sent Secretary of Defense Donald Rumsfeld a 34-page memo, and was furious that Rumsfeld had not responded. Generally speaking, my friend was not alone in demonstrating a remarkable ignorance of how policy-makers operate, in peace or war. Most of the participants did their share of Bush-bashing, violating one of the key principles we teach our students: stereotyping and blaming people you disagree rarely work, because they deepen divisions and make it hard to persuade both sides to talk. One colleague said he assumed that everyone in the room opposed the war; in fact, only about two-thirds of us did.

Eventually, a colleague (who was at the time the leading funder in the conflict resolution field) interrupted with me: we said that we do conflict resolution so that there can be constructive solutions to the world's problems. In the end, the meeting accomplished little. However, I decided to work with an intern whom I met that afternoon, so that together we would write a chapter for a book on terrorism being jointly published by George Mason University's Institute for Conflict Analysis and Resolution, and the Defense Threat Reduction Agency (Hersey and Hauss 2002). That chapter gives my basic answer to Lawrence Wright.

Lessons Learned: Response to Lawrence Wright

First, in our opinion there is no quick solution to terrorism. As we saw in a previous chapter, the outlines of an agreement in Northern Ireland were clear as early as 1974. However, it took a quarter-century to reach a settlement.

Secondly, because all wars have a political end, an end to the war on terrorism means that at some point we must talk to al Qaeda and other terrorists. As I said to Wright, we probably can't do so now. And, as an American and a Jew, I am probably not the right person to be involved, in early discussions at any rate. Rather, I suggested that we find better intermediaries such as Tariq Ramadan—who was appointed to a professorship at Notre Dame University and then denied a visa by the State Department—and the Crown Prince of Jordan, who has been active in conflict resolution circles.

Thirdly, one skill of conflict resolution specialists is to "reframe" the terms of debate, broadening them in a way that makes more "space" for creative discussion. The best example of that so far is the recent report of the US–Muslim Engagement Project (2008) convened by Search for Common Ground and the Consensus Building Institute. The project consisted of 38 prominent American leaders, including a former secretary of state and a former deputy secretary of state. About half are on the left politically, and the other half on the right. There were at least seven Jews (including an orthodox rabbi who is also a conflict resolution professor) and nine Muslims.

I will talk about consensus building as a process in the concluding chapter of this book. For now, it is enough to note that these men and women reached a wide-ranging agreement on what should be American public policy toward the Muslim world. The report's core findings include these:

- make diplomacy our top priority in dealing with Israel, Palestine, Iran, Iraq and Afghanistan
- support efforts to strengthen the state and civil society in the Muslim world
- help create jobs in the Muslim world that could benefit both their economies and ours
- increase mutual respect and understanding between the United States and the Muslim world.

These actions alone will not end terrorism soon. However, they carry the potential for easing tensions and building relationships that could become central to an agreement in the not-too-distant future.

Finally, and perhaps most importantly, we have to do work in the field that will help convince young Muslims (and others) not to become terrorists. It is important to remember that there are few terrorists, and most people who become terrorists do so as a last resort. The best work in this area is being done by the International Center for Religion and Diplomacy (www.icrd.org). As I write, this organization has had considerable success in bringing Hindu and Muslim religious leaders together in Kashmir. As an outgrowth of that work, it has begun consciousness-raising work with the *madrasas* (religious schools) along the Pakistan/Afghanistan border. ICRD has even had meetings with Taliban leaders in both countries.

In conclusion, it must be acknowledged that none of these non-violent options will end terrorism soon, or on their own.

Select Bibliography

Anonymous (Michael Scheuer) (2004). *Imperial Hubris: Why the West is Losing the War on Terror.* Washington, DC: Brassey's.

Banks, William, Renée de Nevers and Mitchell Wallerstein (2008). *Combatting Terrorism: Strategies and Approaches*. Washington, DC: CQ Press.

Coll, Stephen (2008). *The Bin Ladens: An Arabian Family in the American Century*. New York: Penguin.

Cronin, Audrey Kurth (2002/3). "Behind the Curve: Globalization and International Terrorism." *International Security*. January: 20–38.

Dekmejian, R. Hrair (2007). *The Spectrum of Terror*. Washington, DC: CQ Press.

Filkins, Dexter (2008). *The Forever War*. New York: Borzoi/Knopf.

Hersey, Matthew and Charles Hauss (2002). "Addressing the Root Causes of Terrorism." In *Terrorism: Concepts, Causes, and Conflict Resolution*, R. Scott Moore (ed.). Arlington, VA: Defense Threat Reduction Agency.

Hirsch, Susan (2006). *In the Moment of Greatest Calamity: Terrorism, Grief, and a Victim's Quest for Justice*. Princeton, NJ: Princeton University Press.

Lederach, John Paul (2001). "Quo Vadis?" www.nd.edu/~krocinst/sept11/ledquo.shtml (accessed October 24).

Pape, Robert (2005). *Dying to Win: The Strategic Logic of Suicide Terrorism*. New York: Random House.

US–Muslim Engagement Project (2008). *Changing Course: A New Direction for US Relations with the Muslim World*. Available at www.usmulimengagement.org.

Wright, Lawrence (2006). *The Looming Tower*. New York: Random House.

CHAPTER NINE

Iraq

If I make a peace proposal, then I'm the one who will have to make concessions. If the others propose one, then I can obtain concessions.
—*Saddam Hussein*

This will be the longest and most controversial chapter in Part 2. As I wrote in late 2008, the United States was fighting its second war in Iraq in less than 20 years. The second one started with an American-led invasion of Iraq which quickly and easily toppled Saddam Hussein's dictatorial regime. But the war didn't end. Five years later the United States was

Figure 4 Map of Iraq

still occupying Iraq, to all intents and purposes. It was still fighting an insurgency that the Bush administration did not anticipate and had done little to prepare for. By the time I wrote, the Iraq war had become the longest in American history. The security situation improved considerably with the so-called surge that began in early 2007, but there were few signs that it would end soon.

Before We Begin

Because this chapter will be the most controversial for most readers in many ways, let me start with four background themes that will help you see why I reach the conclusions I do.

First, I have been deeply involved in discussions about American policy in Iraq. As will become clear in the next paragraph, I have done most of that with serving and retired military and intelligence officers. All of them know that I opposed the war when the Bush administration strongly suggested it was necessary. But, I have chosen not to take a visible public stand so that I can maintain and build on the relationships I had established after 9/11. Until now, I have not published any of the papers I've written on the war. And even here, I am far less judgmental than I could be. I am often criticized for not using what little leverage I have to attack the Bush administration. That criticism may well be accurate. My decision, however, was based on the assumption that the only viable solution to the catastrophe that is Iraq would require some kind of cooperation between NGOs and the military. I always try to describe political issues simply, and I try to be constructive at all times.

Secondly, not surprisingly, this chapter draws heavily on work I have done with the military and the intelligence community. Most serving officers I know who have spent time in Iraq (and Afghanistan) have serious doubts about how the wars have been prosecuted. Given the soldiers' and civil servants' sense of duty and the provisions of the Universal Code of Military Justice, few of them have been willing to go public at least until they retire. Therefore, I will cite very few of my sources by name, but if you want to see how young officers deal with the contradictions between their duty and their conscience, read the wonderful book by Elizabeth Samet, *A Soldier's Heart* (2007). Samet is a civilian and an English professor at West Point. I first heard her interviewed on the radio, oddly, while driving home from a week's teaching at the academy. Samet covers more than Iraq, but the book's most evocative passages deal with how current and former cadets cope with the rigors of war. I also saw that at first hand. While I was there I had lunch (the cadets are in and out in 25 minutes) with a group of seniors who were going to receive their post-graduation assignments the next day. They all knew they were going to either Afghanistan or Iraq. None seemed happy about it, but since the war had started before they enrolled, they knew what they would be facing for their entire undergraduate careers. One of the things that struck me (and Samet) most forcibly was their profound sense of commitment to their profession, a profession that is changing dramatically as we will see at the end of the chapter and the book.

Thirdly, the literature on Iraq is immense. I haven't had time to read it all; you certainly will not. I have focused primarily on works by journalists who spent time in the country and came back highly critical of American policy. By far the most detailed of these is Bob Woodward's four-volume history of the war, which is far too long for our purposes. What is intriguing about most of the works I cite is that their authors have historically been quite supportive of the military. I have also noted several of the best works by military specialists about the surge, and the counter-insurgency in general.

Fourthly, this is really two chapters in one. It explores why conflict resolution practitioners had such a minor impact both on the first Gulf War and the current one. Also, note that I could have presented the final three chapters of Part 3 in almost any order. I start the three most depressing cases with Iraq because the US actually have made more progress there than with the global war on terrorism or the genocide in Sudan—though admittedly, that isn't saying much.

Theoretical Issues

This chapter's theoretical focus is different from those of the previous four, because win-win conflict resolution and steps toward stable peace were never options in Iraq's ongoing dispute with the international community. Here, though we will concentrate on many of the same explanatory themes that were raised in Chapters 6 through 9, the challenge is to understand why a non-violent solution to the crises involving Iraq has proved elusive during both the 1991 and the 2003 crises. Thus, we will review:

- the way the end of the Cold War made new alliances and other geopolitical arrangements possible
- the weakness of international institutions and the international community in general, except under the most exceptional circumstances
- the assertion made in earlier chapters that it is easy to plan a hypothetical win-win outcome, but that this is rarely a primary goal of foreign policy-makers
- a certain conceptual looseness in the idea of a "hurting stalemate" that makes it a less useful analytical tool than it might have seemed in earlier chapters
- the way that misperceptions and other psychological factors, as well as domestic politics, can reinforce the kind of intransigence shown in the statement by Saddam Hussein that begins this chapter
- a contrast between the heavily multinational effort in the first Gulf War and what amounts to American unilateralism since 9/11
- the difficulties in resolving asymmetrical conflicts in which the seemingly weaker side may actually have more staying power and commitment than the stronger one
- the importance of considering "failed" cases in which the outcomes that we in the conflict resolution community would have preferred did not happen.

That final bullet point may provide the most important reason for considering Iraq, for three reasons. First, it reminds us of just how hard and rare it is to achieve effective win-win conflict resolution. Secondly, and ironically, by considering the causes of the continued conflict between Iraq and most of the rest of the world we can see more clearly that forces able to achieve win-win conflict resolution yield positive-sum outcomes. Finally, the tragedy that has befallen Iraq as a result of the three wars it has fought since 1980 should drive home yet again the normative conclusion that we need to find better ways of settling our disputes.

The Gulf War

In his remarkable speech to the United Nations General Assembly in December 1988, Soviet president Mikhail Gorbachev used the term "new world order" to describe the international relations being born out of the ashes of the Cold War. Then, US president-elect George Bush adopted the term to describe what he—and most of the rest of us—hoped would be a more peaceful world.

Yet, even before the Soviet Union disintegrated three years later, the international community was plunged into a new and costly war following Iraq's August 1990 invasion of Kuwait, a war that led some pundits to call ours a new world *dis*order instead. More than three-quarters of a million soldiers from 35 countries were deployed to the region in Operation Desert Shield, while negotiations to convince Iraq to withdraw from Kuwait continued. In January 1991 negotiations broke down and the war, dubbed Operation Desert Storm, began. Seven weeks of air strikes and a few days of surprisingly easy ground combat forced Saddam Hussein's troops out of Kuwait, and dealt a terrible blow to Iraq's society and economy.

A Common Problem

This chapter will be making a number of conclusions about what happened in Washington and Baghdad before, during and after the two wars. Those conclusions should really be read as assertions because of a problem all international relations scholars face, which is particularly challenging here.

We do not have access to all the factual information we want or need.

As the description of the United States intelligence community later in the chapter attests, surprisingly little was actually known about Iraq before Saddam's overthrow. We do not have in-depth information about the working of the Baath Party's inner circle. Therefore, we are forced to rely on at best educated guesses about what motivated Saddam Hussein and other key Iraqi leaders, and some of the more militant insurgents today.

The United States, other Western governments, and the United Nations are much more open to journalists and scholars than is Iraq. However, even with these more open sources much information remains classified, and the political leaders involved have revealed primarily what they want the public or the academic community to know; and they have withheld other material.

This is, in fact, a problem for all the case studies in this book, but it is particularly problematic here. What I have tried to do throughout is to rely on the most widely respected sources of information, and to draw on works that reflect the varied points of view on these conflicts.

Attention, however, did not subsequently shift to peace-building and other conflict resolution strategies. Indeed, after the fighting stopped, the Gulf war allies and Iraq remained deeply at odds. Sanctions were still in effect. Skirmishes periodically broke out between Iraq and what remained of the UN-led forces of 1990–91.

But at this point it is important to underscore a first and more important conclusion. The Gulf War was clearly a case in which traditional approaches to conflict management and resolution failed, while the new approaches outlined in Part 3 never made it onto the political agenda.

There are many reasons why that was the case. Responsibility for the failure is to be found on both sides. One of the most important explanations for why the Iraqi case is different lies in the statement by Saddam Hussein that begins this chapter. He was certainly reluctant to take the first steps toward reaching an agreement, because he was convinced that doing so would also require Iraq to make the first concessions, something he was never willing to do. Although they would never speak so bluntly, the same case can largely be made for the leaders of the 1990–91 coalition. The Bush and Clinton administrations, in particular, were unwilling to make (m)any conciliatory gestures because they were convinced that, given Iraqi behavior since 1990, they need not and should not do so.

The point is not to cast blame on either or both sides. Rather, you should see that the stances both have taken have done little or nothing to bring an end to the conflict, despite the tragic consequences of both wars.

Iraq and International Relations before the Gulf War

As was the case with the other three case studies, the conflict with Iraq had roots stretching back hundreds of years and including regional issues, the long-term impact of imperialism, and other causes (Hauss 2009).

The region now known as Iraq was almost certainly the birthplace of civilization. The first cities, systems of writing, and irrigation were developed over four thousand years ago in the fertile region between the Tigris and Euphrates rivers. The tower of Babel stood there. As recently as the thirteenth century, Baghdad was one of the world's leading intellectual centers, and the Muslim empire which had its capital there dwarfed anything in Europe at the time (see Table 9.1).

Later, the region, which has no natural defenses, was repeatedly invaded and overrun. In 1900 it was nothing more than a group of provinces in the crumbling Ottoman empire, based in Turkey.

During World War One, the British offered a group of Arab leaders independence after the war if they would help to defeat the Ottoman Empire. The British reneged on their offer shortly after the war ended, and carved up the Arab world from Egypt to Iraq with their allies, the French. The country they called Iraq was put together from eighteen provinces of the old Ottoman Empire but did not include Kuwait, which many thought should have been part of it.

Thus was created a country that is richly endowed with natural resources, but also plagued by ethnic and religious divisions. Over 15 percent of the world's proven oil reserves lie beneath Iraqi soil, enough to last at least 140 years at 1980s levels of production. Despite its location in one of the most arid parts of the world, the area between the Tigris and Euphrates is fertile enough for Iraq to grow all the food it needs.

In short, Iraq was quite well off by regional standards before the invasion of Kuwait. Its cities were among the richest and most cosmopolitan in the Arab world. Literacy stood at 55 percent or more. Most people in the countryside, as well as the cities,

Table 9.1 Iraq and the World before 1990

Date	Event
1919	Treaty of Versailles
1932	Iraq becomes legally independent
1958	Monarchy overthrown
1963	First Baath coup
1968	Baath comes to power for the long term
1979	Saddam Hussein takes control
1980–88	Iran–Iraq war

enjoyed reasonable health care, had adequate housing, and could aspire to a middle-class standard of living. Iraq also offered more professional opportunities and personal freedoms to women than any of the other Arab states.

However, the British decision after World War One made Iraq all but ungovernable by anything but the most authoritarian regimes, because it combined three groups whose histories were antagonistic to say the least. About 95 percent of the population is Muslim. There is a small Christian minority—Tariq Aziz, for instance, who held a number of key posts until he surrendered in 2003, is a Christian. There was also a small Jewish population, though most Jews emigrated after the creation of Israel in 1948.

The apparent homogeneity of Iraq, however, is misleading. Between 55 and 65 percent of the population are Shiites. They are part of a quite devout (and often militant) sect of Islam that is dominant in neighboring Iran. Virtually all the Shiites are ethnic Arabs. The rest of the population are Sunnis, who make up the overwhelming majority of the world's Muslim population. In Iraq, however, Muslims are divided into two roughly equal—and antagonistic—communities. Until 2003, independent Iraq had always been dominated by Sunni Arabs, including Saddam Hussein and most of his entourage. The rest of the Sunni are Kurds, who are part of a wholly different ethnic group. The world's nearly 30 million Kurds are spread across Iraq, Turkey, Syria, Iran and Azerbaijan. The Kurds never accepted their incorporation into any of these states, and various (and often feuding) Kurdish groups have been fighting for their own country since 1919, when their hopes were thwarted by the Treaty of Versailles.

The British compounded the difficulties caused by ethnic and religious differences in Iraq by importing King Faisal I from what is now Saudi Arabia as the country's first head of state. Faisal and his successors were, at best, mediocre rulers who did little to forge a stable or legitimate regime after Iraq gained its nominal independence in 1932. The last king was overthrown in 1958, which began a series of coups and counter-coups that left the country without an effective government for a decade.

By that time, the duplicitous role played by the British and foreign capitalists had reinforced three key Iraqi cultural values:

- a distrust of outsiders
- strong parochial loyalties to family, clan, and region
- acceptance of violence to settle political differences.

In 1968 the Baath Party filled the power vacuum in Baghdad, and ran the country with an iron fist until the 2003 invasion. The party was formed in the late 1940s as a pan-Arab and socialist party, whose primary goal was to unify all Arabs into a single state. The Baath party came to power in Syria and Iraq, but its goal of Arab unity collapsed as those two states became rivals in the 1970s and then combatants in the Gulf war.

The Iraqi Baath party was always composed of a tiny elite, whose rule ranks among the most brutal of the twentieth century. Its regime was always repressive, but after Saddam Hussein (1937–2006) took power in 1979 it became all but totalitarian.

Saddam and his inner circle turned the Baath party into a tool of what amounted to total and personal power. His inner circle, too, was composed mainly of his family and others from his hometown of Tikrit (Dawisha 1999). The party controlled everything, including the press, the schools, all social organizations, and institutions including the Olympic committee and national soccer team, which were run by Saddam's son, Uday. The regime was so powerful and repressive that one observer called it a "republic of fear," even before the invasion of Kuwait brought the country to the attention of the rest of the world (al-Khalil 1990). Four secret police bureaus monitored what Iraqi citizens did at home and abroad. Anyone who spoke against the regime risked arrest, torture and execution. Of the tens of thousands who perished were two of Saddam Hussein's sons-in-law. I could go on and present dozens of specific examples, but the following story told by Elaine Sciolino of the *New York Times* provides good corroboration. She arrived at the airport in Baghdad (named for Saddam Hussein, of course) and hailed a taxi to take her into town. Sciolino asked the driver what he thought of Saddam Hussein. The cabbie replied:

> "This is car," he says, patting his hand on the dashboard. "But if Saddam says this is bicycle, it is bicycle." He looks around anxiously and added: "He could kill me for this." (Hauss 2009: 394)

The Iran–Iraq War

Some academics and policy analysts were well aware that the Baath party had already established an authoritarian regime in the 1970s. Few others cared, since the repression had yet to reach the proportions it would under Saddam Hussein. More important, Iraq was at most a minor irritant in global politics, even in the ticklish relations between Arabs and Israelis.

All that changed when Saddam Hussein seized total control in 1979, and ushered in what turned out to be a quarter-century of personalized and highly despotic rule. That same year, fundamentalist Shiites led by the Ayatollah Ruhollah Khomeini (1902–89) overthrew the Shah's corrupt dictatorship in neighboring Iran.

As the two most powerful countries in the region, Iran and Iraq had long been rivals for control of the Persian Gulf. Iran had also supported Kurdish rebels in northern Iraq. Now, the secular Baath worried that the religious fervor that had spawned the Islamic revolution would spread to Iraq's Shiites. There was good reason for those fears, since Khomeini had lived in Iraq for years until he was thrown out by the Baath regime in 1978. Then, Egypt's signing of the Camp David Accords cost Cairo its leadership role among the militant foes of Israel, a role both Baghdad and Tehran coveted.

The new regime in Iran purged its army of officers who had been loyal to the Shah. Iraq decided to take advantage of the decline in Iranian readiness and morale by invading, on September 22, 1980. Contrary to Baghdad's expectations, the Iranian army held their ground. The war would last eight years. During that time the front barely moved. However, hundreds of thousands of soldiers and civilians were killed on both sides. Iraq used chemical and biological weapons both on Iranian troops and on their own Kurdish citizens, the first time such arms had been used since World War One. Finally, the Iranian government was convinced that it could not win, and on August 20, 1988 agreed to a cease-fire that amounted, at most, to a marginal victory for Iraq.

For our purposes, Iraq's changing relations with the West during the 1980s are more important than the war itself. Policy-makers in the West and the other Arab states had no illusions about Baghdad's intentions. The Baath party was anti-Western, and Iraq had long had fairly close ties to the Soviet Union.

The war against Iran, however, changed the geopolitical landscape. Iraq portrayed itself as defending the Arab world against the Persian and fundamentalist menace, gaining itself an estimated $40 billion in support from the wealthy Gulf oil states. Western governments seemed to adopt the Arab adage "my enemy's enemy is my friend." Arms and development assistance poured into Iraq. For example, in 1987 no country received more agricultural aid from the United States. The West turned a blind eye to Iraq's use of chemical weapons on the Kurds, and other human rights violations. When the war with Iran ended, the Western consensus was that Iraq was run by a reasonably pragmatic leader who could and should be encouraged to reform his regime.

The Gulf War

Iraq emerged from the war with Iran deeply in debt, especially to the other Gulf states it believed it had helped to defend by taking on Tehran. Quickly, it staked its claim to compensation for its effort and its losses from its wealthier neighbors which had not been touched by the war.

At the time, Iraq was not a major focus of Western attention. Like almost everyone else in the world, policy-makers on both sides of the Atlantic were preoccupied by the confusing changes occurring behind the disappearing Iron Curtain. To the degree that Western leaders did worry about the Middle East, they were more concerned with the conflict between Israel and the Arabs as the *intifada* gradually drew to an end.

In short, only low-level political appointees and career analysts in Western foreign ministries and intelligence agencies were paying much attention to Iraq. And, there was no consensus among them about either what Iraq was about to do, or how the West should respond.

Some Western analysts did point out that Iraq was a rogue state, whose unpredictable leadership could lead it to threaten the regional balance of power. However, given the other events sweeping the world, there was little enthusiasm for changing policy toward Baghdad in the United States or Europe. If anything, many of those countries encouraged trade and other contacts with Iraq which, ironically, helped Baghdad to rearm and speed up its programs to develop weapons of mass destruction.

In 1989 the US intelligence community issued a national intelligence estimate that predicted Iraq would not pose a threat to any of its neighbors for a number of years. Indeed, in October 1989 the administration of George H. W. Bush adopted National

Security Council Directive 26, which called for a policy of cooperation with Iraq on the assumption that it would be playing a more constructive role in global affairs (George 1993: 33–89).

As a result, Western governments were slow to respond when Baghdad began sending out ever more ominous signals. On February 24, Saddam Hussein made a major speech in which he attributed hostile intentions to the United States for maintaining its fleet in the Persian Gulf.

Then, in June and July, Iraq demanded $30 billion from the Gulf states as payment for "protecting them" during the war. It also accused them, and Kuwait in particular, of exceeding agreed levels of oil production and driving prices (and hence Iraqi revenue) down. Finally, it raised the old, but widely rejected, claim that Kuwait legally should have been the nineteenth province of Iraq.

At the end of July 1989, Iraqi troops massed near the Kuwaiti border. No one knew what their plans were. The American intelligence community was split down the middle, about half the analysts thinking Iraq would invade, half claiming it would not. The uncertainties went both ways. The Iraqi regime left an (in)famous meeting with US ambassador April Glaspie convinced that Washington would not stand in the way of an invasion.

Saddam Hussein

Toward the end of this chapter, we will see how the demonization of Saddam Hussein and his regime contributed to our inability to prevent two costly wars. Here, however, it is important also to see that the Iraqi regime proved hard to deal with in part because Saddam Hussein *was* a brutal leader of what can only be considered a rogue regime.

Saddam Hussein was born in 1937 in a dirt-poor village 100 miles from Baghdad. His father died before he was born, and he was abused by several of the relatives who helped raise him.

He moved to Baghdad aged 18, and immediately got involved in revolutionary politics. Wounded in the Baath party's first attempt to seize power in 1959, he then studied law in Cairo, the farthest he had ever been from Iraq for any extended period of time. He returned to Iraq, took part in the 1968 coup that brought the Baath party to long-term power, became the second most influential person in the new regime, and rose to the top in 1979, when he forced Ahmad Hassan al-Bakr to resign.

Saddam Hussein was a ruthless ruler who exerted all but total control over his country. Through a series of purges, he turned the Baath regime into what was little more than a personal dictatorship. Thomas Friedman of the *New York Times* described him as a thirteenth-century tyrant whose craving for weapons of mass destruction turned him into the archetypal twenty-first-century threat.

Saddam was removed from power in April 2003, captured that December, and executed three years later.

There was uncertainty on the Iraqi side as well. Saddam Hussein and his immediate entourage seem to have assumed that the international community would not retaliate if he moved on Kuwait. Moreover, the most recent evidence suggests that even people just outside the inner circle in Baghdad did not know what Saddam Hussein had planned.

Tariq Aziz, for instance, apparently thought that Iraq would only seize part of the country to settle an old border dispute, and he tried to talk Saddam out of doing that (Cockburn and Cockburn 1999: 7–9).

In that atmosphere of uncertainty, Iraq's troops poured into its tiny neighbor on August 2, 1990. Within hours, it had taken over Kuwait City. The royal family fled, along with many other prominent Kuwaitis (see Table 9.2).

By taking Kuwait, Iraq had also positioned itself to attack Saudi Arabia. Had it occupied that country as well, it would have controlled upward of a quarter of the world's proven oil reserves.

At that point, the kind of conflict resolution techniques we have concentrated on throughout this book were not on anyone's agenda, nor to all intents and purposes for the 13 years to follow. Instead the UN, the United States, and the rest of the allies engaged in a classic example of coercive diplomacy (Herrmann 1994), combining negotiations with the threat of force in an attempt to stop Iraq from moving into Saudi Arabia and to compel it to pull out of Kuwait.

Within weeks the UN Security Council passed a number of resolutions, the most important of which demanded that Iraq withdraw from Kuwait (Resolution 660), and imposed economic and other sanctions (661). With the end of the Cold War, most of the world united against Iraq's invasion. The United States and the USSR did not completely agree on the tactics to use. Still, the two superpowers worked more closely together than they had at any point since World War Two. Saudi Arabia, Syria, Egypt and a number of smaller Arab states joined in condemning the Iraqi invasion and supporting the coalition's efforts to roll it back.

Table 9.2 Iraq and the World in the 1990s

Year	Event
1990	Invasion of Kuwait
	Operation Desert Storm
	UN authorizes sanctions and use of force
1991	Gulf War
	Uprisings by Kurds and Shi'ites
	UNSCOM created
1992	More violations of UN restrictions on Iraqi program developing weapons of mass destruction (WMD)
1993	Iraq formally accepts UN conditions on WMD
1994	Iraq moves troops close to Kuwait border
1995	Iraq acknowledges major WMD programs
	Saddam and Hussein Kamel and families defect and return
	Saddam and Hussein Kamel executed
1996	Limited oil sales permitted for purchase of humanitarian aid
1997	Iraq tries to deny UNSCOM access to "presidential" and other sites
1998	Iraq stops cooperating with UNSCOM
	UNSCOM leaves
	Latest round of air strikes begins and continues into 1999
1999	Iraq rejects plan for new UN inspection regime

This point is worth underscoring. The end of the Cold War produced a sea change in international relations. The old bipolar division had disappeared, and the United States and United Nations could build a much broader coalition that was prepared to go much farther than at any point during the Cold War. Even though the allies were not able to prevent war, the six months between the invasion and the launch of Operation Desert Storm opened the door to a dramatic expansion of multilateral responses to aggression. The consequent undermining of regional peace has characterized international relations ever since.

Meanwhile, the United States took the lead in putting together Operation Desert Shield. The force, which would eventually top 800,000 soldiers, was designed to prevent Iraq from moving into Saudi Arabia and, it was hoped, eventually persuade it to withdraw from Kuwait.

In retrospect, some left-wing critics have taken the allies to task for their occasional rigidity and their frequent use of heated rhetoric laden with images of Saddam Hussein as an evil human being. Others suggest that President Bush had all but given up hope on the diplomatic front as early as the first week of November. Conservatives, in contrast, argue that Bush was not tough enough in dealing with a leader who emerged from a culture in which toughness is respected, and any sign of meeting one's adversaries halfway is seen as a sign of weakness.

Most observers, however, are convinced that the most serious misperceptions and miscalculations occurred in Baghdad. It was at the height of the crisis that Saddam Hussein uttered the words that begin this chapter, at a meeting with a delegation from the PLO (Cockburn and Cockburn 1999: 8–9). These words could have been used to describe the Iraqi leadership's attitude from 1990 onward. By all accounts, Saddam Hussein (though not necessarily his advisers) was convinced until the very last moment that the allies would not attack and that if they did, his troops would prevail in what he called the "mother of all battles." He was also convinced that most of the Arab world would rise up with him to defeat what he saw as Western imperialism.

After nearly four months without a positive response from Baghdad, the UN Security Council voted on November 29 to authorize the use of force if Iraq did not withdraw by January 15, 1991. The United States and other coalition members engaged in non-stop diplomacy, trying to convince Saddam Hussein to withdraw and avoid war. Other states that were not affiliated with Operation Desert Shield tried to mediate, most notably the Soviet Union, which had a history of good relations with Iraq.

The deadline came and went, and in the early morning of January 17, 1991 (Baghdad time), the allies started what turned out to be a 39-day air war. Despite devastating damage to the country's cities and infrastructure, the air campaign did not lead to an Iraqi surrender. Therefore, on February 24, the allies launched a ground attack. The Iraqi forces crumbled in the face of the superbly led and immensely better equipped coalition forces. Three days later, the Iraqis fled Kuwait, and President Bush announced a cease-fire.

The elder Bush has been severely criticized for not pushing on to Baghdad and removing Saddam Hussein and the Baath party from power. To this day, Bush justifies himself by stating that the UN mandate only extended to liberating Kuwait. Many—though by no means all—observers are also convinced that such a campaign would have been far bloodier than Operation Desert Storm, in which fewer than 200 Americans were killed, most of them as a result of friendly fire.

Useful Websites

The Middle East Network Information Center at the University of Texas provides a good comprehensive site for the entire region: <http://link.lanic.utexas.edu/menic>.

The *Middle East Report* is one of the best journals in the field. Its website has its publications and more: <http://www.merip.org>.

Perhaps the best source is maintained by the United States Institute of Peace: <http: www.usip.org/isg/index.html>

Invasion and Insurgency

It is an open question whether war still fulfils the task assigned to it by Karl von Clausewitz—settling political disputes that could not be resolved otherwise. The Gulf war reached only one of the allies' goals at most, although it was clearly their most important. The allies were able to force Iraq out of Kuwait. However, they were not able to put an end to the tensions between Iraq and the international community. In many ways the inconclusive end to the fighting, as described above, left the parties with a different but still intractable situation. It is possible that the uncomfortable stalemate which emerged in 1991 could have lasted indefinitely, had not the terrorist attacks of 9/11 occurred.

Whatever the actual causes of the war that began in March 2003, the fact is that the conflict inside Iraq has deepened in ways that few of us could have imagined—supporters and opponents of the Bush administration's policies alike. To make matters even less hopeful, the six years since this most recent war began have given few signs that the tools which conflict resolution professionals bring "to the table" will have any chance of working in the foreseeable future.

The Immediate Aftermath of the Gulf War

The United States and its allies in Operation Desert Storm made a fateful decision following the Iraqi surrender. The Iraqi army was in tatters and coalition forces could easily have continued the war, moved toward Baghdad and, conceivably, toppled the Ba'ath regime. President George H. W. Bush decided not to do so in what has turned out to be one of the most controversial decisions of his presidency. The president and his team justified their decision in many ways (Bush and Scowcroft 1998). As mentioned above, they emphasized that the UN's mandate to the coalition only authorized the removal of Iraq from Kuwait. But, probably just as important was the administration's concern that moving on to Baghdad would lead to an unacceptably large number of American casualties.

As a result, Saddam Hussein and the Baath regime remained in power. President Bush and other Western leaders made ambiguous statements about the future of relations with Baghdad as long as Saddam was still in control. The US administration, in particular, issued statements that many Iraqi opposition figures felt urged them to take up arms to overthrow Saddam.

Within days of the cease-fire, Shiites in the south and Kurds in the north rose up against the government in Baghdad. The international community did little to help them overthrow the government. For logistical reasons, little could be done to help the Shiites, who were brutally repressed. The United States and its allies were able to assist the Kurds, who succeeded in setting up their own *de facto* state in northern Iraq, largely outside the control of the central government. No-fly zones that Iraqi aircraft were not permitted to enter were created over the northern and southern parts of the country. But, as 1991 ended, Saddam Hussein was as securely in power as ever.

By no means was the crisis over. For the next 12 years the international community maintained sanctions, and the United States and its allies engaged in short-term military actions whenever it seemed as if the Iraq regime was trying to break out of those constraints. For example:

- January 1993. The United States fired 40 cruise missiles at a factory suspected of being part of the Iraqi nuclear weapons development program.
- June 1993. More cruise missiles were fired at Iraqi intelligence headquarters after reports emerged that Baghdad planned to assassinate former president Bush when he visited Kuwait.
- October 1994. The United States sent aircraft and over 50,000 soldiers to the region after Iraq massed its own troops near the Kuwaiti border.
- September 1996. The United States fired missiles at a variety of targets after Iraqi troops moved into Kurdish areas in the north.
- February 1998. UN secretary-general Kofi Annan defused a crisis over UNSCOM access to "presidential sites" suspected of being used for weapons development.
- December 1998. About 450 cruise missiles and 650 bombing runs by conventional aircraft were launched following Iraq's decision to stop cooperating with UNSCOM, once it became clear that the UN Commission was bringing to light Baghdad's biological weapons program.
- In 1999, repeated attacks by British and American planes were challenged by Iraqi fighters.

Many of those confrontations have revolved around the regime of weapons inspections. In spring 1991 the UN Security Council passed Resolution 687, which stated that economic sanctions would stay in place until Iraq complied with all UN demands. The most important of these was an end to its program to develop nuclear and other weapons of mass destruction (WMD). To that end, the UN created UNSCOM (United Nations Special Commission) to monitor Iraq compliance (or the lack thereof) with its demands. By the middle of 1991, it was clear that Iraq was not providing anything like a full disclosure of its inventory of weapons, or its plans for developing new ones.

For the next seven years, Iraq played a political cat-and-mouse game with UNSCOM. It did whatever it could to deny the inspectors access to possible weapons sites or data on their development. Over the years, UNSCOM was able to document that Baghdad had made more progress than had previously been suspected toward developing nuclear, chemical and biological weapons, as well as medium-range missiles. The Commission provoked tremendous criticism from Iraq, including charges that it was little more than a cover for American officers such as former Marine captain Scott Ritter to spy for the United States. In the light of those accusations and other problems, UNSCOM left Iraq and was dissolved in 1999. Iraq's failure to cooperate with its successor body contributed to the American decision to invade four years later:

- 1991. Iraq made its first attempt to deny UNSCOM officials access to suspected weapons sites, refused to provide documents about its nuclear weapons program, prevented the destruction of some dual-use technologies, and held UN officials for four days.

- 1992. Iraq continued to deny UNSCOM officials access to Department of Agriculture sites and other buildings suspected of being used for weapons research and development.
- 1994. Iraq threatened to stop cooperating with UNSCOM unless the embargo was lifted. The UN refused.
- 1995. The Iraqi government claimed it would refuse to provide material on biological weapons unless the UN terminated its investigations into other weapons systems.
- 1997. Despite its differences over how to respond to Iraq, the Security Council unanimously passed resolution 1115, which ordered Baghdad to allow UNSCOM to complete its work as it saw fit.
- 1997–98. Iraq tried to block UNSCOM access to the "presidential sites," many of which were vast territories containing palaces and, it was alleged, weapons development facilities.
- 1998. Iraq again refused to cooperate with UNSCOM, Richard Butler resigned as head of the Commission, and the UN disbanded it.
- 1999. The UN approved plans for a new inspection system. Iraq refused to cooperate.

The International Community

Operations Desert Shield and Desert Storm were remarkable coalitions that brought together an unprecedented number of countries, some of which would never have cooperated with each other during the Cold War. Although led (some would say dominated) by the United States, the coalition was also unprecedented in that it sought authority and legitimacy for its actions by gaining the approval of the UN Security Council through 1990 and 1991.

The Coalition of the Willing, which the younger Bush assembled, was nowhere near as broad. Of the world's major powers only Britain joined it, and the coalition did not win support for the invasion from the United Nations. The UN did eventually authorize coalition forces to remain in Iraq, to provide security and to help reconstruct the country's infrastructure after the war ended.

The final carry-over from the first Gulf war was the system of economic sanctions imposed by the United Nations. In fall 1990 Security Council Resolution 687 imposed economic sanctions that prohibited nearly all forms of foreign trade with Iraq. With the exception of the sale of some oil, and the purchase of medicine and other humanitarian supplies, the sanctions remained in place until Saddam fell from power.

The sanctions became the most controversial aspect of allied policy because of their impact on Iraq's society and economy. As David Cortright and George Lopez put it for an earlier period:

For more than seven years, since August 1990, the people of Iraq have experienced almost complete economic isolation. The Gulf War with its intensive bombing campaign exacerbated the effects of sanctions and created what a March 1991 UN report described as "near apocalyptic" conditions. (Cortright and Lopez 1999)

Conditions deteriorated dramatically during the next decade. Iraq lost the equivalent of about $130 billion in oil sales. That money *could* have been used to purchase needed food, clothing, medicine and other supplies, and to fund the rebuilding of the country after the destruction of the two wars. The word "could" was emphasized in the preceding sentence because Western supporters of sanctions are quick to point out that there is no reason to assume that the regime would have used the money for those purposes, given its track record both before and after 1991. Indeed, there is evidence that the regime kept much of the money from the limited amount of oil it was allowed to sell, and never bought the food or medicine the program was created for.

The sanctions took a terrible toll. Study after study by the UN and other international institutions have confirmed Kofi Annan's conclusions in a report to the Security Council in late 1997:

United Nations observers regularly report an exceptionally serious deterioration in the health infrastructure: a high infant mortality rate and high rates of morbidity and mortality in general, poor and inadequate storage conditions for supplies, an unreliable supply of electricity and back-up generators, faulty or non-functioning air conditioning, defective cold-storage, interrupted water supplies, broken/leaking sewage systems and non-functioning hospital waste disposal systems. (United Nations 1997)

Critics have also pointed out that the sanctions did not have the desired impact on the regime (Byman 2000). As we saw in 2003, sanctions did little to compel Iraq to reach a final agreement with the international community.

The one thing its allies did not do was to make a concerted attempt to remove Saddam Hussein from power and instigate what President George W. Bush would later call a "regime change." Either London or Washington would have been delighted were Saddam Hussein to have been forced from power and, preferably, killed. Because Iraq was so tightly controlled by the Baath regime, there was no "inside the system" way of changing the leadership. In other words, the United States and its allies had no choice but to try to foment a coup.

It is against American and British law to assassinate the leader of another country, and there is no evidence that either government tried to do so, though allied forces did target buildings Saddam Hussein was rumored to be in during the war. With the aim of encouraging resistance to Saddam, the United States and Great Britain in particular supported a number of Iraqi exile groups (no viable opposition exists or can exist inside the country). The largest of these is the Iraqi National Congress, many of whose leaders ended up in positions of power after 2003 (Di Giovanni 2000). Like most such groups, it is made up of long-standing opponents of the Baath party, as well as more recent defectors. Intelligence agencies such as the CIA and MI6 gave these often-shady groups hundreds of millions of dollars, but they never came close to toppling the regime. There have been some rumors of coup attempts. One group (apparently not supported by either the British or the Americans) nearly killed Saddam Hussein's son, Uday. The most spectacular defection from the regime came when Saddam's cousins and sons-in-law, the high-ranking

Saddam and Hussein Kamel, fled to Jordan with their families. After their attempt to spark the opposition failed, they returned to Iraq, where both men were assassinated by the regime.

Toward War

The second President Bush listened to many of the same men and women who had advised his father on foreign policy between 1989 and 1993. Most had come to regret the decision not to "take out" Saddam following the liberation of Kuwait. However, until the terrorist attacks on 9/11, there seemed little or no probability that more aggressive action toward Iraq could gain the needed political support. Although the administration raised the rhetoric to a degree, and claimed that Clinton's policies had failed, it seemed destined to continue a policy that sought only to contain and weaken the Iraqi government.

The attacks on the World Trade Center and the Pentagon changed everything. Bob Woodward (2004: 23, 53) reports that Secretary of Defense Donald Rumsfeld raised the possibility of war with Iraq on the very day of the attacks. There are rumors that Bush and Vice-president Dick Cheney also discussed the option within the next few days. What we know for sure is that Bush met with his senior advisors at his Texas ranch on December 28 to discuss preliminary plans for a war with Iraq. Woodward, Tom Ricks (2006), and most others who have written about the road to war are convinced that the decision that we would almost certainly "have to" go to war was made at that meeting, and no later (see Table 9.3).

It should also be pointed out that Bush surrounded himself with a very homogeneous group of political and military advisors. Most were part of a group of conservative defense intellectuals known as the "neo-cons." Among them were Cheney, Rumsfeld, Deputy

Table 9.3 Events in the Second US War with Iraq

Date	Event
1999	UNSCOM leaves
2001	Terrorist attacks in New York and Washington
2002	US administration plans for war and makes its case
2003	Invasion and defeat of Baath regime
	Insurrection begins
	Coalition Provisional Authority in power
	Bombing of UN headquarters in Baghdad
2004	Formal sovereignty returned to Iraq
	Elections held
2006	Surge begins
	Saddam executed
2008	Sharp decline in violence
	Plans made for troops to leave by 2011
2009	Inauguration of President Obama
	US troop pullout begins

Defense Secretary Paul Wolfowitz, most of the policy staff at the Pentagon, and informal advisors such as Richard Perle.

Most of the dozens of people who have written on the war have been highly critical of the Bush team. That includes Ricks, and also Kenneth Pollack, who wrote by far the most credible book about the need to remove Saddam but who later changed his mind as the situation deteriorated (Pollack 2001, 2004). Of course, there were books and articles by people long associated with the peace movement, including Noam Chomsky, who would be expected to oppose the war. But Woodward, Ricks, Pollack, and many others are not part of the political left. Ricks, for instance, has a long history as a military correspondent and is generally seen as sympathetic to the military's operations. Pollack had just moved to the Brookings Institution after more than a decade as a Middle East analyst at the CIA.

The criticisms do not focus on the ideological views of the neo-cons. Rather, almost every commentator finds fault with the way the administration made its decisions, in a classic example of what political scientists call "groupthink."

It isn't that the administration didn't get advice from many different sources, including many who were skeptical about the war as either necessary or easily winnable. James Fallows (2004) cites 17 reports sent to the White House from various government agencies, some of which cast doubt on the administration's urgency and optimism. What we know about the internal workings of the administration is that they rarely took views that didn't easily fit their preconceptions. Similarly, they relied on a small group of Iraqi exiles who knew that war was their only route to power. The most notable of these was a banker, Ahmed Chalabi, whose reputation for honesty was, to say the least, shaky.

The administration based its case on three main claims, all of which proved to be inaccurate.

First, it insisted that Iraq had weapons of mass destruction (WMDs) and was prepared to use them. The regime *had* used chemical weapons on its own Kurdish population during the war with Iran. And, despite UNSCOM's unsuccessful efforts to reveal the regime's weapons deployment, it seemed plausible that the regime had kept some and could easily create new ones quickly and hide them effectively, because they are small. The administration also asserted that Iraq was moving faster than previously thought in its efforts to build an atomic weapon. In perhaps the most dramatic speech in the build-up to the war, Secretary of State Colin Powell told the Security Council about the conclusions the administration had reached, and some of the evidence it based those conclusions on.

Powell's speech was especially important because he is held in such high esteem by almost all Americans. Many of my retired military friends initially supported the war because they "knew" that General Powell would not lie to them. Powell himself probably believed in the case he made that afternoon. In all likelihood, he was convinced by the one-sided and dubious evidence he was given, most notably by CIA Director George Tenet, who is said to have called the case on WMDs a "slam dunk." To this day, Powell considers the speech to be one of the worst stains on his otherwise successful and honorable career.

Saddam Hussein did not help his own cause when he strongly hinted that the regime did indeed have some weapons. But as we learned after the regime fell, there were no weapons of mass destruction. — but yellow uranium suits, —> Syria

The Bush administration's second claim was that Iraq still wanted to be the most powerful country in the region. Among other things, that meant it also still wanted to destroy the state of Israel. And to do that, it was willing to give any and all help to militants in the region, including providing WMDs.

It is true that Iraq had fired some highly inaccurate SCUD missiles on Israel in 1991. And, it certainly had given financial and logistical support to the PLO, and to even more radical groups in Gaza and the West Bank (see the previous chapter). After the second *intifada* broke out, Saddam announced that he would send "rewards" to the families of suicide bombers.

This was the most plausible of the three main arguments. However, Saddam's political "bark" was much worse than his "bite." Most notably, Baghdad could have supplied militant groups with WMDs at any point for a decade or more, but had not done so. Why would they start doing so in 2002, when the country was under the closest scrutiny ever?

The administration's third argument, advanced by Vice-president Cheney in particular, was that there were close links between Baghdad and al Qaeda (see the next chapter). The only evidence of any link was a rumored meeting between an Iraqi agent and Mohamed Atta, the leader of the 9/11 teams in Prague in 2000. There is substantial doubt about whether this meeting actually occurred.

More importantly, there is every reason to doubt the existence of any significant links between the Iraqi leadership and al Qaeda. Indeed, the Baath regime was precisely the type that Osama bin Laden and those around him hated the most. Despite an attempt to seem more pious in the 1990s, Saddam was not a religious man. His drinking, womanizing and corruption were legendary. Iraq and al Qaeda may have had a common adversary in the United States, but that was the limit of their affinity.

Clearly, Bush did not have a case for war that was as solid as his father's was. Most of my academic and political colleagues did not altogether rule out the prospect of a war. Given that the various assertions made by the administration, or analysts like Kenneth Pollack, might be correct, many observers were at least somewhat open to supporting a war. But the fact is that long before Powell's speech on February 3, 2003, most of us in the conflict resolution community decided that the case was too weak to justify a war at any point in the foreseeable future.

President Bush did obtain broad bipartisan support from both the House and the Senate. At a closed-door session, senators were told that Iraq had drone aircraft that could reach the east coast of the United States. Publicly the administration rode the wave of anti-terrorist sentiment in the country as a whole, and justified its actions by means of the Iraq Liberation Act passed near the end of the Clinton presidency.

Most of the international community agreed to veto America's plan to wage war against Iraq. Unlike in 1991, the United States could not get authorization from the United Nations. The French, Russians and Chinese made it clear that they would veto any proposal to attack Iraq. In vain hopes of getting their actions approved, the United States, Great Britain and Spain proposed a resolution that would authorize the use of force if Iraq did not comply with all UN sanctions within a month. The United States withdrew the resolution, not wanting to suffer the embarrassment of a defeat.

The War

By the beginning of 2003, war seemed inevitable. Two-thirds of the American public accepted Bush's rationale. About the same proportion of the population wanted a negotiated settlement. They would not get one.

Both Bush and Saddam seemed more intransigent than ever. There were almost no diplomatic channels that held out any hope of success. The peace and conflict resolution communities had little constructive to offer. For example, a group of senior conflict resolution practitioners met in Boulder, Colorado, a few weeks before the war started. We approached Nelson Mandela and George H. W. Bush's friend and secretary of state, James Baker, to see if they could intervene with the two leaders. Both essentially told us it was too late.

In 2002, the United States began deploying troops in Kuwait and elsewhere to prepare for the invasion. On March 20, the coalition launched Operation Iraqi Freedom in a display of force that Secretary of Defense Rumsfeld called "shock and awe." Only six countries participated, each providing a number of troops:

- The United States: 250,000
- Great Britain: 45,000
- Australia: 2,000
- Spain: 1,300
- Denmark: 500
- Poland: 194

As had been the case 12 years earlier, the war began with air strikes directed at bunkers, palaces, and other targets where the leadership was thought to be. The coalition added a ground war component far more quickly than it had in 1991. Baghdad fell on April 9. Less than two weeks later Saddam's home town of Tikrit was captured, the last city to come under coalition control.

The Iraqi army fought less enthusiastically and less effectively than many analysts had expected. Within a month the Baath regime was gone, its leaders either captured or on the run. Saddam's sons were killed in a firefight in July. Saddam himself was captured in December and executed three years later, after a prolonged trial under the Iraqi interim government.

Playing Cards

As it had done in other wars, the military gave troops decks of playing cards. This time they included the names and faces of the top 52 Iraqi leaders. Soldiers could play cards to pass time. And, they could use the pictures to determine what their foes looked like. At the time the cards were issued, most of the top Baath leadership was still at large. Saddam, of course, was the ace of spades.

Critics of the war, of course, issued a separate deck of cards for what they described as "war criminals." Cheney was ace of spades.

On May 1, President Bush piloted a jet fighter onto the deck of the aircraft carrier USS *Abraham Lincoln* off the coast off San Diego. The sailors had made a huge banner reading "mission accomplished." Bush announced that major combat operations in Iraq were now over.

The president was wrong. Already there were signs of trouble. In Baghdad, rioters looted treasure from sites including the historical museum. General Tommie Franks was named commander of the occupying forces, which made him the *de facto* administrator of the country. Plans were underway to move to an American-led civilian authority that would, in turn, prepare the way for a new Iraqi regime.

Nothing turned out the way the administration expected. A central assumption in their war planning was that the troops would be welcomed as liberators, and that within a matter of weeks the US could withdraw most of their soldiers, sailors and marines. Wolfowitz publicly claimed that we would have no more than 30,000 troops in the country by the end of the summer. In fact, they were so certain of this that the administration did next to nothing to plan for the post-war transition. This was despite the fact that most observers, including NGOs, much of the military, much of the State Department, and many analytic teams at the CIA predicted that the occupying force would face something an insurgency like the one that followed.

The Insurgency and the Surge

By summer 2003, American policy and actions in Iraq were in flux. Put as simply as possible, the United States civilian and military leaders were not prepared for what was about to happen.

The fact that post-conflict situations could be messy was not new. The military leaders had been thinking and writing about what they awkwardly called "military operations other than war" since the late 1990s. At that time, marine commandant General Charles Krulak developed the idea of a three-block war. His troops might have to fight rebels, maintain the peace, and rebuild a community, all in the same neighborhood and at the same time.

The American leadership in Iraq was in tatters. Most of the generals who had planned and fought the war left, to be replaced by a smaller team of less competent leaders. Civilian control was initially given to a retired general, Jay Garner. Garner and the administration soon fell out, and he was replaced by former ambassador Paul Bremer as head of the Coalition Provisional Authority.

Bremer was no more successful or competent than Garner had been. Among other things, he purged tens of thousands of former Baath party members from the government bureaucracy, and disbanded the army. All this did was to give those men more reason to hate the American occupation, and do whatever they could to force the coalition to leave.

By fall 2003 at the latest, the United States was facing a full-scale insurgency. As military scholars and officers use the term, an insurgency is a war fought by irregular forces, who are usually urban-based, and use tactics that can only be called terrorist (see the next chapter). Insurgencies also normally pit a much stronger side against a smaller and weaker group of rebels. However, because insurgents don't wear uniforms and can generally blend into the civilian population, they are hard to track down and defeat.

In reality, the United States and its allies faced two insurgencies. The one it paid the most attention to came in the "Sunni triangle" where most Sunni Arabs, and therefore most former supporters of the Baath party, live. Perhaps because most residents of the triangle are Sunni, it was there that al Qaeda in Iraq gained a major foothold, especially in al Anbar province to the west of Baghdad. But there was also considerable if more episodic violent resistance from disciples of the young Shi'ite cleric, Muqtada al-Sadr.

He is the son of one of the most revered ayatollahs in modern Iraqi history, and arguably one of the three most popular leaders in the community. In 2004 and 2005, his Mahdi army staged a series of attacks on foreign troops in the heavily Shi'ite south, and in neighborhoods in Baghdad and other Sunni triangle cities with a significant Shi'ite minority.

The United States did not have much recent experience of planning a counter-insurgency program (except perhaps with the disastrous peacekeeping mission in Somalia in the 1990s). Nonetheless, there is a vast body of literature on the subject of counter-insurgency, mostly drawn from the British experience in Malaya, Kenya and Northern Ireland. From what we know about successful counter-insurgency efforts, the United States did almost everything wrong until General David Petraeus took command of its forces in Iraq in 2007.

The conventional wisdom is that counter-insurgency work has to include social and economic reconstruction and political reconciliation, along with the establishment of physical security. Under Bremer and a series of less than successful generals, the United States emphasized the purely military side of the insurgency. It talked about reconstruction, stabilization and institution-building. In practice it did very little of that.

In fact, in a rare public statement by a serving officer, Lt Col John Yingling wrote a scathing attack on his superiors entitled "The Failure of Generalship" (2007, also see Hashim 2005). Yingling's article was remarkable because he had taught political science at West Point earlier in his career. What Yingling said openly, most other majors and colonels I have worked with have said privately, a point we will return to in the next section.

Well into 2006, the death toll of coalition troops kept mounting. By the time President Obama took office, more than 4,000 Americans and about 500 British soldiers had been killed. Estimates of Iraqi deaths often top 100,000. While these numbers are much smaller than the casualties suffered in Vietnam and other wars, the fact that Americans saw the faces of the fallen on the nightly news and in their newspapers served to reinforce the growing frustration with the lack of progress the coalition seemed to be making. I saw this in the faces of a group of West Point Military Academy cadets I had lunch with, as I mentioned earlier, on the day they were to get their post-graduation assignments. All knew they were going to Afghanistan and Iraq. None were happy about it: they all realized that was part of the bargain they made when they accepted their education, which cost the taxpayers a million dollars for each cadet. They then told me that each time a former cadet was killed in action, the death was announced through the loudspeakers in the dining hall at breakfast.[1] The day before my visit, the fifty-third death had been made public.

Petraeus was named commander of the multi-national force to lead the so-called "surge" in which the United States sent in more than 30,000 additional troops. Like many

---

[1]   One of the curious things about the three major military academies is that the cadets all eat at the same time in the same place. At West Point, the mess hall has three wings, and the noise can be deafening. At the much newer Air Force Academy, the hall is one huge room, but because it is only 40 years old, it has much better soundproofing. It also has wide enough doors so that the cadets can march in for meals. The meals are distributed in hot trays to the tables which have assigned seating. Meals are mandatory. Cadets eat their lunch and talk with each other a bit, all in 25 minutes.

peace activists, I didn't think adding another 30,000 troops would make much difference. I was wrong.

The military side of the surge has received most attention in the press and from the Bush administration, for good reason. Iraq is by no means a peaceful country, as I write in late 2008. But, over the last year it has become a lot safer, and life is returning to some semblance of normality.

Nowhere is this more evident than in al-Anbar province which had been the center of the insurgency and was, for all practical purposes, outside coalition control for much of 2004 through 2006. As noted earlier, it was "home base" for most of the foreign fighters who came to Iraq and took on the mantle of al Qaeda. To some degree, the foreign fighters shot themselves in their political feet. Huge disputes broke out between the fighters and the traditional tribal leaders over whether or not the outsiders could have "access" to local women. So, by 2006 many tribal leaders were growing disillusioned with al Qaeda, and gradually decided it made more sense for them to cooperate with the new government and the Americans. The United States provided massive amounts of aid and other support, and by the end of 2007 al Qaeda in Iraq was a fraction of its former self (Smith and McFarlane 2008).

As I write, more and more authority is being handed over to the Iraqi government. Even though it is still quite fragile and its security forces remain less than adequate, negotiations are underway for a "status of forces" agreement between the United States and Iraq, and a new resolution in the United Nations. Officially, the UN's authorization of American occupation forces was due to expire on December 31, 2008. In October, it became clear that Washington and Baghdad were not going to reach their own bilateral agreement to potentially have all US combat forces out of the country by the end of 2011. The UN authorization was therefore in jeopardy. However, late in October the Russians signaled that they were willing to support a one-year extension of the UN authorization, which most observers felt was a gesture of goodwill to the new administration, whether led by Obama or McCain. President Obama has largely carried through his campaign promises about Iraq, declaring that combat troops will be withdrawn by the end of 2010, although some support and training personnel will remain.

We don't know how to measure these things. But colleagues who have served in Iraq, in a few cases directly under General Petraeus, argue that the surge's "non-kinetic efforts" (military jargon for not using force) were at least as important in forging the improvement that has occurred in Iraq. We will explore the profound changes that their involvement in Iraq and Afghanistan have forced on the American military.

Many readers who have qualms about the role of the military in general will have concerns about the last half of this section. It draws in large part on work I have done at the Alliance for Peacebuilding, and before that at Search for Common Ground, with the military. At first I thought I had just met a bunch of very unusual current and former officers. I am convinced now that the changes the military will go through, as the current leaders retire and the next generation reaches the top, will be profound.

But first, we have a more vexing issue to deal with: the relative lack of NGOs, especially NGOs that specialize in conflict resolution, in Iraq.

The reasons are obvious. The situation on the ground is still dangerous. Unlike some of the larger humanitarian NGOs such as Save the Children or Doctors Without Borders, conflict resolution organizations lack the funds to hire private security firms, only some of which are either effective or ethical.

These dangers were publicized in late 2005 and early 2006 when Tom Fox, a Quaker peace activist (who used to attend my local meeting) was abducted and killed. Tom had spent 20 years in a Marine Corps band. After retiring he became a Quaker and did graduate work in peace-building at Eastern Mennonite University. He joined the Christian Peacebuilding Team, which had been inspired by Mennonites and other Christians from peace-centered churches. Against the advice of many colleagues (including me), Tom went to Iraq. Unfortunately, the insurgents had a hard time differentiating between supporters and opponents of the war. Tom disappeared in December 2005, and his body was found three months later.

More important than the danger they face is the issue of neutrality. NGOs pride themselves on this, and on the distance they keep from governments, and especially from military forces. Few go as far as the organization Doctors Without Borders, which typically refuses to work with any party to a conflict. Still, despite efforts to create protocols in which the work of the military and NGOs can be kept separate while providing opportunities for information-sharing, relations remain tense.

Conflict-resolution NGOs view the neutrality question rather differently. We think that we need to talk with all parties in order to help forge win-win outcomes. And, most members of the Alliance for Peacebuilding have done just that. However, the cases of Iraq and Afghanistan are different, at least for American- and British-based NGOs. Because our governments have played such a major role in causing the conflict in the first place, it is hard for us to find a niche where we can do our work without being seen as a pawn of our governments.

There is a clearing-house for NGOs working in Iraq (www.ncciraq.org). But, to reinforce the points made in the previous paragraphs, it does not list its member organizations. And, except in a short page on civil society, it does not include many activities that conflict resolution groups could do.

Of the few conflict resolution NGOs that are engaged in Iraq, one stands out.

Women for Women International (www.womenforwomen.org) was founded in 1993 by Zainab Salhi who was then a sophomore at George Mason University where, luckily for her, she avoided my classes during her final three years. Zainab had come to the States as a refugee from Saddam Hussein's regime. She is a remarkable woman. Instead of having a traditional honeymoon, she and her husband (a Palestinian-American attorney who was then advising the PA on negotiating with the Israelis) went to Croatia to distribute aid to victims of the war there.

The opportunity to work in Iraq was always something Salhi had in mind, but never thought she could do. But when the regime fell in 2003, her organization was ideally placed to take steps that few other NGOs could. She speaks Arabic well, and has family and other contacts in the region. Women for Women may have been the first American-based peace-building NGO to set up an office in Iraq where, not surprisingly, they focused on the role that women had to play in promoting a successful transition. Perhaps more than most NGOs, they understood, too, that women had played a more important role than their counterparts in other Middle Eastern countries in professional and academic life. In a statement about the dangers that remain in Iraq, the Women for Women website does not list the names of its Iraqi staff, and provides very little information about its projects there.

More remarkable, and potentially more hopeful for the future of peace-building, has been the response of the military. In the conclusion to this chapter and the book a a whole, we will explore whether the military can contribute to peaceful conflict resolution, especially when the military itself contributed so massively to the violence in the first place.

We will look at the changes in the military first through three anecdotes about what American soldiers have done to promote peace during their service in Iraq. I do not want to push this argument too far. We have seen plenty of evidence of the military's failure, ranging from reports of the abuses at Baghdad's Abu Ghraib prison to a PBS video of American troops abusing the family of an Iraqi taxi driver (www.youtube.com/watch?v=VFSzqST83Ywv).

Still, consider three other cases. For reasons of confidentiality I can only identify the third soldier.

First, an army captain was among the first soldiers to enter Iraq. He was in charge of building an airstrip not far from Baghdad. He found what looked like an ideal location, on what looked like an abandoned farm. His team laid down the metal plates used for temporary airstrips. A couple of days later, his team saw a man weeping in the middle of the airfield. He was, of course, the owner of the land who had returned to discover not only the airstrip, but the irrigation system he had painstakingly constructed in ruins. The captain had the man brought to his headquarters, knowing he had to do something fast. He immediately agreed to pay compensation, and asked the farmer how much he wanted. The Iraqi asked for $6,000. The captain said, "How about $14,000?" The farmer was delighted. He and his family moved back to their compound. His wife provided the small detachment of US soldiers with home-cooked meals. His sons helped identify two mid-level Iraqi intelligence officers who were on the run.

A marine colonel was called up from the reserves and put in charge of a civilian affairs unit. One day, a convoy team under his control was attacked with an improvised explosive device (IED). As they had been trained to do, the young marines got out of their Humvees and shot the person who had planted the bomb. He turned out to be an orphan who was no more than nine years old, and had left the bomb in order to make enough money to survive.

The boy was not expected to survive, but the surgeons at the Navy field hospital worked wonders. After a few weeks, he had recovered enough to be released. But someone in the chain of command determined that he was an enemy fighter and insisted that the boy be sent to Abu Ghraib prison. When the marine colonel learned of this, he enlisted the help of a sympathetic military doctor who "convinced" the prison authorities that the boy needed more medical treatment at the hospital. Within a day or two, the marine had found a family outside the country who was willing to adopt the boy, and he was on his way out of the country to a new life in Europe.

The most impressive story is that of Captain Travis Patriquin. In 2006, he was 32 and a veteran of 14 years in the army. In the process he had learned Pashtu, Urdu, and Arabic, and had served valiantly in both Afghanistan and Iraq. Even before the surge, Patriquin understood that counter-insurgency efforts had to include a great deal of people-to-people cooperation. In attempting to convince his superiors of this, he created a PowerPoint presentation using stick-figure representations of American soldiers, Iraqi civilians and terrorists, a sheikh, and a regional Iraqi commander. At first the American, "Joe," was wearing 80 pounds of protective equipment, which meant he had no hope of chasing insurgents. His Iraqi equivalent, the commander, had done little better. Joe decided to talk to one of the sheiks in Anbar, and makes him an offer. The sheikh did not want his men to join the army and be deployed elsewhere. Joe offered to send half of the sheikh's men for training as police officers so that they could stay at home and protect their families. The other half were given other forms of education. Joe could not figure out which stick-figure Iraqis were innocent and which were terrorists—but the new policemen could! (www.youtube.com/watch?v=iMBWpgMTJjs)

How did Joe make it work? He started by simply drinking tea with the sheikh. Then, once he realized that all Iraqis like men with mustaches, he grew one of his own. Gradually, the first sheikh brought others to work with Joe. In the last frame, Patriquin makes it clear that everyone ended up happy—other than the terrorists. But as Joe put it, that's ok because "terrorists suck."

Unfortunately, Captain Patriquin did not get to see the fruits of his labor. He was killed by an IED in late 2006.

In the long term, doctrinal and policy changes came in the wake of US failures in Iraq that may prove to be even more important. I knew something was up shortly after the war started. I was at a meeting of NGO and military representatives at the United States Institute of Peace. One of the colonels and I then had to go for a meeting with an assistant secretary of defense, who was at a meeting about new strategies. As we headed to the Metro in downtown Washington DC, the colonel said, "Chip, you know we're your best audience. If you've ever seen combat in a place like Afghanistan or Iraq, you never want to go back."

An hour later, I learned that the assistant secretary hadn't been able to attend our meeting because he was in the process of helping draft Directive 3000.05, which was formally issued in late 2005 (www.dtic.mil/whs/directives/corres/html/300005.htm). Entitled "Military Support for Stability, Security, Transition, and Reconstruction," it declared that conflict prevention and post-conflict reconstruction would henceforth be as important for the military as combat operations (Wells and Hauss 2007, 2008). The directive was issued over the signature of Gordan England, who had replaced Wolfowitz as the second-ranking official at the Pentagon. A few days later, the White House issued National Security Presidential Directive 44, which created the State Department's fledgling Office for Coordination of Reconstruction and Stabilization, to head civilian and inter-agency efforts to the same end: post-conflict reconstruction.

Remember that these initiatives came from the Bush administration, with very little input from the NGOs or the peace community. Remember, too, that the American military is a massive bureaucracy, and its culture will not change quickly. Nonetheless, like most Western governments and their defense establishments, the United States has committed itself to using the military in new, different, and more peaceful ways.

That the military and NGOs could and should work together became clear a few weeks later, when much of Southeast Asia was devastated by a tsunami. Secretary Rumsfeld ordered an aircraft flotilla to the region, and military and NGO workers realized that they could work together, at least in some circumstances.

Lessons Learned

At this point, you might well be asking what this material has to do with conflict resolution. At first glance, the answer is remarkably little. No matter what your ideological perspectives on the continuing conflict with Iraq, you are unlikely to be able to discern any significant moves toward reconciliation or stable peace since the invasion of Kuwait.

However, if we dig a bit deeper we can see that the failure to make progress toward resolving conflict tells us at least as much about how conflict resolution does occur than the more successful examples presented in the preceding four chapters.

My goal here is not to argue whether or not Western foreign policy, or Iraq policy, have been correct. In particular, I am not going to suggest that the West could or should have tried to move toward reconciliation or stable peace at any point in the years after Saddam Hussein came to power.

Those are touchy and controversial issues, and taking a firm stand on them would make it harder for you to reach your own conclusions. Furthermore, in keeping with the purposes of this book, it is more important to focus on empirical conclusions about the conflict with Iraq and its theoretical implications, of which six stand out.

1. *Opportunities for cooperation in the changing international environment.* The Iraqi case does illustrate at least one of those opportunities for international cooperation, if not conflict resolution per se. The onset of the Gulf crisis marked the first time at least since the Korean War that the international community used an international organization to structure and justify the response to aggression. Indeed, before the Gulf crisis, it was impossible to talk about *the* international community, because Cold War rivalry divided the major powers on almost every issue.

Operations Desert Shield and Desert Storm were led by the United States. However, the first Bush administration went out of its way to ensure that these were international operations of unprecedented breadth, with unprecedented support from the United Nations. In fact, these operations ushered in a period in which the major powers became more willing to intervene in the domestic affairs of rogue states. However, they only seem willing to do so with at least the semblance of support from institutions that are beginning to take on some of the trappings of regional, if not global, governance.

That pattern continued throughout the 1990s, until the impasse surrounding the American plans to invade Iraq. All the major instances of intervention were carried out at least in the name of a regional organization, or with the agreement of the United Nations. Critics are undoubtedly correct that this was often mostly a political fig-leaf to give legitimacy to actions the United States planned to take anyway. Nonetheless, even the limited shift toward the use of international organizations does seem to have set a precedent that can be developed in the future. There is little doubt that the unilateralism of the younger Bush's administration set back the prospects for collaboration. The first signs from the Obama administration suggest that things may change dramatically—and soon.

2. *The weakness of those international organizations.* We should not exaggerate the power exerted by the United Nations or the regional international organizations. After all, the international community's track record since the end of the Gulf war is largely one of failure to persuade or compel Iraq to comply with UN resolutions. What's more, the UN in Iraq, and NATO in Bosnia and Kosovo, have been heavily dependent on a handful of powerful countries, especially the United States.

In other words, the international community can only exert the kind of influence it did in late 1990 and early 1991 under the most exceptional circumstances. It requires political conditions that allow the formation of what amounts to a consensus among the major powers to act quickly and decisively, for instance to raise, fund, deploy, and coordinate troops whether they are sent to keep, make or impose peace. It is probably easier to do this today than it was in 1980 or 1970. However, for all the domestic and international reasons we have seen, that kind of political will is difficult indeed to muster, and has been hard to sustain even with the situation of Iraq. That became obvious with the plummeting support for the war after 2004, and the accompanying decline in the popularity of the Bush administration, which had reached an historic low point when he left office.

3. *The continued importance of traditional geopolitics.* The Iraqi case also reminds us that the changes that have swept the world since the mid-1980s have not eliminated traditional geopolitics. As a result, it shows us more clearly than any of the other cases how traditional theories and issues in international relations remain important, and why it is difficult to achieve non-violent solutions to conflicts that are primarily geopolitical in origin.

The crisis over Kuwait arose out of aggression of the most traditional variety. It wasn't just the invasion of Kuwait that concerned international policy-makers, but it was also that episode's broader implications for Saudi Arabia, and for the fragile balance of power in the Middle East as a whole.

The threat to regional security was complicated by two other issues. First, as many critics of the high-minded rhetoric coming from Washington, London, and other Western capitals pointed out, the conflict was as much about access to oil as about national sovereignty or human rights. Secondly, political leaders in Washington and elsewhere after March 1991 were convinced that they had to take broader regional power dynamics into account. Thus, the Clinton administration felt the need to maintain a policy of "dual containment" against Iran as well as Iraq, which left it reluctant to support Saddam Hussein's Shiite opponents lest they throw their own lot in with the Iranians.

4. *Is there always a win-win solution?* In earlier chapters, I chose my words carefully in stating that it is almost always possible to chart out an intellectually plausible win-win solution to any international conflict. However, as this case makes clear, it is one thing to devise an intellectually plausible proposal. It is quite another to make it politically plausible.

In this case and perhaps others, such as the 1999 war over Kosovo, there has not been a realistic option for a non-violent resolution of a conflict. Furthermore, policy-makers often have to deal with rogue states whose leaders are not very open to the kind of discussion that can take parties toward a negotiated settlement. In such conflicts, when world leaders confront a sudden, and often unpredicted, crisis, they have to act quickly, making it even harder to rely on preventive or coercive diplomacy, which typically take months if not years to make an impact.

This is not to suggest empirically or normatively that we should abandon attempts to seek win-win conflict resolution and stable peace, or that we will not become more adept at doing so over the medium to long term. However, it does seem safe to conclude that whatever "progress" the international community and individual states make, we are likely to face conflicts of this sort in which the use of force may be the only realistic path for one or more of the parties to take.

If, as senior conflict resolution practitioners, we learned anything from our last-minute attempt to intervene following our meeting in Boulder, it is that the earlier you get involved, the better your chances of success. Of course, we already knew that, but had not been practicing what we preach.

5. *Hurting stalemate?* The Iraqi case also shows us both the importance, and some limitations, of the concept of a hurting stalemate.

On the one hand, it is easy to argue that there has been little progress toward a definitive settlement because neither the Iraqi insurgents nor what is left of the Western alliance has concluded that it cannot win, and that the costs of continuing the conflict have grown too great.

On the other hand, we can also see that there is a certain looseness to the "hurting stalemate" concept that may make it a less useful analytical tool than it might have seemed in earlier chapters. In other words, it might seem, at first glance, that a hurting stalemate might be an objective state of affairs: the two sides get to a certain point at which victory is no longer an option, and the costs of continuing to fight are devastating. However, it should be clear from this chapter that the concept has a psychological or perceptual component as well. Thus, the hurting stalemate had not been reached when these lines were written because leaders in Washington, London, Baghdad and elsewhere were not yet convinced that the concept existed.

In short, a hurting stalemate actually can *only* lead to negotiations once the leaders involved accept the possibility that this step could be taken. In the case of Iraq, it has not come despite the deaths of hundreds of thousands of people. In Northern Ireland, it emerged after "only" 3,000 people died during the course of the Troubles, and was strongly encouraged by the 1998 bombing at Omagh that "only" killed 28 people.

This combination of objective and perceived conditions may be a more accurate way of rendering the idea of a hurting stalemate than the way it was used in earlier chapters and is usually presented in the literature. Conversely, it becomes a less useful concept for analytical or policy-making purposes, because it is much harder to predict or explain when leaders reach (or don't reach, as the case may be) the conclusion that a hurting stalemate is possible.

6. *Domestic politics and psychological dynamics.* Finally, this chapter provides us with the best insight into two ways that domestic political dynamics can render a win-win solution difficult, if not impossible.

First and most obvious is how images of the enemy, and similar stereotypes, made both sides more intransigent and less constructive than they might otherwise have been. Leaders on both sides demonized each other. The first President Bush led other Western leaders in branding Saddam Hussein the "second Hitler," while Western rhetoric in general likened Iraqi policies to those of the Third Reich, or the Soviet Union under Stalin. Iraqi attitudes toward the United States were no more conciliatory, and became even more extreme later. For instance, the regime had a picture of President Bush inlaid into the entry to the hotel where Western journalists stayed in Baghdad, forcing them to step on it on their way in and out. Similarly, Saddam Hussein strode onto the balcony of one of his palaces, and fired his pistol in the air in celebration, on the night Bush lost his bid for a second presidential term in 1992.

This is not to say that there is no grain of truth in those stereotypes. The Iraqi regime was among the most ruthless and tyrannical in the world—though it was a far cry from either Nazi Germany or the Soviet Union of the 1930s. As the psychologists who have done the most work on this subject point out, however, the most important factor is that such thinking in and of itself hinders any moves toward negotiation. People who invoke the image of the enemy tend to use rhetoric that sees their own side as "in the right," turns the other side into a caricature rather than a collection of real people and institutions, and places all the blame for the crisis on them. Under those circumstances, it is hardly surprising that such politicians (or ordinary citizens) assume that the other side has to take the first step because it is, after all, responsible for starting the conflict in the first place. Moreover, as the quote that begins this chapter implies, taking the first step toward peace can be viewed as a sign of weakness that one's "evil" adversary will only take advantage of.

Secondly, we can see the importance of misperceptions and other difficulties in making effective judgments, an issue which has been well covered in the mainstream literature on international relations since the 1960s. As we saw above, the United States and its allies lacked reliable intelligence information about the capabilities and intentions of the Iraqi government from the first days of the crisis in early 1990, until the end of the war. That led to an underestimate of Baghdad's expansionist intentions before August 1990, and an overestimate of its ability to resist the Western onslaught in 1991.

For its part, the Iraqi leadership also seems to have reached its share of mistaken conclusions about Western intentions. The (in)famous meeting between Saddam Hussein and Ambassador April Glaspie constituted one of many signals that Baghdad read incorrectly before it decided to invade Kuwait. Similarly, it appears that much of the leadership watched the US Senate debate on authorizing the use of force on CNN and read it as a sign of weakness, indicating that the United States would not have the courage to fight. Finally, after the end of the war, the Iraqi leadership made numerous attempts to divide and intimidate the 1990–91 coalition which, so far at least, have had a minimal impact, at least on the lifting of sanctions.

In short, the combination of stereotypical thinking and other biases, plus frequent misperceptions, combined to reinforce a predisposition against negotiation and win-win conflict resolution on both sides. While it is especially hard to extrapolate from the single, admittedly unusual, case of Iraq, there is enough supporting evidence in the international relations and psychological literatures to indicate that these dynamics are typically obstacles to the peaceful resolution of disputes.

In conclusion, to once again see the importance of domestic politics, conduct a simple mental experiment. Imagine that Al Gore had won the presidential election in 2000, not George W. Bush: American policy toward Iraq, and the Middle East in general, would almost certainly have been very different.

Select Bibliography

Al-Khalil Samir (1990). *Republic of Fear: The Inside Story of Saddam's Iraq*. New York: Pantheon.

Batatu, Hanna (1978). *The Old Social Classes and the Revolutionary Movement of Iraq: A Study of Iraq's Old Landed and Commercial Classes and of its Communists, Ba'athists, and Free Officers*. Princeton, NJ: Princeton University Press.

Bengio, Offra (1998). *Saddam's Word: Political Discourse in Iraq*. New York: Oxford University Press, 1998.

Bush, George H. W. and Brent Scowcroft (1998). *A World Transformed*. New York: Knopf, 2008.

Byman, Daniel (2000). A Farewell to Arms Inspections. *Foreign Affairs* 79 (January/February): 110–32.

Cockburn, Andrew, and Patrick Cockburn (1999). *Out of the Ashes: The Resurrection of Saddam Hussein*. New York: HarperCollins.

Cortright, David, and George Lopez (1999). "Sanctions against Iraq: Facts and Analysis." <http://www.fourthfreedom.org/hottopic/sanctionsagainstiraqfactsanalysis.html>. Accessed January 8, 2000.

Dawisha, Adeed (1999). "Identity and Political Survival in Saddam's Iraq." *Middle East Journal* 53 (Autumn): 553–67.

Di Giovanni, Janine (2000). "The Enemy of Our Enemy." *New York Times Magazine*, February 20, 46–9.

Fallows, James (2004). "Blind Into Baghdad." *The Atlantic Monthly*. January/February.

Fuller, Graham, and Ian Lesser (1997). "Persian Gulf Myths." *Foreign Affairs* 76 (May–June): 42–53.

George, Alexander (1993). *Bridging the Gap*. Washington, DC: United States Institute for Peace.

Hashim, Ahmed (2005). *Insurgency and Counter Insurgency in Iraq*. Ithaca, NY: Cornell University Press.

Hauss, Charles (2009). "Iraq." In *Comparative Politics: Domestic Responses to Global Challenges*. 6th edn. Belmont, CA: Wadsworth/Cengage Learning: 394–427.

Herrmann, Richard (1994). "Coercive Diplomacy and the Crisis over Kuwait, 1990–1991." In *The Limits of Coercive Diplomacy*, ed. Alexander L. George and William E. Simons, 229–66. Boulder, CO: Westview Press, 1994.

Karsh, Efraim, and Inari Rautsi (1991). *Saddam Hussein: A Political Biography*. New York: Free Press.

Pollack, Kenneth (2001). *The Threatening Storm*. New York: Random House.

—(2004). "Spies, Lies, and Weapons: What Went Wrong?" *The Atlantic Monthly*, January/ February.

Ricks, Thomas (2006). *Fiasco: The American Military Adventure in Iraq*. New York: Penguin.

Samet, Elizabeth (2007). *A Soldier's Heart: Reading Literature Through Peace and War at West Point*. New York: Farrar, Straus and Giroux.

Smith, Niel, and Sean McFarland (2008). "Al-Anbar Awakens: The Tipping Point." *Military Review*. September/October.

United Nations (1997). *Report of the Secretary General Pursuant to Paragraph Three of Resolution 1111 (1997)*. November 28.

Woodward, Bob (2004). *Plan Attack: Volume 1 of Bush at War*. New York: Simon and Schuster.

Yingling, Paul (2007). "The Failure of Generalship." *Armed Forces Journal*. www.armedforces journal.com/2007/05/2635198.

CHAPTER TEN

Darfur

If you see a village, you burn that village. If you find a civilian, you kill that civilian. If you find a cow, that cow is your cow.
—Former Sudanese soldier who defected

In 2006, I was invited to hear a friend talk about the Arab–Israeli peace process at one of the largest synagogues in the Washington area. The entrance had a green and white sign with www.savedarfur.org written on it. Later that afternoon, my dog and I wandered past

Figure 5 Map of Sudan

our local synagogue and saw the same sign. I then called my observant Jewish friends, who told me that their synagogues all had the same sign.

I knew a little about the crisis in Darfur, but nothing about why these signs were springing up at synagogues throughout the United States. It turns out that the Save Darfur movement was originated largely by Ruth Messinger, a veteran New York (and Jewish) politician who had learned an important lesson I wish everyone who reads a book like this would take into account.

The Hebrew term "Shoah" means "Never again," and refers to a shared belief among most Jews that nothing like the Holocaust should ever take place again. For good or ill, most Jews (including this author) paid much too little attention to other examples of genocide until Messinger and her colleagues put Darfur on our political radar screens.

What Messinger and others (see Power 2005) did was to help us come to grips with the fact that all genocidal episodes leave us with the same political and moral responsibilities. Yet, as I write two years after discovering Save Darfur, little has changed on the ground. A quarter of a million people have been killed. Even more have been displaced from their homes. And, even though most Americans and Europeans agree that something needs to be done, we remain impotent.

A lot of high-profile people have weighed in on the issue. Don Cheadle (star of the film *Hotel Rwanda*) and John Prendergast, a long-time human rights advocate, have written a book. Olympic gold medal skater Joey Cheek has given much of the money he made at the Olympics to Team Darfur (www.teamdarfur.org), a global organization of athletes that is trying to save a people who have no chance of ever qualifying for the Olympics.

Despite the attention Darfur has gained from the likes of Cheadle, Prendergast and Cheek, we have not made much progress. Prendergast was earlier a supporter of Senator Barack Obama's presidential campaign. However, this is not an issue that sharply divides Americans, or any other electorate in the Western world. The Bush administration declared the actions of the Sudanese government and its Janjaweed allies "genocide." Bush himself met with leaders of the Save Darfur coalition the day before tens of thousands of us assembled on the Mall in Washington.

But despite the bipartisan support for the cause of Darfur in the United States and beyond, again we have been able to accomplish very little to stop the carnage, whether one wants to call it genocide or "merely" ethnic cleansing, as implied in the quotation that begins this chapter. One can find reasons to fault the American, European, and other African governments for their failure to act decisively. However, the fact is that there are impediments, ranging from the isolation of the region to international interference, that have made it all but impossible for the international community to intervene helpfully.

Like many of the countries covered in Part 3, Darfur has a huge emotional importance for me. I wear a green "Save Darfur" wristband to balance my Pentagon lapel pin.

But, for the purposes of this book, it is a challenge to get beyond the horrors of genocide and the failed promise of Shoah, to see why the crisis in Sudan defies solution and what it tells us about conflict resolution in general.

As you will see later in the chapter, I do not agree with everything Save Darfur has done. Nonetheless, Darfur is the human rights disaster of our time, with something like a quarter of a million people dead and as many more who are refugees.

Theoretical Questions

As was the case with the chapter on terrorism, neither traditional international relations theory nor the new approaches developed by conflict resolution practitioners take us very far. In this case, it is not because they do not help us understand what is going on, but neither school of thought does much to help us find solutions that could stem and then end the conflict.

- **The legacy of imperialism.** Like most underdeveloped countries today, Sudan had long been a colony, first under Ottoman and later joint British-Egyptian rule. How has that helped to fan the flames of conflicts during the last few decades?
- **Image of the enemy.** This is one of the core concepts in conflict resolution theory. How has it operated in Darfur, and made a bad situation worse?
- **Role of international law.** Genocide is a new concept but has been prohibited in international law for more than half a century. If so, why hasn't the legal system taken the perpetrators to court?
- **Failure of the international community.** More generally, the international community has had little success in Darfur. Why is that the case?
- **National interests.** This is one of the key concepts in traditional international relations. How have the national interests of distant states such as China and the United States made resolution all but impossible in Sudan?
- **Importance of domestic politics.** Domestic political dynamics play a role in any international conflict. In this case, why did Darfur become an important cause in the United States and elsewhere, and how has Sudan's role as one of the world's weakest states magnified the conflict?

Sudan and Darfur

Sudan is huge. With more than two-and-a-half-million square kilometers of land, it is about one-quarter the size of the United States. But, with only forty million people, it has less than half the population density of the United States. Its population is young: two in five people in the country are under 15 years old.

It is also poor. GDP per capita is under $2,000. Forty percent of the population as a whole, and half of Sudan's women, are illiterate. Eighty percent of the population work in agriculture, although the industrial and service sectors each contribute as much to the country's overall wealth. At the best of times, no more than 20 percent of the people had electricity. Few of the things we take for granted exist there—paved roads, banks, stores. The land is dry and not very fertile. Droughts are common. Cattle are the best measure of a family's wealth.

Half of the population is "black;" 40 percent are "Arabs." The rest come from a handful of other ethnic groups, and a few foreigners. "Black" and "Arab" are in quotation marks here because they describe different cultures, as well as denoting physical differences among the Sudanese. People of the south are clearly black, and many are Christian. The population of the north, which includes the capital city of Khartoum, is predominantly made up of Arabs whose ancestry can be traced to the Middle East. But in the rest of the country, there has been enough intermarriage that some Arabs look black, and vice versa. In Darfur, blacks tend to live in villages and farm, while Arabs are nomads who raise animals while they travel (Jok 2007). And even these numbers are misleading, since anthropologists count anywhere from 40 to several hundred different ethnic groups in a region that had a population of less than seven million before the genocide.

The Arabs have been politically dominant since Sudan gained its independence in 1956. As we will see below, their rule has never been easy, nor has the state ever enjoyed much legitimacy. A decades-long civil war between Khartoum and the south ended in 2005, and the two regions are joined in a power-sharing government at least until elections scheduled for 2009. As we will also see below, the peace between the two feuding parties also made the genocide easier because the government and its militias—the *Janjaweed*—now only had one "enemy" to focus on.

The Conflict in Darfur

Genocide

Samantha Power (2005) entitles her book on genocide *A Problem from Hell*. She reminds us that genocide is a fairly recent phenomenon, both as a political reality and as a subject of international law. The United Nations Convention reads in part:

> In the present Convention, genocide means any of the following acts committed with intent to destroy, in whole or in part, a national, ethnical, racial or religious group, as such:
>
> - killing members of the group;
> - causing serious bodily or mental harm to members of the group;
> - deliberately inflicting on the group conditions of life calculated to bring about its physical destruction in whole or in part;
> - imposing measures intended to prevent births within the group;
> - forcibly transferring children of the group to another group.

For centuries, people have been killing people for these reasons. However, what we now think of as genocide is a fairly recent phenomenon, probably made possible by the invention of ever more lethal weapons that could kill many people quickly—though it should be pointed out that the killings in Rwanda were mostly done by Hutu extremists wielding machetes.

The first "modern" genocide occurred in 1915 and 1916, when the "young Turks" turned on the Armenians who lived in the crumbling Ottoman Empire. The Turks claimed that the Armenians were disloyal in World War One, which was going disastrously for the Ottomans. Therefore, to this day, most Turks insist that only Armenians in the war zone were forced to flee and that there was no genocide. However, the Armenians insist that as many as one-and-a-half million of the two-and-a-half million of their people who lived in the Empire were killed, including almost all of their intellectual and political leaders.

A few years later, a young Polish law student, Raphel Lemkin, asked one of his professors why the leaders of the mass killings had not been arrested. The professor's comment was simple. There was no law under which they could have been arrested. That set

Lemkin off on a crusade that would last until he died. As a Jew, he fled Europe after the Nazis took power, and lived the rest of his life in New York, where he taught law and promoted the cause of preventing mass killings. It was he who coined the term "genocide," and he was its leading advocate at the United Nations, which defined it as a crime against humanity in a series of declarations, the first of which was passed in 1948 and came into force in 1951.

That date was not a coincidence.

World War Two had ended in 1945, only after at least six million Jews and a larger proportion of the Roma (gypsy) population of Europe were exterminated. The trial of Nazi leaders in Nuremberg had been held. There was widespread agreement that something had to be done to prevent such devastation from ever happening again.

A Personal Example

My mother and her sister both have boxes of pictures of relatives whom they never met, because they were all killed in the Holocaust. We know they are close relatives because they look a lot like my grandmother and others who came to the United States in the late 1890s. That is all we know. The captions are in a version of Yiddish which I can read but do not understand.

My father's parents came from a small town in what is now Poland. Their families also emigrated in the 1890s. At that time, the town had a vibrant Jewish community and six seminaries for training rabbis. They are all gone, too.

It should be pointed out that the United States was one of the last countries to endorse the international law on genocide. Indeed, it was only in 1988 that the Senate finally passed a law that still fell somewhat short of a full ratification of the UN accords. That bill is named the Proxmire Act for William Proxmire (D–WI), who gave 3,211 speeches on genocide, one every day the Senate was in session between 1967 and 1986.

The international convention against genocide had come into effect 37 years earlier, and the United States was a signatory to it. However, many US leaders balked at any provision in international law that could limit American sovereignty, an argument that one still hears today—for instance, in opposition to the more recent International Criminal Court. It was also true that the convention and the draft legislation submitted to Congress were both quite vague about how extensive the extermination had to be before the term genocide would be used. And, given the language of the convention, the United States would be expected to join international efforts to punish the perpetrators of genocide if the term was used. It also did not help to sway members of Congress when critics accused the United States of practicing genocide with the atomic bombs it had dropped on Hiroshima and Nagasaki, and the violence it used against African and Native Americans. In sum, as Power concludes, the United States has rarely summoned the political will to take a strong stand against any instance of genocide. Instead, it more often decided that its national interests, as defined in realist terms, trumped humanitarian obligations.

As a result, American policy-makers have rarely called mass killings genocide. During the "killing fields" period in Cambodia, when 1.7 million of 7 million people died, the United States implicitly supported the Cambodian government. As Secretary of State Henry Kissinger put it at the time, "You should also tell the Cambodians that we will be friends with them. They are murderous thugs, but we won't let that stand in our way. We are prepared to improve relations with them." Kissinger, the most influential realist of his time, argued that Vietnam posed a much greater threat to the United States, and that Cambodia and Vietnam were hostile to each other. As one Arab cliché puts it, "My enemy's enemy is my friend."

The United States was also slow to respond to the mass killings, evictions, and rape of Bosnian Muslims by Serbs following the collapse of Yugoslavia. The United States eventually did intervene after the massacre of thousand of Bosnian men and boys at a United Nations-run safe haven in Srebrenica. It did respond more quickly to the Serbian ethnic cleansing of Kosovo. And, it supported the International Criminal Tribunal for the former Yugoslavia, where former Serbian President Slobodan Milosevic died before his trial concluded.

The United States' record on Rwanda in 1994 is therefore not surprising. While President Clinton acknowledged that the killings of 800,000 Tutsi and moderate Hutus was despicable, he always avoided using the term genocide. Had he done so, the United States would have been under some obligation to act, something he had no intention of doing in the aftermath of the failed humanitarian mission in Somalia the year before. Clinton also pressured the United Nations not to send a peacekeeping mission to Rwanda, even though the Canadian general in charge of the small force there claimed he could have stopped the killing with a few thousand soldiers.

Therefore, as we will see, the American response to Darfur has been unusual. As early as 2004, Secretary of State Colin Powell used the term genocide. American authorities endorse sending the Sudanese leaders to stand trial at the International Criminal Court, even though they oppose our own membership of the court. President Bush sent a message of support to the 2005 rally on Darfur on the Mall in Washington, even though virtually every participant disagreed with the president on just about every other foreign policy question.

As we will also see, the problem is that there is little that the United States can do on the ground to improve the conditions in Darfur.

The Evolution of Sudan

Like Iraq, Sudan is an artificial country. Its borders were set by a series of colonial rulers. In other words, if the people in today's Sudan had been free to define their own borders and their own state, Sudan as we know it would almost certainly not exist.

Foreign influence in the region that became Sudan began centuries ago when Egyptians traveled up the Nile (which branches into two rivers in Sudan) and established contact with the largely Arabic population along its banks. Egyptian influence ebbed and flowed from 2,700 BC onward. Christianity took hold in Nubia, the region along the Nile in southern Egypt. The term Sudan itself probably derives from commentaries by Arab intellectuals of the time, referring to the "land of the blacks."

After the Muslims arrived in Egypt in the middle of the seventh century, they progressed southward. Within a few decades most of the people had converted to Islam, but the fighters who came to the region did not find much wealth and largely left it alone. By 1000, most of the north was Muslim, and most people spoke Arabic (see Table 10.1).

Table 10.1   Events in the History of Sudan and the Darfur Conflict

Time	Event
Fourteenth century	Arrival of Islam
1821	Egyptian/Ottoman takeover
1898	British/Egyptian condominium
1956	Independence
1983	Civil war with south fully underway
1989	NIC takes power
2004	Outbreak of genocide
2005	Comprehensive peace agreement

That was not true for Darfur and the south (which we can ignore for the moment). Darfur was independent from the middle of the sixteenth century until the British solidified their hold on the region in the early twentieth century. That does not mean that Darfur was something we would recognize as a state today. It was a monarchy whose strength varied with the quality of the leaders. Its borders continually shifted. And, perhaps most importantly of all, it was a collection of different ethnic groups only some of whom were Fur (Darfur literally means "the home of the Fur"). Although most people in the region had converted to Islam by the fifteenth century, there was also tension between Arabs and Africans, especially when the latter had control of the region. Modern-day Darfur was also isolated from the center of what was to become Sudan's power base, the regions bordering the banks of the two branches of the Nile River. As a result, Darfur was largely self-sufficient politically and economically into the nineteenth century and, in some ways, beyond that time.

The Egyptians (as part of the Ottoman empire) tried to seize control of what is now northern and western Sudan, and had occupied most of the Arab north by 1821. It was not an easy struggle, and led them to suspend efforts to take over Darfur as well. Fifty years later, conflicts between Darfur and the Egyptians and their Sudanese allies led to the collapse of the kingdom in Darfur.

Egyptian domination was not to last, however. There was always considerable resistance to it. Meanwhile, the Europeans were staking claims to all of Africa. It took longer for them carve up East Africa than other regions, but in 1898 the British and Egyptians agreed to a "codominion" or joint rule of Sudan, which now included the south as well as Darfur. The British were really in charge, and decided to give Darfur considerable autonomy until after World War One. The British had little or no interest in the development of what became Sudan. Rather, they were primarily interested in maintaining order in a volatile part of a volatile continent.

Because Darfur and other peripheral regions of Sudan were not important to the colonial rulers, they neglected it economically and in other ways. The region, for instance, only received about 5 percent of total investment funds for the entire colony, which did not get a great deal in total. In 1935, Darfur had only four elementary schools, and no educational facilities beyond that. There were also no trained agricultural scientists.

From then on, the British helped prepare Sudan for independence. Little of their effort had to do with the interests of Sudan, let alone Darfur. Rather, the UK was preoccupied with the fate of Egypt, and especially the Suez Canal, which would be invaded and produce a major international crisis shortly after Sudan was granted its political freedom. One of the consequences of the independence process was that Sudan and the countries on its borders argued over the populations and regions between them.

Sudan gained its independence on January 1, 1956, without much of a struggle with either the British or the Egyptians. From the beginning the new regime was dominated by Arabs and by Khartoum. In the mid-1960s some Sudanese in Darfur and in the south began to protest against their continued neglect by the national government. They found it hard to grant legitimacy to a government that disdained them culturally, and diverted almost all of the country's limited resources to an increasingly militant and vengeful Arab leadership, comprising a handful of families and clans based in or near Khartoum.

Useful Websites

Conciliation Resources has done the best research on the entire country, although its work has been mostly in the south: www.c-r.org/our-work/accord/sudan/contents.php

Concordis International is a small British-based NGO that has tried to bring at least moderates from both communities together: www.concordis-international.org.

Save Darfur is the largest and most influential advocacy group working on Darfur and the issues that eddy around it: www.savedarfur.org.

Team Darfur was created by Olympic gold medalist Joey Cheek, and is made up of athletes from around the world who are committed to improving the situation in Darfur: www.teamdarfur.org

---

Civil War with the South

The Sudanese government was never very effective because it faced opposition not only from the non-Arab regions of the country, but from the Arabs in the north themselves. Within two years of independence, control of the government had been handed over to the military, and for a decade the country was led by a succession of weak governments, some of which were civilian. In 1969, devoutly Muslim officers led by a young colonel, Jaafer Nimeiri, took over.

The situation worsened when the National Islamic Front (now the National People's Congress) seized power in Khartoum in 1989 under the leadership of the current president, Omar al-Bashir. If anything, the NIF/NPC was even more committed to strict enforcement of strict Islamic principles throughout the state. Bashir's regime turned Sudan into one of the most Islamicized countries in the world which was controversial even among the Arabs—many of whom were secular and opposed to *sharia*, for example. As we saw in Chapter 10, the Bashir government allowed Osama bin-Laden to operate his businesses and his terrorist training camps in Sudan for a number of years in the 1990s.

In fact, southern opposition began even earlier, within days of independence. Northern arguments that the country had to stay unified to show their common opposition to their former colonial masters and slave traders frequently fell on deaf ears.

The resentment grew after the first government handed over power to the military in 1958. That government decided to make Arabic the language of instruction in schools throughout the country, and expelled missionaries from the largely Christian (and non-Arabic-speaking) south.

Americans are used to hearing about a supposed military-industrial complex that wields tremendous influence on political and economic life. In a play on words, Jok Madut Jok (2007: 49) refers to Sudan as a military *Islamic* complex in which a theocracy is more than willing to use force to impose its values on the rest of the country. The development of radical Islam in Sudan parallels what Fawaz Gerges (2006) has documented in Egypt, Afghanistan and Iran, which he labels "the journey of the jihadist." Bashir and his predecessors, in fact, had close ties with the Muslim Brotherhood and other extremists in Egypt. In other words, the Bashir regime drew support from two groups that already existed: devout but poorly educated soldiers, and radical and increasingly religious students and intellectuals.

Even before Bashir came to power, Khartoum tried to isolate the south. Thus, the region was not allowed to participate in the 1965 elections because Khartoum deemed the situation there too insecure. It was true that there was already some fighting. Nonetheless, the government's actions only exacerbated the resentment. As has been the case in many other countries, the desire for hegemony by one group in a multi-ethnic society only fuels resentment among those excluded from power.

The same thing happened after Nimeiry seized power in 1969. Three years later, he decided to change course and seek a settlement with the south. That led to the first and only decade of relative calm in this new country. In retrospect, the south probably made too many concessions to make the peace last.

Southern resistance flared up again in 1983, when the government imposed *sharia* on the entire country. The southerners, being Christians, opposed the use of Muslim law and the repression of their people that came with it. They claimed they were not fighting for the right to secede, but for national unity around secular principles that would treat all Sudanese equally and with dignity.

They were fortunate to have an effective and charismatic leader, John Garang, who headed the Southern People's Liberation Army (and Movement), which he led until his death in a helicopter crash in 2005. That does not mean that the SPLA/M was unified. Ethnic divisions among southerners emerged in the early 1990s. That did not stop the carnage. According to most estimates, two million southerners were killed. Another million lived in exile. The devastation led the exiled political leaders to unite behind John Garang in 1995.

Tensions mounted, too, after the 1998 discovery of large oil reserves in the Arab-controlled parts of the country. Khartoum's decision to use most of the revenues to support development in the north only reinforced southern (and Darfurian) resentment about resource distribution that dated back to colonial rule.

Shortly thereafter, the two sides grudgingly came to the conclusion that they had reached a hurting stalemate. The north could not subdue the south. The south had no real chance of either gaining independence, or achieving their vision of a more secular and unified nation. The toll had been immense. No one knows how many people died. The best estimate is that more than four million were living in camps for internally displaced persons inside Sudan, and another half million were in refugee camps in neighboring countries.

That made it possible for international mediators to facilitate what came to be called the Comprehensive Peace Agreement (CPA) in July 2005. It called for a power-sharing government between NPC and SPLA, the drafting of a new constitution, and elections by 2009. Garang joined the government as vice-president. He died less than a month later, but the tenuous peace has held.

However, there is no reason to assume that it will continue to do so. The violence and insensitivity of the north throughout the civil war leave many in the south still interested in secession. The 2009 election will tell us a lot about the short-term possibilities for peace, but little about longer-term prospects for reconciliation.

The war with the south also revealed the weakness of the Sudanese state. It has not been a classic "failed state" that lacks the capacity to govern effectively. Instead, it has relied on racism and repression to solidify its hold over governmental and economic institutions centered on the Arab minority.

Ironically, the strengths of the Sudanese state may actually turn it into a failed one if it completely loses control in Darfur and the south. Most international observers doubt that the CPA (the details of which are not important for our purposes) will survive (see www.c-r.org/our-work/accord/sudan/contents.php). If so, the combination of government failure in both regions could well result in a failed state and continued violence and anarchy. As one southerner put it:

> This country of ours is like a highwayman, it robs our resources and never gives anything back. It says: "Give me your money, your loyalty, your identity, or you will lose your life." (Jok 2007: 28)

One of the short-term consequences of the fighting and subsequent negotiations about the south was that two parties and the international community decided not to include Darfur in the peace negotiations. It would have just made things more complicated and an agreement more difficult.

Put as bluntly as possible, as we are about to see, the reduction in fighting between north and south, and then the introduction of the CPA, made it possible for the government in Khartoum to turn its attention westward.

The Ambiguous Genocide

My two favorite books on Darfur have very different titles. Julie Flint and Alex de Waal (2008) subtitle theirs *A History of a Long War*. Gerard Prunier (2007) calls what happened an "ambiguous genocide." The two books put forward slightly different interpretations of the conflict. Both help us realize that the dispute has roots that go back decades, if not centuries—hence the notion of a "long war." Both help us see that armed rebellions early in this century by groups in Darfur allowed the government to justify the genocide that draws our interest to this isolated and impoverished part of the world.

Whatever the disagreements among analysts, there is a consensus that the peripheral regions, including Darfur, the South and others, were not involved in the process that led to independence and the creation of a Sudanese state. They were always wary of the intentions of whoever led the government in Khartoum, especially as the leadership became increasingly Arabized and Islamist, and intolerant of everyone else.

As Khartoum's attention turned away from the South, it became involved in two overlapping disputes with fellow Muslims which it found doubly vexing.

First, the leadership in Khartoum was divided. As the 1990s wore on, the two dominant personalities, President Bashir and Hassan al-Turabi, had a falling-out. Turabi is devout and rather intolerant. He is often given most of the credit for the imposition of *sharia*. Though not from Darfur, he had developed close ties to the Justice and Equality Movement by early in this century. To complicate matters further, the Bashir government decided to improve relations with the West after 9/11, by taking a stronger stand against terrorism and a softer position on Islam. In fact, al-Turabi was arrested again and spent a few more years in prison.

Secondly, the main Darfurian groups complained about their economic and political discrimination. The long-standing poverty in the region was magnified by the decade-long drought discussed above. Meanwhile, Khartoum focused on what it saw as their impiety and, increasingly, their impudence.

The conflict that gave rise to the genocide was, thus, not new. In 1983, a clash between Arab herders and African farmers left at least 3,000 dead. Meanwhile, Darfur (roughly the size of France) had been gripped by a drought for 30 years, a drought which reached new levels of severity in 1984 and 1985. Later in the decade and in the early 1990s, the SPLA attacked Darfur as well.

Complicating matters further, the Arabs had claimed title to the land with the most access to water, leaving the Africans with the least fertile and most arid croplands. In other words, an ethnic division was also turning into a dispute over very scarce resources.

Things only degenerated over the next few years. Sudanese on both sides began using racial epithets in dealing with each other—"the image of the enemy," in conflict resolution theory terms. Chad, Libya, Eritrea and other neighboring countries weighed in on one side or the other of the dispute, further complicating matters. There had been sporadic raids by armed Arab militias throughout the 1980s and 1990s, but they received little attention given the intensity of the conflict in the south. But in the last years of the 1990s the raids intensified, prompting at least 100,000 Darfurians to flee to Chad.

In 2000, a group of intellectuals published a *Black Book* documenting human rights abuses and poverty in the region. The next year they joined with traditional leaders to form a number of dissident movements, the most important of which became the Sudan Liberation Army (SLA) and the Justice Equality Movement (JEM).

To make a long story short, rebels from Darfur began launching attacks on the army and government offices in the region, with February 26, 2003 usually given as the start of a revolt that had begun in more limited ways years earlier (see Table 10.2). It was at best a disjointed rebellion, since most of the different ethnic groups did not talk to each other. Nonetheless, if we focus on 2003 alone, the opposition in Darfur attacked first, at least from Khartoum's perspective, thus giving rise to Prunier's notion that this is an "ambiguous genocide."

The government declared a state of emergency in Darfur. It also began making plans to coordinate government actions with those of the *Janjaweed*, which already existed to some extent.

On May 1, members of parliament from Darfur visited President Bashir and documented almost 200 attacks that had killed more than 450 people. They were rebuffed by the central government authorities, and consequently the violence continued.

In sum, both sides played a role in starting the violence in Darfur. However, given the ferocity of the regime's response, it is most certainly a genocide and thus unacceptable by any international or ethical standard. That is the case because the regime responded in

Table 10.2 Key Dates and Events in the Genocide

Date	Event
1987–1989	First modern Arab–Fur war
1989	Bashir takes power
2000	Publication of *Black Book* decrying conditions in Darfur
2003	First attacks by JEM and SLA *Janjaweed* become more organized
2004	Attacks intensify First use of term "genocide"
2005	Comprehensive Peace Agreement between Khartoum and SPLA/M UN refers Sudan to ICC
2006	Peace negotiations with rebels fail
2007	African Union peace-keepers arrive First indictments by ICC
2008	Government declares cease-fire, rejected by rebels
2009	Indictment of al-Bashir by ICC

ways that could not be justified in terms of a state's defending its sovereignty or integrity. In no way can the government's response be seen as equal to the threat it faced from the rebels in Darfur.

By early 2004, Sudan had cut Darfur off from the rest of the world. By the middle of the year, almost a million and a half people had been forced into camps either in Sudan or in neighboring Chad. No one knows how many people died in the year before Secretary Powell called the killing "genocide." What makes it doubly tragic is that it built on the "experience" of the violence in the South, doing as much damage but in far less time.

In the meantime, the communities of Darfur divided along several lines. First, their ethnic divisions prevented them forming a united front. Secondly, some of the organized political groups chose to attack the government. In addition, the JEM and the SLA, the two largest rebel groups, were never able to cooperate before the genocide broke out. Thirdly, some of the leaders had been forced into exile in neighboring countries, which meant there was a split between them and those inside the country who were far more at risk.

None of the leading groups in Darfur advocated secession. Rather, the SLA and JEM called for more national unity, a presidency that would rotate among the regions, and more democracy. They were further divided because their leaders came from different clans and were highly suspicious of each other. Also, while these groups and others did launch attacks before the genocide, they were poorly trained and organized, lightly armed, and forced to deal with disagreements within their own ranks.

The genocide was "ambiguous," too, because it was not directly carried out by the government for the most part. Rather, the regime armed and equipped the *Janjaweed*. *Janjaweed* is a generic term used to refer to armed fighters. Traditionally, they operated with horses and camels. Today, they also use Land Cruisers and airplanes. The *Janjaweed* were recruited from the Arabized, mostly nomadic residents of the region.

They were and are the immediate perpetrators of the genocide. But make no mistake, they have operated with the support of the regime, which has turned a blind eye to their attacks, even if it has not ordered all of them. Most observers are convinced that the authorities in Khartoum knew exactly what the *Janjaweed* would do, given their fears that the blacks had largely taken up arms against them rather than the central government. Their local leader, Musa Hilal, sent a memo to his aides stating: "You are informed that directives have been issued to change the demography of Darfur and empty it of African tribes" (Flint and de Waal 2007: 128)

The current crisis began in earnest on April 25, 2003, when a small convoy of SLA and JEM fighters destroyed all the airplanes at a government-controlled base in Darfur. Until then, Khartoum had not paid much attention to the fighting in Darfur, thinking it was largely about issues internal to the region. However, this attack did more damage than anything the SPLA/M had done in their generation-long war.

During the course of the next year, the government made a momentous choice. Rather than relying on its own ground troops, it would count on the *Janjaweed* to strike fear and cow the population of Darfur.

That the government was committed to crushing resistance in Darfur became clear on February 27, 2004, when several hundred men on horses and camels attacked the town of Tawila. Seventy-five people were killed. Hundreds of women were raped and/or abducted while the men of the town watched helplessly. Attacks continued throughout the year with strong support from the air force, which the villagers could do nothing to stop.

Proportionality and Targeting Non-combatants

There are dozens of versions of "just war" theory that hold that under certain circumstances, war can be justified. Typically, those definitions list four criteria, one of which is proportionality. This means that if it is justified for one side to retaliate, that force should be commensurate with, or proportional to, the damage it has suffered.

Similarly, it is generally considered unethical and even illegal to target civilians who are not involved in the fighting. It is in the nature of warfare that there is always some of what the military calls "collateral damage." But, every version of just war theory I know of prohibits the explicit targeting of non-combatants (think again about the attacks on the World Trade Center on 9/11).

Clearly, Khartoum violated these principles by several orders of magnitude.

The government denied any responsibility for the attack. Nonetheless its leader, Musa Hilal, had close ties to the leaders in Khartoum. He was also heir to the leadership of a long-standing clan of influential nomads who were, themselves, threatened by the drought, and by the expansion of the Sahara desert which had been taking place for several decades.

Musa's supporters and others who formed the *Janjaweed* also had access to arms. In 1990, for instance, a Kalashnikov semi-automatic weapon could be bought for $40, and the issue of cheap weapons has also figured in many other conflicts in Africa and beyond.

By the end of 2004, most of the region where the rebels were based was in utter ruin. But by then, the destruction had been expanded to include all of Darfur. The government and the *Janjaweed* may have eliminated the immediate threat the rebels posed, but the human suffering continued.

The devastation went beyond guns and bombs. More people probably died of disease and starvation than from the physical attacks. As the quote at the beginning of the chapter suggests, the government explicitly tried to make traditional agriculture in Darfur impossible, and often made it difficult for relief supplies to enter the country.

The statistics on the genocide are at best approximations. Also, they convey a sense of abstraction and generality that does not adequately convey the horror of the last five years. No one has done that better than Halima Bashir (2008). Bashir (a pseudonym) is a doctor currently living in exile in London.

Her family was wealthy by the region's standards; her father was a prosperous farmer who even owned a Land Cruiser. That meant that the parents could send their most precocious child to secondary school, and then to the university. That required her to leave the village and go to larger towns, where she was subjected to discrimination as an African long before the fighting broke out.

As the situation deteriorated, she was forced out of a job in the maternity ward at a hospital, and went back to her village to live and work. Although she had never chosen a political affiliation, she did treat wounded rebels, a fact that was widely known on both sides of the conflict.

Government airplanes and *Janjaweed* militiamen came close to her village many times. Finally, they attacked. Her father and many other members of her family were killed. The village was utterly destroyed. The survivors fled. She became separated from the members of her family who were not killed. She still does not know if they are living or dead.

She made her way to London, where she faced yet another hurdle. The British government was reluctant to grant her and her new husband asylum, and let them remain in the country. Bashir knew that because of her work with the rebels, a return to Sudan was a certain death sentence.

The genocide did not just devastate people. Some analysts estimate that 40 percent of the livestock in pre-war Darfur was killed. Another 20 percent was stolen, but before let 30 percent died for lack of food or water. Not much was left.

The situation has barely improved as I write in early 2009. There may be fewer killings and less ethnic cleansing than in 2003 and 2004. But, that is hardly encouraging news since there are not many people left to kill or drive away.

More discouraging yet is the unsurprising fact that many young people in the camps keep getting angrier, and are defying the authority of the traditional sheiks whose influence was predominant in the first phase of the move from the villages to the camps. The so-called *shabab* have led protests in many of the camps which have led to the expulsion of tens of thousands of refugees, and the deaths of an unknown number of these angry young men (see The *New York Times*, December 21, 2008, p. 8).

The *shabab* do not make the prospects for negotiations any brighter. While they do not appear to be very well organized, many have made it clear that they would only support negotiations if, among other things, the *Janjaweed* were dissolved and President Bashir agreed to turn himself over to the ICC.

The Failure of the International Community

The fact that the genocide reached tragic proportions almost exactly ten years after the disaster in Rwanda was not lost on the international community. But as Prunier notes (2007: 125–30), the crisis in Darfur was well known to African specialists before the end of the 1990s. Virtually no one else seemed to pay attention. It took the events of 2003 and 2004 to rivet world attention on the region. By then, it may well have been too late: the start of the counter-insurgency campaign had made it clear that Darfur was already in the midst of a major humanitarian crisis.

The international community has been able to provide considerable aid, although nowhere near enough. Sudan now has more internally displaced persons—people who have fled their homes but stay in their own country—than any other state in the world. The United Nations created Operation Lifeline Sudan as early as 1989. Its goal was to work with all parties in Sudan and neighboring countries to ensure that relief supplies could get through to the camps peacefully, and be distributed to the people who needed help the most. OLS enjoyed a modicum of success over the next decade. But, the fighting in this century outstripped its capacity. To make matters worse, the UN, which coordinated much of the relief work, was rarely able to raise even a third of the money it needed each year from the member states.

The same worries about the safe flow of medicine, food and other goods persist today. The Sudanese government has made it as difficult as possible for NGOs and international agencies to reach and support the camps in Darfur itself. Conditions have improved in refugee camps abroad, where the death rate is similar to that of the camps run elsewhere by the UN and other international agencies.

The international community has had even less success in trying to find a negotiated solution to the conflict. There have been periodic negotiations between the government and the rebels, often mediated by third parties from elsewhere in Africa. Many felt that Bashir's government never took the mediators seriously, used them as a stalling tactic, and only dealt with them in an effort to improve Sudan's international reputation. Meanwhile the SLA, in particular, has been reluctant to support any cease-fire, let alone a comprehensive agreement to reduce or end the fighting.

Very few conflict resolution NGOs have been involved in Sudan. Few have been allowed. Two exceptions are the British Conciliation Resources (www.c-r.org/our-work/accord/sudan/contents.php) and Concordis International (www.concordis-international.org/story4.php). Conciliation Resources' work in the region has largely been in the south, and has focused on the Lord's Resistance Army which plagues southern Sudan and northern Uganda. CR has published the best single analysis from a peace-maker's perspective on Sudan; that is the "url" listed above. Concordis has been active in Darfur since 1999. Unlike the advocacy groups we will consider later in the chapter, Concordis has tried to be a neutral broker. Depending on what is possible at a given moment, it has made itself available to facilitate dialogue to promote peace and reconciliation in Sudan and abroad.

The African Union and the UN have also taken an interest in defusing the dispute. A small AU mission (African Union Mission in Sudan) has been in place since 2004 and has some limited authority to protect civilians. AUMIS was in place until it was succeeded by the United Nations UNAMID at the end of 2007. At its peak, AUMIS never had more than 3,000, mostly poorly trained, soldiers whose rules of engagement all but completely ruled out their use of force. In 2007, the Security Council passed Resolution 1769, which authorized a UN force of 20,000 troops and 4,000 police officers for deployment in Sudan. It was intended to be largely African, but Canada, Sweden and other countries with extensive peace-keeping experience have contributed troops and advisors. What is probably more important is that the Sudanese government has resisted the efforts of the UN to the point that only about half of the planned personnel had been allowed in by the end of 2008.

Senior politicians from Europe, North America and Africa have all tried to mediate. As of late 2008, no agreement has shown any sign of lasting. Officials of many other countries, including the United States, have not been allowed in the region at all. The United States does have an embassy in Khartoum, but there has not been a serving ambassador since 2007.

The successful deployment of UN or other peace-keepers and peace-makers has been hindered Sudanese politics on both sides. Many leaders in Khartoum have been willing to try to buy off potential interlocutors on the Darfurian side. Many rebels have been unwilling to cooperate at all. The few cease-fires that have been reached have been honored in the breach. Thus, in 2005 and 2006, the two sides negotiated in Abuja, the capital of Nigeria. The fighting continued and even escalated at the same time.

It is also clear to most observers that some form of military intervention will be needed, including a force that far exceeds even the most ambitious plans for UNAMID. There are two seemingly insurmountable obstacles in this respect. First, the Western powers have not been able to agree on what should be done, let alone on who should do it. Second, the Chinese would almost certainly veto any Security Council resolution authorizing the use of force because of their dependence on Sudanese oil.

The United States has played an ambiguous role in the international discussions about Darfur. In the late 1990s and early 2000s, its primary concern was the conflict between north and south, not Darfur, which received very little attention from American officials. After 9/11, the fact that Bashir was taking a strong stance against terrorism (despite the government's ties to bin Laden a decade earlier) led Washington to try to maintain links with Khartoum in what was expected to be a volatile region on a volatile continent. The United States also is concerned about inroads China is making through its purchase of large quantities of oil from Sudan.

The International Criminal Court (ICC) has tried to intervene. In 2007, it indicted Ahmed Haroud, the man responsible for security in Darfur, on 42 counts of crimes against humanity for his role in coordinating the genocide. The court's prosecutors have recommended indicting Bashir and others. So far, no one has been turned over to the court. Instead, the threat of legal action has only intensified the government's resistance to anything approaching peaceful change.

Save Darfur

If there is any good news about Darfur, it has been the growth of a global grassroots effort to persuade governments to do more to stop the genocide. As noted earlier, the movement began in the American Jewish community and has spread from there to the rest of America, and the world.

The Save Darfur Coalition reached its peak after the physical violence had lessened considerably. Still, it did remarkable work in raising awareness of the plight of the region. In preparation for its April 29, 2006 rally in Washington, the movement gathered more than a million postcards and emails which were sent to the White House.

SDC also assembled an unusual coalition. Speakers at the event included some of the "usual suspects," such as the film stars Mia Farrow and George Clooney, long-time supporters of progressive causes. But, speakers also included the Rev. Richard Cizik, then the policy director of the National Association of Evangelicals. By that time, the Save Darfur Coalition included more than 130 faith-based organizations, from all the major religious traditions in the United States.

The movement also brought together some strange political bedfellows. By presenting itself as non-partisan and inclusive, the coalition drew support from many conservatives. After all, they argued, who could favor genocide? Conservative Senator Sam Brownback (R–Kansas) was the cause's strongest supporter in Congress. President Bush sent a message approving of the rally and its initiatives.

The coalition has been particularly effective in attracting popular celebrities to its efforts. *Sixty Minutes*, for instance, covered the trip by African activist John Prendergast and actor Don Cheadle into the camps which the two men then turned into a best-selling book reflecting why they had become so deeply involved (Cheadle and Prendergast 2007). The fact that they subtitled their book "The Mission to End Genocide in Darfur *and Beyond*" (emphasis added) reflects the understanding throughout the movement that their task extended to genocide wherever and whenever it occurred.

Team Darfur is somewhat different and considerably less visible. It was co-founded by Olympic speed skater Joey Cheek, and former UCLA volleyball player Brad Greiner. The movement got off to a flying start when Cheek announced that he would be giving his bonus for winning the gold medal to the cause of Darfur. In the next months, he raised over $1 million to create an organization in which elite athletes would use their popularity to support Darfur. As of early 2009, the "team" had more than 400 athletes on its "roster" from more than 25 countries. Cheek did his organization a world of good by stating early in 2008 that he had no intention of organizing protests at the Beijing Olympics out of respect for the spirit and rules of the Games. Nonetheless, China denied him a visa to attend.

Team Darfur is not the only example of athletes working for peace. Indeed, Cheek is not the first speed skater to do so. There is a joint Israeli-Palestinian soccer team. Benetton sponsored summer camps for teenagers from all six Yugoslav republics as that country was falling apart. Search for Common Ground sponsors inter-ethnic soccer tournaments in Burundi, a country that does not have a professional league of its own.

But there is little doubt that Team Darfur is by far the most successful organization of its type.

There are criticisms of these and other advocacy movements. Although these kinds of organizations agree with Conciliation-Resources and Concordis on most issues, they have slightly different goals. Conflict resolution groups may not be able to work with all parties to a dispute, but they do try to bring at least some people from both sides together, typically the men and women who are most open to dialogue and to long-term, peaceful solution. As the term "advocacy group" suggests, the Save Darfur Coalition and similar groups are more interested in raising awareness and, with it, pressuring governments to act to protect the people of Darfur. By taking uncompromising stances and working with some of the more militant representatives of the Darfur community, they may have made it harder for either conflict resolution practitioners or government officials to make inroads toward peace. Some have even argued that activism makes it harder for relief workers—some of whom had been in Sudan for 20 years—to do their jobs.

Conflict resolution and advocacy groups know they need to work together, and we have exploring ways of exploring together our slightly different goals and tactics. Darfur is so complicated and so divisive that it is probably not the place where our breakthrough will happen first.

Lessons Learned

The conflict in Darfur is still far from resolved. Yet, we can draw some at least tentative lessons to answer the questions posed at the beginning of the chapter.

1. *Imperialism.* As we also saw with Iraq, the legacy of imperialism in Sudan stretches far beyond its domination by the British for a half-century. The ethnic divisions within the country are in large part the product of invasions that stretch back at least to the arrival of the Arabs, if not Islam.
2. *Image of the enemy.* The degree of hatred at the grassroots level is unmatched anywhere else covered in this book. Alas, it is a common theme in almost all of the other examples of genocide we could have turned to.
3. *Law and the international community.* International law does offer legal remedies for the victims of genocide and their advocates. The problem is enforcing those laws, and forcing the perpetrators of genocide to face the International Criminal Court.
4. *Domestic politics and national interests.* That is a key factor because domestic politics and the pursuit of the national interest get in the way. In this case, China has a vested interest in supporting the government of Sudan. The attention of the United States was focused elsewhere at least until Save Darfur launched its campaign. In particular, this case illustrates the fact that any one of the five permanent members of the United Nations can paralyze the one global institution that could act in the name of humanity.

Select Bibliography

Bashir, Halima (2008). *Tears of the Desert: A Memoir of Survival in Darfur.* New York: One World/ Ballantine Books.
Cheadle, Don and John Prendergast (2007). *Not on Our Watch: The Mission to End Genocide and Beyond.* New York: Hyperion.
Flint, Julie, and Alex de Waal (2008). *Darfur: A New History of a Long War.* London: Zed Books.
Gerges, Fawaz (2006). *Journey of the Jihadist.* New York: Harcourt.
Jok, Madut Jok (2007). *Sudan: Race, Religion, and Violence.* Oxford: OneWorld.
Power, Samantha (2005). *A Problem from Hell: America and the Age of Genocide.* New York: Basic Books.
Prunier, Gérard (2007), *Darfur: The Ambiguous Genocide.* Ithaca, NY: Cornell University Press.

PART 4

Conclusions

CHAPTER ELEVEN

Intellectual Conclusions

We need to know the destination—if not in a precise way, at least in a generalized way. Before we actually translate something into reality, we must be able to dream about it. If we do a good job in identifying our destination, more innovations and changes will take place to help us reach it.
—Muhammad Yunus

As noted in Chapter 1, this book is based on the premise that a student of international relations can make tremendous progress in understanding general trends in the field by considering theories and case studies together. Now, having examined samples of both, we return to that premise both empirically (in this chapter) and normatively (in the next).

The process of shuttling back and forth between theory and examples while writing this book has worked well for me. In particular, focusing on traditional theories and "unsuccessful" cases like the dispute with Iraq led me, first, to challenge some of the conventional wisdom in the field, and then to deepen my understanding of conflict resolution.

Ten Empirical Conclusions

It is impossible to reach anything approaching definitive conclusions about international conflict resolution—at least at this point. Nonetheless, the following ten points do seem to emerge from the discussion in this book so far.

1. There Is No Blueprint for Conflict Resolution

Some of the more simplistic descriptions of win-win conflict resolution leave the impression that there is almost a step-by-step approach to conflict resolution. Everything we have seen in the first ten chapters of this book demonstrates that such impressions are misleading at best.

The conclusions that follow do present some general principles that seem to affect the likelihood of win-win conflict resolution. However, they cannot be applied in anything like a routine manner, for what should be an obvious reason. All conflicts are different, and those differences matter.

Consider, for example, that the parties involved in the conflict in South Africa all agreed that they had to share the same territory. Such an agreement has not been in place for most of the history of the Palestinian–Israeli conflict.

Along similar lines, we have also seen the importance of "historical accidents," which make any step-by-step approach all but impossible. These may have a permanent effect, such as the way the borders of Darfur or Iraq were drawn, or a short- term effect, such as the Supreme Court decision that made George W. Bush US president in the year 2000.

2. Non-violent Conflict Resolution May Not Always Be Possible

In an earlier book, I agreed with colleagues who argue that non-violent conflict resolution is always possible (Hauss 1996). That may be true in theory. However, each of the cases in Part 3 suggests that being able to identify the outlines of such an agreement is very different from actually implementing it.

In the best circumstances, turning the dream of non-violent change into reality can take a depressingly long time: under the worst circumstances, a negotiated settlement is either impossible in practice, or would be unacceptable if it were possible.

In Chapter 9, we saw that the Western powers might have eventually forced Iraq out of Kuwait by maintaining its sanctions after the January 1991 deadline. Similarly, stiffening of sanctions may have forced Iraq to cooperate in the run-up to the 2003 war. However, there is no guarantee that these results would have been achieved; in fact, it is more likely that the US-led coalition itself might have begun to splinter first, in either situation.

More important, it is hard to see how the international community and Iraq could have come to a workable agreement at any point in the history of the conflict as long as the Baath regime remained in power in Baghdad. In particular, there was simply too much mistrust and hatred for any US administration to find common ground with Saddam Hussein and his colleagues.

Nowhere is this clearer than with the war on terror. As I noted in Chapter 10, we in the peace-building community had precious few alternatives to offer in the days after 9/11. As I also noted, we have made little progress in generating ideas that could be used in non-violent responses to terrorism: but we also know that the forms of terrorism considered in that chapter will exist for a long time—whether we respond with forces, or conflict resolution strategies, or both.

3. Reconciliation Is Critical

All analysts working on international conflict resolution stress the importance of agreements that end or ease the fighting, reached by the parties involved. However, as we look deeper into the whole peace process, it becomes clear that formal agreements are never enough. For stable peace to be achieved, reconciliation at the grassroots level—not just the elite level—must occur.

This is not an original point, indeed it is central to the burgeoning literature on new forms of conflict resolution discussed in Chapter 4. What emerges from this study is the need to stress the importance of reconciliation more than most international relations specialists have done.

What we have seen in the six case studies is that efforts at reconciliation (in terms of conflict resolution) or civil society-building (in terms of comparative politics) are just beginning to get the attention they deserve. But from both a normative and an empirical perspective, reconciliation needs to play a more important role in our thought and action in the context of international conflict resolution.

Here, the work of David Bloomfield (1997) on Northern Ireland has far-reaching implications. He draws the distinction between the structural attempts to reach peace through formal, governmental agreements, and cultural initiatives that stress change in the values of all parties to the dispute. Focusing only on the former often leads to what Fen Osler Hampson (1996) calls "orphaned agreements." In those circumstances, leaders reach an agreement as they did in Northern Ireland in 1998 and 1999. But, without social pressure to go further, they find it increasingly difficult to find the additional common ground needed to push the peace process further. At least so far, the parties and the people in Northern Ireland have managed to avoid that trap. But the Israelis and Palestinians have not . . .

4. Incremental Steps Can Be Enough . . . For Now

At first glance, this point might seem to contradict the previous one.

Critics attack the Good Friday Agreement or the Oslo Accord as half-measures that raised as many problems as they solved. That is not just true of international politics. To cite one example, the limited gun control legislation passed in the United States since the mid-1990s is often scoffed at because it has so many loopholes and was never intended to get existing weapons off the street.

The case studies here suggest a somewhat different interpretation. To begin with, full-blown agreements to end the kind of conflicts discussed in this book are virtually impossible to reach in a single negotiating cycle. There is simply too much tension, mistrust and division for leaders to bridge all their differences.

That said, limited incremental steps can produce major progress if two other factors are in place:

- The step makes the return to violence considerably less likely.
- The step opens the door to reconciliation, even though the completion of the process takes a long time.

Unfortunately, as the events of the Middle East since 2000 show so painfully, the negotiations that lead to a first agreement provide no assurance that any subsequent steps will occur.

5. Leadership and Domestic Politics Matter

There is no mistaking Nelson Mandela for Saddam Hussein. The conciliatory attitude of the former and the hostile one of the latter go a long way toward explaining why the conflicts in South Africa and the Persian Gulf turned out so differently.

The role of individual leaders, however, may be seen as just part of a much broader phenomenon that, as noted earlier, is usually minimized in analyses of international relations—domestic politics. When viewed through that lens, the emergence of a conciliator or an antagonist seem less like historical accidents. To be sure, the political viewpoints and personalities of the individuals considered in Part 3 mattered, and they cannot always be explained satisfactorily. However, domestic politics does make the emergence of certain types of leaders more or less likely, in ways that echo the above conclusion about incremental steps.

The type of political system that operates in a country is very significant. One version of the widely cited but controversial theory about "the democratic peace" holds that democracies tend not to go to war with each other because of the way politics is conducted in democratic countries. Emphasis is placed on such values as compromise and coalition-building. It should therefore come as no surprise that democracies tend to produce leaders who are flexible and conciliatory. That is not an invariable rule, since Nelson Mandela certainly did not emerge from a democracy, and the two branches of Ulster unionism have controlled part of one of the world's oldest democracies.

Much the same holds for a country's culture. As Raymond Cohen (1997), in particular, has argued, some cultures do not lend themselves readily to the give-and-take of negotiation. Cohen has pointed out that there are languages in which there is no linguistic term even roughly equivalent to the word "reconciliation."

There is not a one-to-one match between democracy and the kind of culture that lends itself to non-violent conflict resolution. To cite the most important example, there are scholars who argue that Mandela's willingness to reach out to the National Party leadership reflected both traditional African leadership patterns which stress respect for one's opponents, and the shared love of the country seen by Mandela among blacks and Afrikaners alike.

In short, I am not arguing that the "wrong" kind of culture or political system dooms a peace process—there are too many examples to the contrary—but rather that a democratic regime, and a culture that stresses compromise or accepts diversity, can facilitate the end of fighting and the movement toward stable peace.

6. Third Parties Help, But Not All Third Parties Are Alike

Virtually everyone who writes about international conflict resolution stresses the vital role that dispassionate third parties can play in brokering agreements. There are precious few cases like South Africa, where adversaries of long standing can hammer out their differences largely on their own.

The case studies, however, take the analysis of third parties further than one finds in the theoretical literature, in two overlapping ways.

First, there are different types of third parties. George Mitchell is a classic example of a conciliator. As we saw in Chapter 7, he based his entire political career on his ability to treat friend and foe alike with dignity and respect, skills he was able to use to build coalitions in the fractious United States Senate. Much the same is true of former US president Jimmy Carter, whose successful conflict resolution interventions were possible mainly because he gained the personal and political respect of the opposing parties.

Richard Holbrooke is very different. Even his supporters refer to him as a "bulldozer." His critics use harsher terms, like "bully." Holbrooke would not have been an effective mediator for the Northern Ireland conflict. However, his pressurizing and, some would say, intimidating style was probably critical to the success of the Dayton Agreement after four years of tragic fighting.

The contrasting personalities of these two men may have significant implications for the assignments they were given by President Obama two days after he took office.

He immediately sent Mitchell to the Middle East and told him to listen, something the former senator does extremely well. Holbrooke's task will be different. He will have the full array of diplomatic and military tools of the US government at his disposal in dealing with Pakistan and Afghanistan.

Secondly, third parties need not always be neutral. Indeed, there are times when it is impossible or inappropriate for them to be. Many of Holbrooke's predecessors from the UN and the European Union (EU) had tried to walk a fine line between the Serbs and their adversaries. That did not work, partly because the Serbs were so much more powerful than the Croats and Bosnian Muslims, and were intent on clinging to their plans for a Greater Serbia; and partly because the Serbs were responsible for the lion's share of the atrocities committed as Yugoslavia fell apart.

Put simply, sometimes the international community has to intervene on one side or the other, as it has in both Darfur and the Persian Gulf. Sometimes a commitment to neutrality or to the sovereignty of a state can paralyze the international community and prevent it from getting involved—one of the main reasons there was no massive intervention to stop the killing in Rwanda, even though most observers agreed that such an intervention could have done so relatively quickly and easily.

7. Open or Secret?

These cases offer a mixed picture as far as one of the classic questions in the study of diplomacy is concerned. Should negotiations be held in secret, or should they be open to public scrutiny?

Here, there is no question that the secrecy of the Norwegian channel was vital for the Palestine–Israel situation. Without secrecy it seems highly unlikely that the Palestinian and Israeli leaders, who barely acknowledged each other's existence, could have gotten together, let alone made any progress toward peace. To be sure, some Jews and Palestinians had met informally before. But, the mere fact that it was illegal for Israelis to meet with members of the PLO until 1993 posed an all but insurmountable obstacle to any kind of public negotiation.

The same was true, to a lesser degree, in preparing the ground for formal negotiations in both South Africa and Northern Ireland. Thus, virtually no one in the African National Congress leadership—let alone the country at large—knew that Mandela had been meeting with top-level government officials in the late 1980s. Similarly, little news leaked out of meetings between Sinn Fein leaders and British civil servants until the last few days before the Downing Street Declaration was issued.

Secrecy is probably most useful in the early stages of negotiations. At that time, public awareness of even "talks about talks" might scuttle the possibility of progress by strengthening opposition to them from hard-liners on one or both sides. Similarly, as the Dayton negotiations also showed, a news blackout can give highly antagonistic leaders more room for maneuver than they would otherwise have.

This is certainly true of the question Lawrence Wright asked me about how I would deal with al Qaeda. That cannot be done openly, nor even legally, given US law at the beginning of 2009. Americans cannot meet with any organization on the State Department's list of terrorist groups, which includes, of course, the Taliban and Hamas. For all I know, some such discussions are already occurring. But to be effective, they must be secret.

That said, at a later stage in negotiations the glare of the news camera or pressure from average citizens can also make an agreement more likely. In some cases such scrutiny is unavoidable, as in Northern Ireland, where leaks appear on an almost daily basis.

More often, however, openness can help when the visible intervention of national leaders, or the public imposition of a firm deadline, both builds up the pressure and also increases the possibility of reaching a deal. Both these effects certainly occurred in the weeks before the Good Friday Agreement was reached. But, they did not help the efforts of Tony Blair, Bertie Ahern and others to keep Northern Ireland's new institutions in place in early 2000.

8. The New World (Dis)order Matters

In the late 1980s, both Presidents Bush and Mikhail Gorbachev claimed that the end of the Cold War could usher in a new world order. With the Iraqi invasion of Kuwait and the other problems that have beset international relations since then, the pundits are more likely to talk instead of a new world *dis*order.

Whatever term you choose to describe the world we live in today, there is no question that the changed international environment has made humanitarian intervention and new forms of conflict resolution more common than ever before. That does not mean that the international community always gets involved. It has largely stayed out of either conflicts in which solutions seemed unlikely, or conflicts where the interests (however defined) of the major powers were not involved. Intervention that *has* occurred has not always been particularly effective, something Americans saw most tragically in Somalia.

But the kind of approaches to international conflict discussed in this book are easier to employ, for two main reasons.

First, there are no overriding security issues to preoccupy the states that can most readily intervene in conflicts. The Cold War is gone, and no such superpower confrontation has taken its place. Not even the threat of terrorism comes close to rivaling the potential of global annihilation that we lived under for the best part of half a century.

Secondly, the end of the Cold War division of most of the world between East and West means that the United States and the Russia no longer use their power of veto routinely in the Security Council to keep the UN from intervening in a crisis. And, perhaps most important of all, intervention does not carry with it the risk of escalation to a broader war, as was often the case before the collapse of the Soviet Union.

9. The International Community

The previous conclusion includes one of the greasiest terms used in this book—the "international community." It was rarely used before the 1990s, since the very idea of a world community made little sense during the Cold War years. Optimists think we have made major strides toward acting multilaterally. Indeed, virtually every instance of intervention, if not every attempt at international conflict resolution, was at least nominally organized through an international body. Critics point out that "the international community" is often little more than a code word, or a euphemism to describe the United States' self-assigned role as the world's policeman.

Wherever you come down on such issues, it is impossible to deny that international organizations are at least somewhat more important than they were before the end of the Cold War. The United Nations had a major spurt of peacekeeping and related activity in the mid-1990s. Then declining support from the United States, the UN's related budget crisis, and difficulties on the ground, all cost the organization most of the momentum it had achieved. In particular, the UN now finds it impossible to mount the massive efforts that would be needed for effective intervention in Darfur.

In other words, whenever intervention is on the agenda, the world's leading powers have to be involved, because only they have the personnel and other resources to deploy tens of thousands of soldiers. That has shifted attention away from the UN to the EU and especially NATO which, coincidentally, was already seeking a new role in the post-Cold War world. Attention has clearly been focused on NATO's role, given the two wars in the former Yugoslavia. Since Oslo, the organization has also had a formal role in the Middle East peace process, focusing on issues involving refugees and water. It is now part of the not very effective "quartet" with the US, Russia and the UN which has spearheaded many initiatives in the last few years. After retiring as British Prime Minister, Tony Blair became NATO's special envoy.

It is not only European organizations that are important. The West African ECOWAS achieved in the final three cases. Whether the blame lay in those countries or outside of them (especially in the United States) really does not matter. The fact is, there were few plausible or practical strategies that could have been used to avoid violent conflict or end it even after years of fighting.

To be sure, the United States has been the most powerful (and perhaps most arrogant) actor in most instances of intervention and conflict resolution. That should not, however, keep us from noticing some important, albeit tentative, steps taken toward giving international organizations limited power that transcends, and sometimes limits, the sovereignty of individual states.

10. The Uncertain Role of Force

The final conclusion is the most uncertain. More important, it is the most troubling for someone like this author, who came to international conflict resolution with an ironclad commitment to non-violence.

As noted earlier, it is hard to see how a non-violent win-win outcome could have been produced in at least three cases. Whether the blame lay primarily in the mountains of Afghanistan, Baghdad or Washington really does not matter. The fact is that there were few plausible or practical strategies for avoiding violence in dealing with ethnic cleansing in the former Yugoslavia, or the behavior of Iraq either before or after the Gulf war.

For a traditional international relations specialist or policy-maker, military intervention is predictable. For ill or good, force is part and parcel of international life. But for someone from my background, the use of force is troubling indeed, since the major work on such issues as reconciliation inside the academic community has always ruled out force of any kind, violent or otherwise.

But, as we saw in passing, wherever you come down on the ethical aspects of the use of force, its implementation *as a part of the peace-building process* is increasing. We will discuss those initiatives in the next chapter.

Here, it is enough for us to wonder if a country that was a party to a dispute and imposed a military solution can subsequently become an effective peace-builder. As the experience of Iraq and Afghanistan suggest, that is especially true when the invading force is extremely powerful, like the American military.

The Role of Dreams and Passion

I began this book with a statement by Philip Gourevitch about the passions which the study of conflict and its resolution provokes. I wish to end this chapter, and build a bridge to the next one, by returning to the importance of passion and the normative issues that eddy around it.

As everything in the last few chapters has suggested, writing this book has left me less optimistic about the short-term possibilities for non-violent international conflict resolution. However, analyzing these issues has not reduced my commitment to this ideal as a practical long-term goal.

It is hard to find a scholar from any intellectual school of thought who does not consider the various situations of carnage described in this book to be unacceptable. You do not have to be an idealist to demand that we find a better way of settling our disputes. That said, it would be easy to read the more pessimistic cases in Part 3 as reinforcing the realists' argument that the goal of non-violent conflict resolution is a utopian fantasy.

However, the more successful cases in Part 3 suggest that what seem to be idealistic goals can be meshed with the harsh realities of international life. To envisage this, consider the words of Muhammad Yunus that begin this chapter.

Yunus does not work on international conflict resolution—although he did win the Nobel Peace Prize because he could see the overlap between economic development and peace-building. Rather, he is the founder of the Grameen Bank, which is widely (but not universally) thought to hold an important key to development—not just in the Third World, but in poorer sectors of the industrialized democracies as well. It is a concept supported by the more visionary writers in the corporate world.

As Yunus suggests, it is easy to focus on—and sometimes be depressed by—the specifics of daily political life. However, real progress—especially progress toward something new—requires a combination of what he calls "dreaming" about one's goal and empirical analysis.

It is the goal that grabs our attention, and this provides us with the motivation to continue even when the "real world" is providing us with a mixed message about ever reaching it. That is the normative aspect. The goal also offers us a benchmark against which to measure progress, and enabling us to learn to do things better the next time. That is the empirical aspect.

The point about the interplay between passion and the harsh realities of day-to-day politics was driven home to me by the last paragraph of George Mitchell's (1999) book on the peace process in Northern Ireland. The book affected me deeply. I had long been an admirer of Mitchell. I lived in Maine during his years in the Senate, and I even had a small part in one of his campaign ads. Then I lived in the United Kingdom for the first three years of Mitchell's involvement in the peace talks. During that time, a conflict I had paid little attention to became a part of my daily life, as well as his. I had been at the site of two IRA bombings just a day or two before the blasts went off. I twice had to leave shopping malls because of terrorist bomb threats.

Thus, I was delighted by the way George Mitchell had helped turn dreams into tangible progress in Northern Ireland, and I dashed out to buy his book the day it was published. Even so, I was not prepared for its last lines.

Mitchell became a father at one of the low points in the talks. In the book, he frequently muses about the world he was leaving to his new-born son Andrew, and the 61 children born on the same day in Northern Ireland. He ends his book with a description of his dream:

[t]o return to Northern Ireland in a few years with my young son, Andrew. We will roam the countryside, taking in the sights and smells and sounds of one of the most beautiful landscapes on earth. Then, on a rainy afternoon (there are many in Northern Ireland) we will drive to Stormont and sit quietly in the visitors' gallery of the Northern Ireland Assembly. There we will watch and listen as the members of the Assembly debate the ordinary issues of life in a peaceful democratic society: education, health care, agriculture, tourism, fisheries, trade. There will be no talk of war, for the war will have been long over. There will be no talk of peace, for peace will by then be taken for granted. On that day, the day on which peace is taken for granted in Northern Ireland, I will be fulfilled. (Mitchell 1999: 188)

Select Bibliography

Bloomfield, David (1997). *Peacemaking Strategies in Northern Ireland*. Basingstoke: Macmillan.

Cohen, Raymond (1997). *Negotiating across Cultures: International Communication in an Interdependent World*. Rev. edn. Washington, DC: United States Institute for Peace.

Hampson, Fen Osler (1996). *Nurturing Peace: Why Peace Settlements Succeed or Fail*. Washington, DC: United States Institute for Peace.

Hauss, Charles (1996). *Beyond Confrontation: Transforming the New World Order*. Westport, CT: Praeger.

Mitchell, George (1999). *Making Peace*. New York: Knopf.

CHAPTER TWELVE

Political Conclusions

There are three legs to the stool of American foreign policy: defense, diplomacy, and development. And we are responsible for two of the three legs. And we will make clear as we go forward, that diplomacy and development are essential tools in achieving the long-term objectives of the United States.
—Secretary of State, Hillary Rodham Clinton

A Rational Basis for Hope

One of the first articles I wrote on conflict resolution was entitled "a rational basis for hope." Few of the specific arguments I made in 1988 hold in the same form today. In fact, rational or otherwise, there probably is less basis for hope today for the short term than there was a decade ago when I wrote the first edition of this book, especially regarding the final four cases.

However, my reading of the evidence and my own experience over a quarter-century as a conflict resolution practitioner is that there are hopeful signs. Hope could start with the discussion of Muhammad Yunus that ended the previous chapter. Yunus was the little-known president of a little-known bank in Bangladesh that engaged in the little-known business of micro-credit, when he uttered the words that began our last chapter:

> Before we actually translate something into reality, we must be able to dream about it. And we must do a good job in identifying our destination.

Since then, Yunus has won the Nobel Peace Prize. Most readers of this book already knew about the Grameen bank before opening the cover. The United Nations declared 2005 to be "the year of micro-credit," and listed 60 countries where such programs had already been launched (www.yearofcredit.org). That number is closer to 100 today, including the United States. There is now even a website that allows individuals to search data on the track records of dozens of these programs, and then invest in one or more of them (www.kiva.org). Muhammad Yunus himself not only continues to support micro-credit projects but is also working to help women get larger loans to build medium-sized businesses.

Furthermore, micro-credit is not the only positive sign. In ending this book, I will explore three others before returning to the passion that led most conflict resolution practitioners to be interested in this subject.

New Goals and Tools

Yunus was right a decade ago. We needed to know the destination we were headed toward. We probably did, in some important ways. At the very least we understood the importance of building win-win solutions. Now, from both our successes and our failures, we have come to define the goals more clearly, and develop or redefine the tools that can help us achieve them.

Most importantly, the conflict resolution community now knows more than ever that a single "deal" to stop the fighting isn't enough. As we saw in the chapter on Israel and the Palestinians, far too many countries and regions return to violence within five years of an initial settlement. Some estimates put that number as high as a half.

All my colleagues in the NGO community understand that no dispute can be ended with a single agreement. True resolution of conflict does not come quickly or easily. John Paul Lederach once asked people who attended one of his workshops how long it would take to achieve reconciliation in Northern Ireland. He asked how long the conflict had been going on. Three hundred years, he was told. He told the audience to plan on that much time to heal those long-lasting wounds. Lederach knew his answer was wrong, that we could speed up the healing. But he made the comment so that his audience of peace-builders would realize that they had to be in it for the long haul.

We have also realized that in another respect stopping the fighting is not enough. All the conflicts considered in this book, and all the others I could have included, are marked by deep social and economic inequalities. A decade ago, conflict resolution practitioners did not pay anywhere near enough attention to what our colleagues in the rest of the NGO world called "social justice." The conflict resolution NGOs themselves are too small to directly engage in economic development and related work at this time. However, we have been working with colleagues in much larger NGOs such as World Vision, Catholic Relief Services and Mercy Corps, who have added conflict resolution and peace-building programs to bolster their primary mission of providing humanitarian assistance and development aid. From their perspective, too much money and too many other resources have been lost when a hospital or school they have built is destroyed in fighting.

To add to our capacity for conflict resolution, dozens of new NGOs have been formed. Consider two.

Combatants for Peace (www.combatantsforpeace.org) was formed in 2005 by Israeli and Palestinian war veterans, some of whom had personally fought against each other. They had concluded that peace was necessary, and that no group was better suited to advocate it than men who had seen combat in any of the wars that go back to the 1940s. The former soldiers started out by meeting among themselves. In the last two years or so they have also supported other projects, most notably helping rebuild houses, schools and playgrounds that were destroyed by either Israeli or Palestinian rockets.

Concordis-International is not an entirely new organization. Until the late 1990s it was part of a broader, relationship-building NGO associated with the Church of England (www.concordis-international.org). In 1999 it became independent, choosing its new name five years later. It is small, with a staff of five or six full-time employees. Nonetheless, it has had a major impact on conflicts in Sudan, the Democratic Republic of the Congo and Afghanistan. It is also unusual because its president is a retired Royal Air Force pilot, and in most of its work it makes clear its ties to the often conservative Anglican Church.

Apart from new "tools," the conflict resolution community has strengthened those we were using a decade ago. For instance, we have used the media to foster reconciliation by eliciting apologies from perpetrators of conflict, and forgiveness on the part of their former victims.

As should be clear from the chapters on South Africa, Northern Ireland and Israel–Palestine, reconciliation can be a long and wrenching process that historically has progressed by involving a few people at a time. Conflict resolution NGOs have therefore been experimenting with film, television and radio in an attempt to expand those efforts, promoting reconciliation more rapidly than we have been able to in the past.

The leader in this respect is Search for Common Ground (www.sfcg.org). Search (SFCG) is by no means the only agency in working with the media—compare, for example, the Truth and Reconciliation Commission in South Africa, Holocaust survivors who have forgiven the late Dr. Josef Mengele for the experiments he conducted on Jewish twin children, and the Invisible Children project on the plight of child soldiers.

What sets Search apart is the systematic way it has approached the use of the media, in two overlapping ways.

Search began by creating print, radio and television news services that stress cooperation among people from all sides of a dispute. The most extensive of these are studios that produce programs for radio stations throughout much of Africa. Search for Common Ground chose radio as a key medium because relatively few Africans have access to television.

One of its most successful projects was a documentary series, *The Shape of the Future*, which explored the "final status" issues standing in the way of lasting peace between Israelis and Palestinians. The series aired in prime-time in Israel and Palestine, and on one of the Arabic satellite channels beamed throughout the region. An hour-long version aimed at American audiences is also available. The series even has some biting humor about a region that rarely induces laughter. In one episode John Marks, Search's founder and president, is interviewing an old man who has been living in a refugee camp since 1948. Marks asks the man if he would be willing to give up his "right of return" to his village in exchange for peace. The man asks Marks where is from. Marks tells him New Jersey. The man then pointedly asks, "Would you give up New Jersey for peace?"

Search has even experimented with a version of reality television. In 2007 it followed two families from Egypt and the United States as they spent two weeks visiting each other, all the while discovering how much they had in common and how inaccurate were many of the preconceptions each held about the other.

In the late 1990s, the organization began developing radio and television (again, limited by television access in each country) dramas that focus on conflict resolution themes, but without ever using that term. The first and perhaps most successful of these was *Nashe Maalo* ("Our Place"), which aired on several Macedonian television stations from 1998 through 2003. It is based on an implausible scenario, with three teenagers living in the same apartment complex in the capital city of Skopje. What is implausible is that one is a Macedonian, one an Albanian, and one a Roma (gypsy). It is highly unlikely that people from each of the country's three main ethnic groups would live together, let alone be friends. The three cope with problems faced by teenagers around the world—school life, parents who lose their jobs, balancing schoolwork and play, and of course dating. Like teenagers around the world, the young people in *Nashe Maalo* don't do a very good of coping with life's everyday difficulties. That's when the truly implausible happens.

The apartment house comes to life in the form of an animated character, Karman, who helps the young people work through their difficulties.

Search has also brought conflict resolution back to the United States. The modern field of conflict resolution began in the US a quarter-century ago, but at that time most American, Canadian and British NGOs operated primarily abroad.

In 2000, Search's board of directors suggested that if it could make major progress in Israel or Burundi or Ukraine, it could also help solve the political disputes in this country, which are rarely as violent or even as acrimonious as those in Africa or Asia. Therefore, SFCG established a United States project. Once we (I was on the staff at the time) realized that Search could not simply import the tools and techniques we had used internationally, we focused on a technique that better suited the American political situation: consensus-building.

Shortly after the amazingly divisive 2000 election, Search was approached by two of the leading politicians who had been involved in the Florida furor—the controversy over the "hanging chads," and the disputed ballot which finally delivered George W. Bush to power as US president. These politicians did not like what they had seen or done. Both had experience as bridge-builders between Democrats and Republicans. Together with Search for Common Ground, former Montana Governor Marc Racicot, and former Congress member and cabinet secretary Dan Glickman, Search developed the idea of creating a United States Consensus Council (USCC).

The USCC would have extended what Racicot had done as governor in creating the Montana Consensus Council, which is still alive and thriving. The MCC and a dozen or so similar state-level groups around the country would convene all the parties ("stakeholders," in conflict resolution terms) to a dispute, and help them hammer out an agreement which was in many cases then turned into legislation—because all the interest groups involved were involved with, and supported, the consensus council's proposal.

We came close to getting federal legislation passed to create the USCC, but we could not overcome the opposition of a handful of representatives and senators who felt it would intrude too much on their "turf." Therefore, Search convened a series of consensus-building projects on the "faith-based initiative," which would have allowed the federal government to fund religious organizations that provided social services, prisoner re-entry, health care, and American policy toward Islam. Each project brought well-known policy-makers and politicians together in off-the-record discussions, produced widely respected reports, and moved Americans closer to agreement on issues that have divided and vexed the country for decades.

By the time this book is published, the USCC will exist as a stand-alone NGO, operating in a much more favorable political climate. We are hoping, as well, that the Obama administration will make consensus-building an integral part of its political agenda.

There has also been growing interest in determining which techniques work—and which do not. The governments, foundations and individuals that fund conflict resolution work have come to insist that they will not waste their money, and the NGOs themselves want to avoid making mistakes.

For example, Search for Common Ground developed a television series aimed at young people in Cyprus. The show could only be filmed off the island and had to be set somewhere else, in this case London. It was by far the most expensive and ambitious project Search's production unit had taken on. The program was well received, but Search was unable to get it aired on both Greek and Turkish Cypriot television, and the project was abandoned after a single season.

Most major NGOs now set aside funds to hire outside experts to evaluate their projects. Thus, an independent media consulting group conducted a survey to measure the impact of *Nashe Maalo*. The evaluation showed that over 90 percent of young people in Macedonia had seen the program more than once, and that regular viewers were open-minded in their attitudes toward other ethnic groups. An unpublished evaluation of Search-USA's first consensus-building project on President Bush's faith- based initiative led us to make major changes in the way we conducted subsequent efforts.

Perhaps more promising yet is the ongoing Reflecting on Peace Practice (RPP) project conducted by the Boston-based Collaborative for Democratic Action, which has long been a leader in encouraging NGOs to act more effectively and more responsibly (www.cdainc.com). The authors studied conflict resolution programs in Northern Ireland, Cyprus, Burundi, South Africa and Sri Lanka. Further case studies are currently under way.

I am not going to discuss their findings here, because they have already been incorporated into the body of the previous chapter. Suffice it to say that their research has led NGOs to develop more "whole of system" and long-term strategies, two of which will be examined next.

The Changing Role of the Military

One would not normally think of the military as an ally for conflict resolution practitioners. Few of us have been in the military. I was a conscientious objector during the Vietnam war, as was the male co-author of the RPP project. Yet, there are important changes taking place in the militaries in all the advanced industrialized countries where there is collaboration between conflict resolution NGOs and the armed forces.

NGOs have long known that they have to work with the military in the countries where they operate. The security system as a whole almost always is part of the conflict, and almost always has to be an integral part of a solution to it.

But, most of us never thought about working with our own armed forces until quite recently. There were some exceptions. Colleagues in Canada and the Scandinavian countries did have extensive contact with their militaries, because they were deployed almost exclusively as peace-keepers.

Changes in the last decade or so in other countries have come more gradually and sporadically. But the same trend that we are seeing in the United States has emerged in Britain, France, Germany, and beyond.

The most important change came within the military itself, and predated both the terrorist attacks of 9/11 and the difficult wars in Afghanistan and Iraq. Although there is no single cause for the military's evolution, a good starting point is the work of General Charles Krulak, who served as Commandant of the Marine Corps in the late 1990s. He argued that the United States could expect to fight many "three-block wars" in the future in which it would fight insurgents, maintain law and order, and rebuild communities—at the same time, and in the same place (www.au.af.mil/au/awc/awcgate/usmc/strategic_corporal.htm). Interestingly, Krulak became a leading critic of the Bush administration's alleged use of torture.

Similarly, Secretary of Defense Donald Rumsfeld (not usually someone whom conflict resolution practitioners speak highly of) asked the Defense Science Board to devote its annual summer study to the subject of transition to and from hostilities (www.acq.osd. mil/dsb/reports.htm). In that long and, frankly, not very readable document, published in late 2004, the board concluded that the US should expect to be involved in three to five conflicts at any one time for between five and ten years, a concept that later became known as the "long war." Remarkably, the report echoes much of what we have seen in this book, though the authors had little or no exposure to the literature on conflict resolution.[1]

The DSB report was followed a year later by Defense Department Directive 3000.05 (www.dtic.mil/whs/directives/corres/html/300005.htm), entitled "Military Support for Stability, Security, Transition, and Reconstruction (SSTR) Operations." It focuses on the role the military should play in what it calls Phase 4 and the rebuilding of countries such as Iraq or Afghanistan that had been through a brutal war. But, it also hints that the military should focus on Phase 0 or conflict prevention, too. Indeed, within weeks it had become clear that conflict prevention and reconstruction would be as important as combat operations for the American military.

The military aspect of peace operations was echoed in a civilian context about a week later, when the White House issued National Security Presidential Directive (NSPD) 44. It named the State Department's Coordinator for Conflict Reconstruction (S/CRS) as the head of all such efforts for the US government, including the military (www.state. gov/s/crs).

These were remarkable directives to be issued by any American government, let alone one that had been severely criticized by many in the peace-building community. We had never seen the Pentagon as anything like an ally. We had a more natural affinity with the State Department. However, S/CRS was a new organization troubled by a lack of financial and political support at the top level, reflected in a rapid turnover of staff whose careers could best be promoted elsewhere in the department.

Still, the Bush administration was calling for a sea change in American foreign policy, one no one could have predicted before 9/11. An administration that came to power opposed to anything that smacked of "state building" had come to the conclusion that it had to do just that.

Admittedly, it will take time for these new values to fully take root, especially in the military. However, many senior officers who have served in Iraq or Afghanistan returned knowing that they have to cooperate with NGOs and others to undertake their Phase 0 and Phase 4 responsibilities. Some even understand their obligation for an unofficial Phase 5, to focus on reconciliation.

Frankly, the NGO community was slow to respond (Wells and Hauss 2007 2008). Humanitarian and development NGOs were actually hostile to cooperation with the military, for two main reasons. First, their notion of neutrality requires maintaining distance from all parties to a dispute. Secondly, they felt that their ability to function, and even their physical security, is often threatened if they are seen to be cooperating with any armed forces. That includes the American military, which can make at least US-based

---

[1]   The report's primary author is a family friend, who was surprised when I first told him about the eerie parallels between his work and that of several of my friends.

NGOs appear to be a puppet of the government. The United States Institute of Peace (www.usip.org) facilitated a series of discussions between the Defense Department and the humanitarian and development NGOs which led to a 2007 agreement on such issues as the need for military aid providers to be in uniform, so that they are not perceived as part of civilian relief efforts.

The conflict resolution and peace-building NGOs were quicker to respond, though they are far smaller and less influential. The two concerns raised by Interaction (the umbrella organization for development and humanitarian NGOs) apply less in the conflict resolution world. Our sense of neutrality is that we have to work impartially with all parties to a dispute. Thus, organizations like Search for Common Ground have been able to work with the armed forces in war-torn countries such as Sierra Leone and Liberia. If such organizations can work on security sector reform abroad, working with the US military will be far easier. In addition, unlike most Interaction members, conflict resolution NGOs tend to have their greatest impact during conflict prevention and reconstruction periods, and are rarely "on the ground" when the fighting is at its peak.

Cooperation between conflict resolution NGOs and the American military has taken a number of forms. Most importantly, we have simply found times and places to meet, get to know each other, and build some measure of trust. In my own case, I started working with the Highlands Group (www.highlandsgroup.net), which was created by a retired Navy Captain (and nursery school friend) to help the Pentagon "think outside the box." I learned to speak Pentagon, which truly is a foreign language. In fact, I developed good personal relationships with people I didn't agree with to the point that I refer to the most conservative of my colleagues as my younger, Catholic, right-wing brother. But more importantly, I found that my new friends in and around the Pentagon and I agreed on a great deal. We may, for instance, have disagreed on the US invasion of Iraq, but there is widespread agreement among us that we need to chart a new course in our foreign policy.

So I work with a dozen or more colleagues (see, in particular www.3dsecurity.org), with the focus on combining defense, diplomacy and development in precisely the way Secretary of State Clinton suggested in her first address to the department staff that begins this chapter. I doubt that Clinton knew about 3D Security, but was joining a growing group of people in business, the NGO world and government who are talking about "human security," or an integrated approach to ensuring the safety and welfare of people around the world.

My colleagues and I keep getting asked to informal meetings and formal conferences. I have been to three military academies in the last year and a half. In the writing I have done with former Assistant Secretary of Defense Linton Wells, we easily found common ground on most issues that mattered to us most.

Frankly, our initiatives have been largely hit-or-miss, and are based on personal relationships that extend beyond the DoD/NGO world. But NGOs have helped the United States Military Academy create a course called "Winning the Peace," which is a popular elective for junior and senior cadets. Three or four of us routinely do guest lectures each year at West Point. It is now common for NGO staff to attend the annual conferences that the military academies arrange for undergraduates from around the country. We are exploring ways for NGOs, the military, and US government civilians who are likely to be deployed together to train together, although that aim has been hampered by the fact that only one senior NGO staffer (that I am aware of) has a security clearance.

In sum, in our work with the military we have relearned the importance of a statement by the late General Andrew Masondo which is used by Search for Common Ground as a signpost in determining what it should do. Masondo had been the head of the African National Congress's guerilla army. After the end of apartheid, he became the head of what Americans would call "affirmative action" for the South African military. As he so pithily put it: "Understand your differences, act on your commonalities."

My friends who are in the military, or hold senior civilian positions at what I jokingly call the "funny five-sided building," have to be careful about what they say in public (for an exception, see Yingling 2006). In private, many express qualms about our policy in Iraq since the invasion. More importantly, most of us have decided that there is no point in rehashing the debate over the invasion. Whatever we may have felt in 2002 or 2003, the invasion happened: it is history. We must now move on, taking Masondo's words to heart. And, more importantly, military veterans understand the need for peace better than we in the peace community do.

Peace through Commerce

I first became involved in conflict resolution work in the 1980s through the Beyond War movement (www.beyondwar.org). At the time, I never even looked at the business (or military) sections of bookstores.

But, most of the senior leadership of Beyond War had made amazing amounts of money in the early years of the Silicon Valley boom. My mentor Gene, for instance, had invented the payload for the first geosynchronous satellite when he was aged 23. He then formed a company that manufactured telecommunications software which he and his partners sold to IBM for something like $1.5 billion when Gene was in his late thirties— so he could focus on Beyond War full-time.

Gene and his friends kept giving me business books to read. Many of their themes undergird Parts 1 and 2 of this book, and I soon developed a life-long interest in organizational development, microeconomics, and other business matters.

But, the Beyond War team saw their corporate and peace work as largely separate from each other. Of course, they brought the knowledge and expertise from their years in business to the peace work. Nonetheless, we almost never considered how business could contribute to peace.

As I write a quarter-century later, that is changing. There is a loosely organized but growing movement known as "peace through commerce" that is taking hold in the corporate world, including the leading business schools.

I only began working with these colleagues as I was writing this book. Their work was so fascinating and illuminating that I delayed completing the book by three or four months!

Unlike my friends from the early Beyond War days, these activists and scholars are trying to make peace-building a conscious part of business life. There are two important strands to this work, and potentially a third.

The most sophisticated contributions to this book come from the work of Ashraf Ghani and Clare Lockhart (2008), and Paul Collier (2007). Ghani and Collier were both senior economists at the World Bank. Collier's book on the "bottom billion," the people who live on less than a dollar a day outlines their plight, and also underlines that pulling people out of poverty requires a vibrant corporate sector which creates stable and profitable markets among the poorest of the poor (see also Prahalad 2004). That means, in turn, addressing the conflicts that are associated with, and partly caused by, poverty.

As soon as the Taliban fell, Ghani and Lockhart were both sent to Afghanistan on short-term assignments by the World Bank. They stayed four and five years respectively. Ghani was born and raised there, but had lived in the West since the Soviet invasion in 1979. Lockhart is British and a generation younger. They saw in Afghanistan that the conflicts which have destabilized that country for the better part of a half-century cannot be settled unless we can "fix failed states." Echoing Collier, they are convinced a viable state can only exist if there is also a working market economy which the government and the private sector manage effectively. Unlike Collier, Ghani and Lockhart have decided to play an activist rather than a scholarly role, creating the Institute for State Effectiveness in 2005 and initiating projects in other countries (www.effectivestates.org).

The second school focuses more on the business than the conflict-resolution aspect of the "peace through commerce" process. That is not surprising, since most of the proponents are either corporate leaders or business school professors (Fort 2007). What almost all of them argue is that it is in a corporation's self-interest to conduct its business in a socially responsible manner. Some argue that it is detrimental for a company's "bottom line" not to do so (Wineberg and Rudolph 2004, and also www.globalchallengenetwork.com). Socially responsible corporate behavior may not necessarily involve peace-building, but it does involve protection of the environment, sustainable development, the status of women, poverty, and other issues that create a context for peacebuilding.

Some companies have been doing this kind of work for almost a generation (Hauss 1995), but these were typically small firms that were either in the high-tech world or catered to upper-middle-class customers. Ben and Jerry's, and Tom's of Maine, each gave their employees half a day off a week to work in their communities.

Ben (Cohen) and Jerry (Greenfield) are typical of this generation of entrepreneurs. They were childhood friends, and had early "ice cream experiences": Ben drove an ice cream truck after he dropped out of college, while Jerry dished out ice cream in one of Oberlin College's cafeterias. Neither ever expected to be an ice cream mogul. But, having failed in a number of other jobs, they took a Penn State University extension course on ice cream-making. Each got a perfect score; they admit that the test was "open book," and it only cost them $5 each. The next year, they opened their first ice cream store in a converted gas station in Burlington, Vermont. By 1985, the company was doing so well that they created the Ben and Jerry Foundation (www.benjerry.com/foundation), which gives grants of up to $15,000 for socially responsible causes. In 2000, business difficulties led Ben and Jerry to sell the company to Unilever, the most socially responsible of the companies that tried to take it over. The company retains the same ethos (including "free scoop day"), and its commitment to social change has continued.

At the high-tech end of socially responsible business the early leader was the ROLM corporation, co-founded by my friend Gene. The company pioneered digital telephone devices after deciding it no longer wanted to make computer products aimed at the military market. In fact, the first time Gene came to my office he took my telephone apart to see if it had ROLM innards; it did not.

What set ROLM apart from other Silicon Valley start-ups was its labor–management relations. The owners did not want to have to deal with unions, and determined that the best way to do so was to make ROLM a wonderful place to work. They did not go as far as

Google has in this decade, with free gourmet food and nearly-free day-care provision. Nonetheless, ROLM was one of the first companies to have an in-house gym and a quality cafeteria with no special space for the top executives. Pay differentials between senior executives and assembly-line workers were kept very low, though this did not extend to stock options. All workers were given a three-month sabbatical every four years. When IBM bought ROLM in the mid-1980s and imposed its more top-down management style, morale collapsed, and the company could not keep up with innovations from competitors.

The bottom line here is clear. Ben and Jerry's and ROLM did very well by treating their employees and their communities well. Having good products helped too, of course. Ben, Jerry and Gene are now all worth hundreds of millions of dollars. Gene, who is nearing 70, has retired after devoting 20 years to the Beyond War movement and its successor, the Foundation for Global Community. Ben has been a founder and funder of a number of progressive causes, including supporting Dennis Kucinich's unsuccessful bid for the 2004 Democratic presidential nomination, and assisting True Action, an organization which works on poverty, health and foreign policy issues. Jerry spends much of his time with the foundation, and is also on the board of the Peace Company to be discussed shortly.

In recent years, three companies epitomize what corporate social responsibility could and should be, on issues that include conflict resolution. All are much bigger than ROLM or Ben and Jerry's, and all are much more a part of the corporate mainstream. All have chosen to act differently.

First is Whole Foods. Founded in 1978 by the 25-year-old John Mackey and his girlfriend, it was the first supermarket-size natural food store in the country. It now has almost 300 stores in the United States and the United Kingdom, and controls about 40 percent of the natural and organic food market. Corporate policy includes buying locally as much as possible, and even allowing "farmers' markets" to be held in their parking lots.

Whole Foods has also established the Whole Planet Foundation, which is funded through contributions from corporations and employees (referred to as "team members"). The team members are probably more interesting for our purposes here. Almost half of Whole Foods' American employees are immigrants and, like everyone else in the industry, not very well paid. Nonetheless, many contribute a dollar or two from their biweekly paycheck to support the company's programs, some of which are located in their home countries. Indeed, many immigrant "team members" are clamoring for the foundation to expand its work to include their home countries, if it does not yet work there.

The Whole Planet Foundation has focused on micro-credit in ten countries outside the United States. Although building businesses is its core goal, every one of those countries have been devastated by violent conflict at some point in the last generation. John Mackey has also been actively involved in creating Flow, a non-profit organization that tries to foster peace through commerce, especially by empowering women entrepreneurs.

In short, Whole Foods represents the best of what is coming to be called "social entrepreneurship," both in its core business and its philanthropic efforts.

The second company is Google. It is one of the greatest success stories in modern corporate history, which began as a research project by two Stanford computer science engineering students, Larry Page and Sergey Brin. Google's rise to all but total dominance in the search engine and online advertising markets should be well known to any reader of this book. When Page and Brin (already ludicrously rich) decided to take Google public in 2004, they informed potential shareholders (alas, I did not buy any) that they intended to give at least one percent of income and equity, including employee time, to a variety of social causes.

In 2007 that led to the creation of google.org, an unusual philanthropic organization because it is not a traditional non profit. The funds all come from Google, as do many of the staff. By September 2008 it had donated $100 million to programs in health care, conflict and disaster response, and the environment. When it went public, Google also used 10 percent of the three million shares it sold to create a separate Google Foundation, which enjoys tax exempt status and is managed by google.org. According to its 2007 tax filing, the foundation is worth close to $100 million on its own.

My own involvement with this work has been with a colleague, Dr Eric Rasmussen, who is the Chief Executive Officer of INSTEDD. Rasmussen was a doctor in the US Navy for more than 20 years. During that time, he did what you would expect a military physician to do: he served in almost all the world's combat zones, including Iraq and Afghanistan, while maintaining his regular work as a staff doctor in Navy hospitals. Eric also pioneered a form of cooperation between the military and NGOs which is now known by the name of a series of exercises, Strong Angel. When Eric retired from the Navy he was hired by Larry Brilliant, the head of google.org, to create INSTEDD, which Google was spinning off as a separate NGO to deal with relief of disease and disaster.

The last company to consider is Microsoft. I am not a fan of the company. I bought my first Mac in 1984, and apologize whenever I have to tell people that we actually own a Windows machine. Like almost everyone else who is not a "techie," I have to use the Microsoft Office program, but I don't like Microsoft's near-total domination of the personal computer software market, built up over the last 25 years.

But, I also have to appreciate some of Microsoft's achievements beyond their business acumen. Most readers will know about the work that the Bill and Melinda Gates Foundation has done on AIDS and other health issues, economic development, and education in the United States.

Far less known is a new initiative the foundation has undertaken on humanitarian affairs, which parallels INSTEDD in many ways. This is intended to become a profit-making business center within Microsoft under the responsibility of its new chief software architect, Ray Ozzie, whose former firm Groove was a major funder of programs such as Strong Angel.

When Ozzie joined Microsoft he brought his commitment to humanitarian relief and conflict resolution with him. The assumption was that the company would create something like INSTEDD in the non-profit world. Instead (no pun intended), they created a new core business unit within the company to create and market software that the military, NGOs, health care providers and relief workers could use far more effectively than software they had used during humanitarian crises such as the 2004 Asian Tsunami and Hurricane Katrina. To head the division Microsoft brought in Nigel Snoad from the United Nations, a veteran of the tsunami who also knew Strong Angel and its predecessors.

It is by no means clear that Microsoft will ever make money from its humanitarian division. What is clear is that doing the work realizes the vision that Gates, Ozzie and Snoad have brought to the company.

Our final example is the only company that I'm aware of that is trying to make money through merchandising peace—The Peace Company (www.peacecompany.com). Operating almost completely online, the company was created several years ago by a colleague looking for ways to sell her own books and curricula, and those of people close to her. As a result, the site has the feel of something created by and intended for those of us who came to the conflict resolution community through 1960s-style activism.

In 2007, the company was bought by two people with extensive experience as mainstream corporate entrepreneurs. They have approached me to help them turn The Peace Company into a "one-stop shop" for all kinds of products that promote peace: but a company that is easier for people to navigate through than Amazon or GreaterGood, because its products are limited to peace-related material. With luck, the new version of the company will be in place by the time this book is published.

We do not expect The Peace Company to make a lot of money. However, in the jargon of the internet, we expect it to combine "pull" and "push" features that do not yet exist in the conflict resolution world. Of course, it will *push* products, but just as importantly it will try to *pull* or lure people who have little or no exposure to conflict resolution to the site, enabling them to combine buying books or videos or presents with learning some new insights into what this field is all about.

Obamamania

We in the conflict resolution community have a lot of hope for the Obama administration. New and constructive steps have been taken in the Middle East and Iran. We are also optimistic because the rest of the world thinks so highly of him. To give a simple example, the day I wrote this paragraph I had lunch with a French conflict resolution and political science colleague. He said that politically active people in his country used to look at American politics through a lens that focused on George Bush, and what they saw as his gaffes. Now, they expected great things from Obama and looked forward to more cooperative problem-solving initiated by our two governments.

Some Prophetic Words

I had not thought about President Lincoln's second inaugural address very much until I was driving home from West Point one day, and I heard Lincoln's words being discussed on the radio. On March 4, 1865, Lincoln stood under the newly completed Capitol Dome of the White House after weeks of rain had turned the lawn into a field of mud. Nonetheless, thousands of people came to hear the president, who knew that the Civil War would soon be over. President Lincoln obviously did not know that he would be killed five days after the Confederate surrender at Appomattox, barely a month after the date when he was sworn in. What he did know is that the reunited United States had to bind its wounds, and this led him to end the address with words we should all take to heart:

> With malice toward none, with charity for all, with firmness in the right as God gives us to see the right, let us strive on to finish the work we are in, to bind up the nation's wounds, to care for him who shall have borne the battle and for his widow and his

orphan, to do all which may achieve and cherish a just and lasting peace among ourselves and with all nations.

Select Bibliography

Ghani, Ashraf and Clare Lockhart (2008). *Fixing Failed States*. New York: Oxford University Press.

Myers, Winslow (2009). *Living Beyond War*. Tarrytown, NY: Orbis Press.

Prahalad, C. K. (2004). *The Fortune at the Bottom of the Pyramid*. Philadelphia, PA: Wharton School Publishing.

Wineberg, Danette, and Philip Rudolph (2004), "Corporate Social Responsibility: What Every In-house Corporate Counsel Needs to Know." *ACC Docket 22*. May. http://www.lexmundi.com/images/lexmundi/PDF/Rudolph_ACC.pdf.

Index

CPSIA information can be obtained
at www.ICGtesting.com
Printed in the USA
LVHW080224241219
641491LV00024BA/362/P

9 780826 489111